Arms for Africa

Arms for Africa

Military Assistance and Foreign Policy in the Developing World

Edited by
Bruce E. Arlinghaus
United States Military Academy

LexingtonBooks
D.C. Heath and Company
Lexington, Massachusetts
Toronto

Library of Congress Cataloging in Publication Data
Main entry under title:

Arms for Africa.

   Bibliography: p.
   1. Munitions—Political aspects—Africa, Sub-Saharan.
2. Military assistance—Africa, Sub-Saharan.   3. Africa, Sub-
Saharan—Military relations.   4. Africa, Sub-Saharan—Foreign
relations.   I. Arlinghaus, Bruce E.
HD9743.A4382A75   1982   382'.456234'0967   81–48668
ISBN 0–669–05527–1

Copyright © 1983 by D.C. Heath & Company

Published simultaneously in Canada

Printed in the United States of America

International Standard Book Number: 0–669–05527–1

Library of Congress Catalog Card Number: 81–48668

in memory of

Ruth Keiser Arlinghaus
(1908–1979)

Contents

Figures and Tables

Preface and Acknowledgments

An increased awareness of the strategic and political importance of sub-Saharan Africa has made it the setting for an emerging confrontation between East and West. A principal instrument of foreign policy in the region has been the transfer of conventional arms and the provision of military assistance to African nations, and this aid has increased both quantitatively and qualitatively over the past decade.

This book relates the arms-transfer practices of six principal suppliers to their foreign policies, and examines their effectiveness in influencing the actions and attitudes of recipient nations. The contributions in this volume, while not all-encompassing and exhaustive in their treatment of the subject, do define and analyze past, current, and future trends in military assistance to Africa and, most critically, evaluate just how influential arms transfers have been in furthering foreign-policy objectives.

As a result, this book focuses primarily on suppliers rather than recipients; while demand factors may be more significant for the dynamics of the international arms trade with Africa, the various exporters of arms attempt to manipulate this demand for their own ends. Since the majority of African nations remain almost totally dependent on the industrialized countries for their military equipment and technical training, at least in the short term, the supplier nations will continue to perceive arms transfers as one of their most viable and available foreign-policy options. In addition, since the demand for arms is so great and the competition to supply them so intense, there is a growing belief that the dynamics of international politics compel suppliers to transfer arms because military assistance not rendered is influence lost far out of proportion to the influence that such transfers potentially might gain.

The majority of chapters in this volume originated in a panel on conventional-arms transfers to Africa, held at the annual meetings of the African Studies Association in Bloomington, Indiana, October 1981. I would like to thank those who participated in that panel—Dave Albright, Roger Kanet, Ed Kolodziej, Ed Laurance, Bokanga Lokulutu, and Joe Smaldone—since it was their effort and expertise that inspired this book. I owe a special debt to the other contributors since their collective response to a barrage of letters and telephone calls produced papers of equal merit, which complement those of the panelists.

Funding for my participation and research was provided by the Faculty Development and Research Fund of the Association of Graduates, U.S. Military Academy, and the editor's portion of the royalties from this book is being donated to them to, in some small way, repay their generous support throughout. I would be remiss if I failed to acknowledge the support and assistance of my colleagues in the Department of Social Sciences, United States Military Academy, and the Department of National Security Affairs, Naval Postgraduate School, where I was a visiting faculty member during the preparation of the manuscript. Finally, I would like to thank Marilyn Weinstein and Susan Lasser of Lexington Books for their good faith and patience in bringing this book together.

Finally, I must advise the reader that several contributors and I are employees of the U.S. government and that our statements, interpretations, and recommendations are like those of our nongovernment colleagues—totally our own and in no way representative of official positions or policies of the U.S. government, or any of its departments or agencies.

Part I
Introduction

1 Linkage and Leverage in African Arms Transfers

Bruce E. Arlinghaus

In a recent issue of *Time* magazine, an unidentified senior White House official was quoted as saying that "Our foreign policy is in large part arms sales; that's true. Every other week we are selling something to someone."[1] What this statement reveals about American foreign policy should be no surprise to the reader, since virtually every developed industrial state engages in the transfer of arms, and does so under the control and direction of its government. That the foreign policies of these countries, especially in relation to the developing world, should so focus on the supply of weapons as an instrument of international diplomacy should be equally unsurprising, since world military expenditures annually exceed $450 billion, while economic aid totals only $20 billion.[2] In short, as Andrew J. Pierre has recently written: "Arms sales have become, more now than ever before, a crucial dimension of world politics. They are now major strands in the warp and woof of international affairs. Arms sales are far more than an economic occurance, a military relationship or an arms control challenge—*arms sales are foreign policy writ large.*"[3]

While the transfer of arms represents only one part of what has come to be generally understood as military assistance,[4] it forms the most significant portion in terms of both expense and political influence. Increasingly these transfers, regardless of source or means of financing, have come to shape all other aspects of military aid and assistance, since the acquisition of weapons systems determines both the form and the scope of military growth and modernization in recipient countries.[5]

While compared with activities in the Middle East, military assistance and arms transfers to Africa appear insignificant, there are a number of growing trends that contradict that impression. First, the arms trade with Africa has increased steadily over the past decade, and every indication is that it will continue to do so. Second, there is a growing awareness that, demand factors aside, the strategic importance of Africa to the superpowers and to other industrialized states has also steadily increased. Third, Africa, together with the rest of the Third World, is undergoing a wave of military modernization, a trend that is likely to continue throughout the decade as weapons systems become obsolete and regional conflicts increase in frequency and ferocity.[6] As a result, African states have increased dramatically, over the past decade, both the level of their military expenditures and their acquisition of more sophisticated military hardware. While their defense expenditures represent only a minute fraction of the world total, the trend toward military development and military-force modernization has caused the region to import fully one quarter of the arms transferred annually, with indications that such trade will continue to grow rather than recede over the next decade.[7] Furthermore, the fifty sovereign nations of Africa are some of the poorest in the world.[8] Their defense expenditures, especially for modern weapons, stand in stark contrast to the poverty and human suffering that demand foreign economic assistance and investment, and that are the root causes of unrest and insecurity in the region. Most African nations cannot afford arms purchases on anything less than a grant-aid basis, or, at the very least, on extremely concessional terms. Military aid and assistance are therefore even more potent instruments of political influence. Unlike the Middle East, where the buyers of weapons control the marketplace, African recipients seek the best weapons at the least financial expenditure. The difference between dollars and defense is most often made up through concessions of political influence to suppliers—providing them linkage and leverage in international relations.

That, in essence, is what the contributions to this volume are all about: How the suppliers of arms to Africa use that trade as an instrument of diplomacy to achieve their foreign-policy goals. Each supplier and each recipient nation varies in its motives and methods, and ultimately in the effectiveness of that instrument. Yet the desire of the recipient for arms continues unabated, and, as such, constitutes what appears to suppliers as the greatest potential means of influence in the region. It is indeed unfortunate that defense rather than development assistance provides this influence, but in an area of the world where, as one analyst has put it, power grows from the barrel of a gun,[9] it is arms transfers that predominate.

Arms Transfers, Linkages, and Leverage

Both supplier and recipient nations appear to recognize that there are both potential costs and benefits to the transfer of arms and the provision of military assistance. They may summarized as follows:[10]

Arms provided to allies may improve their internal security and external defense, but they may also exacerbate regional tensions and lead to conflict and internal discord.

Arms transfers to one side of a regional conflict may restore a local balance of military power and thus deter external aggression, but they may also spur local arms races that could lead to war as neighboring nations may feel threatened, or feel the need for preemptive military action to retain regional dominance.

Although arms transfers may provide suppliers with a means of political influence over the recipient, they may also result in political and military relationships that could be embarassing to the supplier or lead to unwanted commitments in the region.

Military assistance may enhance internal security, providing a measure of personal protection for the inhabitants of a recipient nation, but they may also be used for repression of its citizens in their pursuit of democratic process or recourse to corruption.

The stability that arms and assistance may create might lead to increased foreign investment and economic growth, but military aid and expenditures represent sizeable diversions of both money and manpower from the civilian economy, thus retarding economic development.

Since arms transfers and military assistance enhance the growth and modernization of local military forces, they contribute to the development and perception of national sovereignty of the recipient nation. But if the political price of such aid is basing rights, agreements on oil or other commodity prices, or political support elsewhere in the world, these may be viewed as reductions in sovereignty, a jealously guarded commodity in Third World politics.

Finally, arms sales represent for suppliers a means of easing balance-of-payments difficulties and indirectly subsidizing their own defense industries and requirements; yet provision of state-of-the-art weapons may detract from their own military readiness, and require substantial numbers of technicians and support to insure the absorption of such weapons by the recipients.

These costs and benefits are assessed and acted upon, thus creating linkage and leverage between supplier and recipient. *Linkage* is a mutually understood and accepted quid pro quo in which the supplier provides arms to the recipient in exchange for a specific goal, for example, basing rights for naval units. *Leverage*, on the other hand, is not so well defined, and its goal is the creation of influence with the recipient for use at a

later time.[11] Most African and other nonaligned nations studiously avoid
linked arms transfers, since they increase dependency upon the supplier
nation, reduce their freedom of political action, and are liable to alle-
gations of neocolonialism.

They are willing, however, to permit a supplier a degree of political
leverage because they are in fact dependent upon one industrialized nation
or another for military assistance, and are in reality seeking to manipulate
the growing multitude of competing suppliers to not only get the most
favorable terms, but also to create a degree of reverse leverage with the
supplier. They do so, for example, by agreeing to access rather than
basing arrangements, and then using one or a combination of several
strategies to bargain for further assistance, on better terms, in the future.
One such strategy is simply to threaten to seek another supplier, with a
consequent loss to the present one of considerable political influence.
Another is to capitalize on local discontent concerning the presence of
foreign troops or the size of domestic military expenditures, stressing that
more aid on more concessionary terms is critical to placate critics or to
suppress political opposition. Finally, there is the possibility of allowing
the supplier considerable access at very little initial cost, permitting him
to invest heavily in facility development and fostering a kind of reverse
operational dependency, and then renegotiating the terms of the agreement
when he has a considerable economic and political investment to protect.

These problems of reverse leverage are growing in importance as so-
called mini-states recognize their importance to the major industrialized
states, not only as support for their actions in the United Nations,[12] but
also strategically. Both recipients of arms and their neighbors recognize
the significance of military assistance and the fact that it effectively ties
supplier nations to them. As Julius Nyerere has said,

> the selling of arms is something which a country does only when it
> wants to support and strengthen the regime or group to whom the sale
> is made. Whatever restrictions or limits are placed on that sale, the sale
> of any arms is a declaration of support—an implied alliance of a kind.
> You can trade with people you dislike; you can have diplomatic relations
> with governments you disapprove of; you can sit in conference with
> those nations whose policies you abhor. But you do not sell arms without
> saying, in effect: ''In the light of the receiving country's known policies,
> friends and enemies, we anticipate that in the last resort, we will be on
> their side in the case of any conflict. We shall want them to defeat their
> enemies.''[13]

As a result of this interpretation of the symbolic nature of arms transfers
by their recipients, the question is raised of whether or not it is the supplier
who in fact has the most influence in the relationship. While it is clear,
as will be shown below, that the demand for arms and assistance on the

part of African nations is much stronger than the need of the supplier nations to provide them, the growing competition among suppliers in the Third World has created a situation in which being the recipient of a nation's arms may be as politically advantageous as supplying them, and where some supplier nations, in their desperation to gain access to or the support of selected African nations, will be more influenced than influential, at least in the short run.

Finally, military assistance may play an important part in access to strategic facilities in Africa without regard for linkage or leverage in arms-transfer diplomacy. Many of the current basing agreements negotiated with African and Middle Eastern nations are predicated on the right of those nations to deny or grant access selectively, on a case-by-case basis. While having met their individual demands for aid and assistance beforehand might conceivably predispose these nations to grant access during a crisis, these decisions will be made by the respective leaders when such occasions arise, and they will be based on their own international and domestic political situations. Just as many NATO allies refused access or overflight privileges to American aircraft resupplying the Israelis in 1967 and 1973, so too might our staunchest African friends deny use of their facilities because it might jeopardize their own interests.

It is in this context that military assistance is so critical. Imagine, for example, a scenario in which the American Rapid Deployment Force is dispatched to the Persian Gulf Region to counter a Soviet or Iraqi takeover of oil facilities in the region. The United States desperately requires the use of both Mogadishu and Berbera, and appeals to the Somali government for access. Foremost in the minds of the Somali leadership would be their ability both to insure the integrity of their borders from Ethiopian incursion, and to maintain order in the streets should any popular unrest emerge as a result of their aiding the United States. The degree of their confidence in their nation's internal and external security will be largely determined by the status of their armed forces, which is in many ways based upon prior provision of adequate and appropriate military aid.

Supplier Considerations

Each of the nations supplying arms and military assistance to Africa utilizes this instrument of diplomacy in characteristic ways, consistent with its objectives in the region and its overall foreign policy. Using arms transfers as an index of interest and influence regionally, it is possible to identify trends in the flow of arms and also the linkage and leverage that apply in the relations between supplier and recipient. Table 1–1 summarizes the cumulative supply of arms for 1974–1978 by major

Table 1-1
Value of Arms Transfers to Africa, 1974–1978, by Major Supplier and Recipient Country
(million current 1980 dollars)

Recipient	Total	Soviet Union	France	Federal Republic of Germany	Italy	United States	Poland	Czechoslovakia	United Kingdom	People's Republic of China	Canada	Others
Africa	13,100	7,400	1,500	575	550	480	240	230	160	120	50	1,800
Algeria	1,500	1,200	10	280	10	—	20	10	10	—	—	40
Angola	725	410	10	10	—	—	—	—	—	—	—	280
Benin	30	20	10	—	—	—	—	—	10	—	—	5
Botswana	10	—	—	5	—	—	—	—	—	—	—	—
Burundi	10	5	5	5	—	—	—	—	—	—	—	—
Cameroon	30	—	—	—	—	10	—	—	—	10	5	—
Cape Verde	20	20	—	—	—	—	—	—	—	—	—	—
Central African Emp	—	—	—	—	—	—	—	—	—	—	—	—
Chad	10	10	5	—	—	—	—	—	—	—	—	—
Congo	40	30	—	—	—	—	—	—	—	10	—	—
Equatorial Guinea	10	10	—	—	—	—	—	—	—	—	—	—
Ethiopia	1,600	1,300	10	5	20	100	10	30	—	5	—	140
Gabon	30	—	10	—	10	—	—	—	—	5	—	10
Gambia, The	5	—	—	—	—	—	—	—	—	—	—	—
Ghana	90	—	—	10	20	—	—	—	10	—	—	60
Guinea	50	50	—	—	—	—	—	—	—	—	—	—
Guinea-Bissau	10	10	—	—	—	—	—	—	—	—	—	—
Ivory Coast	90	—	70	5	—	—	—	—	—	—	—	30
Kenya	100	—	—	5	—	50	—	—	40	—	5	—
Lesotho	—	—	—	—	—	—	—	—	—	—	—	—
Liberia	—	—	—	—	—	—	—	—	—	—	—	—
Libya	5,000	3,400	270	140	330	5	220	180	20	—	—	350
Madagascar	30	20	5	—	—	—	—	—	—	—	—	10
Malawi	10	—	—	—	—	—	—	—	—	—	—	—
Mali	110	100	—	—	—	—	—	—	—	5	—	—
Mauritania	80	—	40	—	—	—	—	—	—	—	—	40

Country												
Mauritius	—	—	—	—	—	—	—	—	—	—	—	—
Morocco	950	20	470	50	40	170	—	5	5	5	—	200
Mozambique	180	130	—	—	—	—	—	5	—	—	—	30
Niger	10	—	5	10	10	10	—	—	30	—	—	—
Nigeria[a]	200	80	40	10	10	20	—	—	—	30	—	10
Rwanda	10	—	—	—	—	—	—	—	—	—	—	10
Sao Tome and Principe	—	—	—	—	—	—	—	—	—	—	—	—
Senegal	40	—	40	—	—	—	—	—	—	—	5	20
Sierra Leone	—	—	—	—	—	—	—	—	—	5	—	—
Somalia	500	300	20	10	20	20	—	—	5	5	5	150
South Africa	600	—	380	—	7	30	—	5	—	—	—	120
Sudan	110	30	10	30	—	—	—	—	5	5	5	10
Swaziland	—	—	—	—	—	—	—	—	—	—	—	—
Tanzania	180	110	—	—	5	—	—	—	—	30	—	40
Togo	40	—	10	5	—	—	—	—	—	10	10	20
Tunisia	80	110	10	10	5	20	—	—	10	10	—	30
Uganda	120	—	—	—	—	—	10	10	10	—	—	5
Upper Volta	10	—	10	10	—	—	—	—	—	—	—	5
Zaire	260	—	120	—	—	20	—	—	30	30	20	70
Zambia	140	40	—	5	10	—	—	—	—	20	20	20
Zimbabwe	20	—	5	—	—	—	—	—	—	—	—	20

Source: U.S. Arms Control and Disarmament Agency, *World Military Expenditures and Arms Transfers, 1969–1978* (Washington, D.C.: U.S. Government Printing Office, 1981).

supplier and recipient. While the chapters in this volume will deal in more detail with the patterns and trends of these transfers, and how they relate to the policies of individual suppliers, it is useful to note one significant feature of the table to illustrate the relationship between arms transfers and foreign policy.

Although the United States ranks first or is tied with the Soviet Union for leadership among suppliers of arms (33 percent and 34 percent, respectively), it supplies only 3.6 percent of the arms transferred to Africa. Traditionally, the United States has not viewed Africa as critical to its security interests,[14] and has practiced a policy of restraint insofar as arms transfers to Africa are concerned, supplying, instead, larger amounts of economic assistance and aid. The Soviets, French, and Italians have siezed shares of the African market that greatly exceed their portions of the world supply of arms, and although the United States has increased its security assistance to African countries in the past five years, the likelihood of a significant change in market shares is low.

The resurgence of American interest in using arms transfers as an instrument of policy in Africa may be attributed more to the demands of strategic concerns peripheral to Africa. The first, and most significant, is instability in the Persian Gulf region, and the need for American access to facilities in Eastern Africa. Here again, the question of influence and reverse linkage seems to obtain, since it is clearly the United States that requires the cooperation of recipient nations—more than their specific need for arms of American manufacture.[15] In the second area of strategic concern—access to key mineral resources—it is again American dependence on African strategic minerals and the perception of many officials in Washington that southern Africa is "the Persian Gulf of minerals" that has led to the meeting of African demands for arms and military assistance.[16]

Recipient Considerations

Although there is evidence that many suppliers—the Soviets and French in particular—are quite aggressive in the marketing and provision of arms and military assistance, research into who is supplying what and how much to whom has led to the conclusion that the single most potent force in the trade in arms to Africa has been the demand for them by African nations.[17] Characterized as "pull factors," both the increase in the frequency and intensity of intra-African conflict, and the expanding resource base of African nations have led to the dramatic growth in the supply of arms to the region.

As one analyst has put it, "The increase in Africa's arms imports are caused by the conflict behavior of many African nations, including various internal conflicts. . . .''[18] Although much of the conflict in Africa may be attributed to the failure of the Organization of African Unity and African solidarity, the resurgence of tribal and ethnic factors, the instability wrought by military intervention in domestic politics, and the failure of many African nations to achieve sufficient economic progress, these essentially internal factors have been displaced. There has been an increase in civil war, expansionist nationalism, foreign intervention, and transborder military intervention by neighboring states.[19] While domestic issues remain unresolved, clearly the African demand for arms is meant to meet these other threats rather than to suppress internal discord.[20]

In peacetime, or the absence of viable threats to the security of African nations, the military plays a special role in reinforcing perceptions by leaders and citizens of both independence and sovereignty. As President Hamani Diori stated at the inauguration of the new army of Niger: "Henceforth, in the eyes of the world and of the whole of our people, you are the visible sign of our political independence and of our proclaimed will to defend it against all aggression."[21] An understanding of this symbolic component of African security concerns is essential, especially since the demand for arms has largely been determined by it rather than by what would be a developed nation's interpretation of genuine defense needs and the appropriate means to meet them.

This is especially true since the transfer of arms has increased not only quantitatively, but qualitatively as well. There is very little interest on the part of African leaders in what they perceive as surplus, obsolete, export-only, "junk weapons,"[22] and most African nations seek to modernize their forces with weapons that will provide them a state-of-the-art military capability into the 1990s and beyond.[23] This desire has manifested itself in African interest not only in such systems as the F–14 and F–18,[24] but also in Western-produced systems in general, commonly perceived to be technologically superior to those provided (although at much lower cost) by the Soviets and other Communist nations. As one Chad official has said, "We accept Russian weapons because we have nothing else. But we would much rather have American made weapons if we could get them."[25]

Limitations of Arms Transfers

There are a number of factors, however, that effectively limit the usefulness of arms transfers in creating linkage and leverage with African nations. The first, quite simply, is that given the increase in interstate conflict in the region, supplying arms creates reverse linkage and leverage, which prevents a supplier from exerting much influence over rival recipients. A good example of this was recent Kenyan dissatisfaction with American supplies of air-defense weapons to Somalia. As one Kenyan official put it, ''You supply us with the planes and the Somalis with equipment to shoot them down.''[26] Such perceptions may lead to increased tension and conflict, and even greater demands for more arms in a more timely manner.[27]

Second, there is the question of the negative impact of arms transfers and military expenditures on the economies of African nations.[28] Given the serious economic conditions of most African nations, their low per-capita incomes and the associated human suffering, there is a growing scepticism that military assistance is either appropriate or necessary. While many Africans recognize that the Soviets emphasize military assistance because they can offer little else in the way of aid,[29] they are disturbed that America and the West may, in fact, be substituting security assistance for the more traditional economic aid.[30] As one local Sudanese official has put it: ''We do not need arms from America, we need roads and economic help. This is much more important.''[31] While most arms transfers are on a credit basis, and thus do not represent a direct expenditure of financial resources, such sales do add to the external debt of African countries, thus causing political and economic difficulties in the form of financial reforms; these, in turn, cause internal unrest and the inability of many nations to acquire further credit.[32] Ultimately, these problems may undermine the very security that arms and military assistance are designed to promote. As Robert McNamara has said, ''The point is not that a nation's security is relatively less important than other considerations. Security is fundamental. The point is simply that excessive military spending can reduce security rather than strengthen it.''[33]

The issue of the appropriateness of military assistance has another dimension as well. There is some concern that the increased sophistication of the weapons transferred to African countries will exacerbate problems of technology absorption generally, and specifically create a situation in which either the weapons will not be operational, or will require significant numbers of foreign technicians to operate and maintain them.[34] The problem of the absorption of military technology stems from deep-rooted historical, social, cultural and lingustic issues that will not be easily overcome without a sizeable diversion of financial and human resources from the private to military sectors.[35] The criterion of applicability has seldom if ever been considered by arms suppliers[36] and is largely ignored by recipients, because of their desire for weapons with the greatest prestige potential and because of implicit assurances by suppliers to overcome any recipient inadequacies as necessary. These assurances reinforce recipient perceptions of the linkage and leverage they possess with suppliers. This situation is further complicated by the tendency of African nations to have multiple arms suppliers, causing what can only be considered a logistical and operational nightmare.[37] Viewed from the perspective of the recipient nation, such a strategy has political advantages that far outweigh potential military consequences. By having more than one supplier, a country is able to develop links to a number of supplier nations and effectively play one off against the other. The strategy also insures against a dependence on one supplier that would subject that nation to "spare-parts diplomacy"[38] such as that experienced by the Egyptians and Somalis with the Soviet Union.

The final limitation of arms transfers as an instrument of foreign policy is perhaps the most telling. Given the competitive nature of the international arms trade and the ability of many recipients nations to shrewdly manipulate the markets and the desires of supplier nations, it is questionable whether it is as useful a diplomatic tool as is commonly believed. A recent study conducted by the Congressional Research Office concluded:[39]

> The American experience in Vietnam, Iran and Ethiopia graphically illustrate that arms transfers, and even the use of American troops, do not ensure "stability" in a country or region or guarantee the continued good will and cooperation of the recipient nation. The Soviet Union has had similar setbacks in the use of arms sales as an instrument of foreign policy in nations such as Egypt, Somalia, and even a fellow Communist state, the People's Republic of China. In short, arms transfers are an unwieldly instrument of foreign policy and they do not always provide the results expected.

Problems of Measurement

While arms transfers and military assistance may be unwieldly and somewhat unreliable as instruments of foreign policy, it is unlikely that supplier nations will forego the opportunity for influence in Africa by restricting their transfers of arms; yet unrestrained responses must be tempered not only by the limitations of arms transfers described above, but also the realization that there are physical and fiscal limits to the amount and type of arms that will be supplied. Furthermore, when measuring the costs and assumed benefits of military assistance to African nations, one must recognize that such calculations are inherently subjective—that the measurement of the effectiveness of arms transfers is at best uncertain, especially in determining to what extent a favorable political outcome is in fact due to military assistance.[40]

A similar situation confronts those who attempt to analyze arms transfers, and understand their role in the foreign policies of supplier and recipient nations. The available data are imperfect and can only suggest the direction and scope of the international supply of arms and military assistance. These problems are further complicated by qualitative issues regarding the arms themselves, and the inefficiencies and secrecy surrounding defense bureaucracies in both supplier and recipient nations.[41] Ultimately, however, the analysis of arms transfers by both policymaker and academician is dependent on intuitive as much as empirical appreciation of the process of military assistance and the role it plays in international relations.

Notes

1. "Divisions in Diplomacy," *Time* (1 March 1982): 12–14.

2. Luther J. Carter, "Global 2000 Report: Vision of a Gloomy World," *Science,* 209 (1 August 1980): 575–6; U.S. Arms Control and Disarmament Agency, (USACDA), *World Military Expenditures and Arms Transfers 1969–1978* (Washington, D.C.: U.S. Government Printing Office, 1980).

3. Andrew J. Pierre, "Arms Sales: The New Diplomacy," *Foreign Affairs,* 60, no. 2 (Winter 1981/82): 266–286.

4. Military assistance also includes activities such as provisions of advice, construction of facilities, and the training of both cadres and individuals at home or abroad. See Major General K. Perkins, "Winning Friends: A Military Strategy in the Third World," *Royal United Services Institute* (June 1981): 39–41.

5. See Mary Kaldor, *The Baroque Arsenal* (New York: Hill and Wang, 1981).

6. Andrew J. Pierre, *The Global Politics of Arms Sales* (Princeton, N.J.: Princeton Unviersity Press, 1982).

7. USACDA, *World Military Expenditures* 1969–1978, pp. 3–8.

8. "Africa's Growing Pains," *The Economist* (10 October 1981): 88–90.

9. Ruth First, *From the Barrel of a Gun* (London: Pantheon, 1970).

10. This summary is based in part on that in the introduction to Andrew J. Pierre, ed., *Arms Transfers and American Foreign Policy* (New York: New York University Press, 1979), pp. 4–5.

11. See Henry A. Kissinger, *The White House Years* (Boston: Little-Brown, 1979), p. 129: "Linkage existed in two forms: first, when a diplomat deliberately links two separate objectives in a negotiation, using one as a leverage on the other; or by virtue of reality, because in an interdependent world the actions of a major power are inevitably related

and have consequences beyond the issue or region immediately concerned.''

12. Kathleen Teltsch, ''Reporter's Notebook: New Flag and Old Wars at the U.N.,'' *New York Times* (21 September 1979), p. A2.

13. Julius K. Nyerere, *Freedom and Development: A Selection From Writings and Speeches 1968–1973*. (Dar es Salaam: Oxford University Press, 1973), pp. 247–248.

14. See Bruce J. Palmer, Jr., ''U.S. Security Interests and Africa South of the Sahara,'' *AEI Defense Review*, 2, no. 6 (1978), and William H. Lewis, ''How a Defense Planner Looks at Africa,'' in Helen Kitchen, ed., *Africa: From Mystery to Maze* (Lexington, Mass.: D.C. Heath and Co., Lexington Books, 1976.), pp. 277–304.

15. See Dale R. Tahtinen, *Arms in the Indian Ocean: Interests and Challenge* (Washington, D.C.: American Enterprise Institute, 1977), U.S. Congress, House of Representatives, Committee on International Relations, *United States Arms Policies in the Persian Gulf and Red Sea Areas: Past, Present, and Future* (Washington, D.C.: U.S. Government Printing Office, 1977); ''U.S., Somalia Move Toward Pact on Access to Military Facilities,'' *The Washington Post*, 12 August 1980, and ''Arms in the Ocean,'' *South* (November 1980): 19–20.

16. Richard Sales, ''The Core of Modern Conflict,'' *Defense and Foreign Affairs*, (June 1981): 20–21, and James Ridgeway, ''Strategic Minerals Down Under,'' *Defense Week* (3 August 1981): 5.

17. William P. Avery and Louis A. Picard, ''Pull Factors in the Transfer of Conventional Armaments to Africa,'' *Journal of Political and Military Sociology*, 8, no. 1 (Spring 1980): 55–70.

18. Feraidoon Sham B., ''American Policy: Arms and Aid in Africa,'' *Current History*, 77, no. 448 (July/August 1979): 9–13.

19. See Raymond W. Copson, ''African International Politics: Underdevelopment and Conflict in the Seventies,'' *Orbis*, 22, no. 1 (Spring 1978): 227–245, and Colin Legum, I. William Zartman, Steven Langdon, and Lynn K. Mytelka, *Africa in the 1980s* (New York: McGraw-Hill, 1979).

20. See Ernest W. Leferer, *Spear and Scepter: Army, Police and Politics in Tropical Africa* (Washington, D.C.: Brookings Institution, 1970).

21. Quoted in Stockholm International Peace Research Institute, *The Arms Trade with the Third World*, revised and abridged edition (New York: Holmes and Meir, 1975), p. 232.

22. Peter Grose, ''Third World Nations at U.N. Show Interest in Curbs on Arms Sales,'' *The New York Times*, 4 October 1976.

23. Gregory Copley, ''Africa Begins the Change,'' *Defense and Foreign Affairs Digest*, 7, no. 10 (1979): 6–13.

24. "Armed Forces a Cash Priority," *Financial Times*, 2 November 1981, p. 2, section II.

25. Defense Marketing Service, *Intelligence Newsletter*, 22 September 1980, p. 3.

26. "U.S. Arms Accord With Somalia Alarms Rival Neighbor Kenya," *The Washington Post*, 20 October 1980.

27. "Somalia Peeved About 'Slow' Pace of U.S. Military Aid," *The Christian Science Monitor*, 7 December 1981.

28. See David K. Whynes, *The Economics of Third World Military Expenditure* (Austin, Tex.: University of Texas Press, 1979).

29. Richard Tunsar, "Angola Has Second Thoughts About Help It Gets From East Bloc," *The Christian Science Monitor*, 2 February 1982.

30. Robert I. Rotberg, "Sudan Needs Butter More Than Guns," *The Christian Science Monitor*, 7 December 1981.

31. Alan Cowell, "In Sudan, 220 Miles Can Last Forever," *The New York Times* 2 November 1981.

32. I.M.F. View of the African Economy," *African Business* (July 1981): 15–17.

33. Quoted in James Reston, "The Meaning of Security," *The New York Times*, 25 May 1979.

34. Geoffrey Kemp, "Arms Transfers and the 'Back-End' Problem in Developing Countries," in Stephanie Neuman and Robert Harkavy, eds., *Arms Transfers in the Modern World* (New York: Praeger, 1979), pp. 264–275.

35. Anthony Pascal, *Are Third World Armies Third Rate? Human Capital and Organizational Impediments to Military Effectiveness* Report No. P-6433 (Santa Monica, Calif.: Rand Corporation, 1980).

36. Michael R. Gordon, "Competition With the Soviet Union Drives Reagan's Arms Sales Policy," *National Journal* (16 May 1981): 868–873.

37. See for example, "America's Newest Ally," *Newsweek* (26 October 1981).

38. Anthony Sampson, *The Arms Bazaar* (New York: Viking, 1978).

39. U.S. Congress, House of Representatives, Committee on Foreign Affairs, *Changing Perspectives on U.S. Arms Transfer Policy* (Washington, D.C.: U.S. Government Printing Office, 1981), p. 45. See also a related document from the same source: *Military Assistance Training* (1970) in which Ross K. Bohen states that: "I would submit that there is no way of assuring stability, supporting friendly regimes, or irrevocably winning the support of the military in Africa, let alone making formidable fighting machines out of the armies," (p. 114).

40. Major General K. Perkins, "Winning Friends."

41. See Robert E. Harkavy, *The Arms Trade and International Sys-*

tems (Cambridge, Mass.: Ballinger, 1975), Edward A. Kolodziej, "Measuring French Arms Transfers: A Problem of Sources and Some Sources of Problems," *Journal of Conflict Resolution,* 23, no. 2 (June 1979): 195–227; Edward T. Fei, "Understanding Arms Transfers and Military Expenditures: Data Problems," in Stephanie Neuman and Robert Harkavy, eds., *Arms Transfers in the Modern World* (New York: Praeger, 1979); and Edward J. Laurance and Ronald G. Sherwin, "Understanding Arms Transfers Through Data Analysis" (pp. 87–106) and Amelia C. Leiss, International Transfers of Armaments: Can Social Scientists Deal with Qualitative Issues?", (pp. 107–117) in Uri Ra'anan, Robert Pfalzgraff and Geoffrey Kemp, eds., *Arms Transfers to the Third World: The Military Buildup in Less Industrial Countries* (Boulder, Colo.: Westview Press, 1978).

Part II
Communist Arms Transfers and Military Assistance to Sub-Saharan Africa

2 Overview of Communist Arms Transfers to Sub-Saharan Africa

David E. Albright

Over the years since the late 1950s, the Communist states have become significant suppliers of arms to sub-Saharan Africa. Their activities in this realm began in late 1958 with a grant by Czechoslovakia of about $3 million in military aid to newly independent Guinea.[1] By the opening of the 1980s, the cumulative value of arms agreements that they had signed with sovereign African countries alone had reached more than $5,400 million.[2] This total, of course, did not include the substantial but unknown amount of arms that they had contracted to furnish various "national liberation movements" in the region during the period. Perhaps more important, the bulk of the arms agreements came after 1974. Prior to 1975, for example, the USSR had consented to provide only $715 million of arms to states in sub-Saharan Africa; in 1975–1979, the figure was $3,920 million.[3]

Deliveries, to be sure, have fallen somewhat short of commitments. Through 1979, for instance, the Soviet Union had handed over just $3,530 million of the $4,635 million of arms that it had contracted to supply to independent African countries.[4] Nevertheless, Communist performance in this regard has improved considerably in recent years. Up to 1975, for example, the USSR had delivered barely half, $410 million, of the $715 million of weapons and equipment that it had promised to African states, but by the end of 1979 the proportion had risen to more than 75 percent.[5]

A breakdown of the general totals reveals that the involvement of individual Communist states in these arms transfers has differed greatly. The smaller, less-developed Communist countries of Asia and Latin America have furnished virtually no arms of their own to sub-Saharan Africa, although both Cuba and North Korea have sent appreciable numbers of military advisors and even combat troops to the area. Indeed, Cuba had an estimated 33,045 military technicians in the region in 1979. This figure included more than 30,000 troops in Ethiopia and Angola.[6] The USSR has been the chief Communist arms supplier. It accounted for $4,635 million of the more than $5,400 million in Communist commit-

The views expressed in this chapter are those of the author and do not necessarily reflect those of the U.S. International Communication Agency or the U.S. government,

ments to sovereign countries of sub-Saharan Africa through 1979, and, as already noted, it had actually turned over $3,530 million of weapons and equipment to these countries by the end of that year.[7] China has run second, though far behind the Soviet Union. Through 1979, it had contracted to provide about $400 million of arms to states of the area, but it had a fairly poor record of follow-up on these promises. During 1964–1978, for instance, it transferred only $191 million of weapons and equipment to independent countries of sub-Saharan Africa.[8] The East European states (including Yugoslavia) have furnished the remainder of the arms. While there are no unclassified data available on their individual pledges, they in aggregate by the close of 1979 had agreed to supply roughly $425 million of weapons and equipment to sovereign countries of the area. The information at hand, however, suggests that their deliveries have been well shy of their commitments. Over the years 1964–1978, for example, Czechoslovakia handed over only $61 million of weapons and equipment to the states of sub-Saharan Africa; Poland, just $20 million. Aside from the German Democratic Republic, these two countries are the most advanced in Eastern Europe and therefore would presumably have made a large share of the promises of arms to the region.[9]

In keeping with the increase in the value of Communist arms transfers to sub-Saharan Africa, the list of recipients of these transfers has expanded substantially. The number of states on it grew from one in 1959 to twenty-two during the 1974–1978 period. Of the twenty-two, ten constituted major recipients—that is, of $50 million or more. They were Angola, Ethiopia, Guinea, Mali, Mozambique, Nigeria, Somalia, Tanzania, Uganda, and Zambia.[10] In addition, a variety of national-liberation movements obtained weapons and equipment from the Communist countries over the years. Although many had won their independence and were among the sovereign recipients of Communist arms transfers by the late 1970s, those in Zimbabwe and Namibia were still carrying on guerrilla struggles with the help of Communist arms.[11]

While for the Communist countries as a whole the pace of expansion of the roster of recipients has appeared to remain relatively constant in recent years as compared with earlier ones, that for most individual Communist states for which data are available seems to have quickened. The case is perhaps least strong for the USSR. In 1974–1978, Moscow supplied arms to nineteen sovereign African countries, whereas the figure for 1964–1973 had been only eleven. However, national-liberation movements in four of the additions—Angola, Cape Verde, Guinea-Bissau, and Mozambique—had obtained weapons from the Soviet Union prior to the mid-1970s, so these states should not be counted as new recipients. At the same time, one country on the 1964–1973 list—Ghana—dropped off in 1974–1978. Hence, there was a net increase of five recipients of Soviet arms in the 1974–1978 period. The number of African states to which China sent arms rose from six in 1964–1973 to eleven in 1974–1978. Although one of the new recipients—Mozambique—had received weapons from Beijing previously as a national-liberation movement and should therefore not figure in the total, two of the countries to which China had supplied arms in 1964–1973—Burundi and Guinea— were no longer receiving shipments from Beijing during 1974–1978. Thus, there was a net of six additions to the Chinese roster during the period. The sum of African states that obtained weapons and equipment from Czechoslovakia fell from five in 1964–1973 to four in 1974–1978, but only one of the four in the latter period—Uganda—was a repeat. Moreover, all three of the others probably qualify as new recipients, even though two—Angola and Mozambique—did not attain independence until the mid-1970s. It is doubtful that national-liberation movements in these countries got arms from Prague during 1964–1973. As for Poland, it dispatched no weapons and equipment to African states in 1964–1973; however, it supplied arms to two states—Angola and Ethiopia—in 1974 1978. In all likelihood, these two countries meet the criterion of new recipients, for Polish arms seem not to have gone to Angola in the 1964 1973 period to support the struggle of a national-liberation move- ment there.[12]

Reasons for Transfers

The explanation for this rising flow of Communist arms to sub-Saharan Africa is complex. To a considerable extent, it lies in alterations in circumstances on the African side. Here two interrelated factors have been key.

To begin with, the level of conflict in the area has been mounting steadily since the late 1960s.[13] This conflict has had intrastate, interstate, and black-versus-white dimensions.

The intrastate ones have stemmed from shifts that have taken place in many of the countries of the region since they acquired independence in the 1960s. Initially, broad national fronts assumed control of the new governments, but by the 1970s, more narrowly based, often authoritarian, regimes had replaced them in most of the states concerned. This devel- opment has had profound effects on domestic politics in these states. In the absence of channels for open political competition, politics have typically become an extralegal contest between rulers and those seeking to oust them, with a heavy emphasis on the use of violence. As force has grown increasingly important in the competition, both the "ins" and

"outs" have tended to seek outside support to wage their battles effectively, and the result has been a further escalation of internal strife.

As for the interstate aspects, the 1970s and the 1980s have witnessed
a substantial weakening of the commitment to resolve border disputes
and other disagreements without resorting to force evinced by the drafters
of the Charter of the Organization of African Unity (OAU) in the 1960s.
Perhaps the most spectacular example of the trend has been Somalia's
effort to wrest the Ogaden region from Ethiopian control in 1977–1978,
but it by no means exhausts the list. Others have included Uganda's
invasion of Tanzania in 1978 during the final months of Idi Amin's rule
and Tanzania's counterattack to overturn the erratic Ugandan dictator.
Such actions would probably have been unthinkable in the atmosphere
of the 1960s.

To make matters worse, the OAU, even though it did approve the
dispatch of an African military contingent to Chad in 1981 to put an end
to the intervention of Libyan troops there, has generally proved highly
ineffectual in dealing with contentious issues between states. Hence,
countries throughout the continent have more and more turned to non-
continental sources for backing to help sustain their positions on questions
in dispute among them.

With respect to the black-versus-white struggle, the demise of the
Portuguese empire in Africa after the April 1974 military coup in Lisbon
has had major consequences. It permitted the Portuguese colonies on the
continent and especially those in the white redoubt of southern Africa to
become independent under black-majority rule, and this development
heightened the hopes of black Africans for the elimination of white dom-
ination everywhere on the continent in the not too distant future. Thus,
there was an intensification of black-African efforts to topple the remaining white-minority regimes in Rhodesia, Namibia, and South Africa.
For their part, the substantial number of whites in the three entities
demonstrated a high degree of resolve to maintain their political control.
The inevitable outcome was rising strife in southern Africa. To be sure,
the political settlement between contending forces in Rhodesia in late
1979 and the ensuing emergence of a black-governed state of Zimbabwe
in 1980 greatly reduced tensions there. At the same time, these events
served to exacerbate conflict between blacks throughout sub-Saharan
Africa and the white government of South Africa, which administers
Namibia as well as runs the affairs of the Republic proper.

Recognizing from the outset of the new situation that they lacked
sufficient assets themselves to compel recalcitrant whites to accept change
but nonetheless sensing expanding possibilities for such change, black

Africans have looked increasingly for assistance from outside the region to hasten the process along. That search has extended well beyond the confines of the continent.

Hand in hand with the mounting conflict in sub-Saharan Africa has gone a decrease in the reluctance of black Africans to have military dealings with Communist states.[14] This trend has reflected both practical and ideological considerations.

The former have involved growing perceptions of a need for arms and a lack of alternative sources of supply for the weapons and equipment desired. During the 1950s and 1960s, the struggle for independence took essentially political form in most sub-Saharan African countries, and movements uniting diverse local elements under a single umbrella led the struggle. Moreover, it was these movements that constituted the first postindependence governments. Under such circumstances, the acquisition of arms did not fall high on the list of priorities of many African political forces—especially in light of the concern with achieving rapid economic advance. As the 1960s waned and the 1970s dawned, however, it became increasingly apparent that the white rulers of Portuguese and southern Africa would not follow the British and French examples and hand over power to blacks peaceably; therefore, blacks displayed mounting resolve to forge the means to wrest it from them by force. Furthermore, internal and interstate conflict, for reasons previously noted, escalated in those portions of the region that had already won their sovereignty. In the eyes of many local political elements, this escalation, too, placed a new premium on obtaining weapons and military equipment. Yet a lot of African political forces found it hard to get arms from the West. The Western powers, for instance, showed little inclination to back guerrilla undertakings against white-minority regimes, no matter how repugnant they deemed the policies of these regimes to be. Nor did the West manifest any greater enthusiasm for attempts to overthrow established black governments by resort to violence. In still other cases, traditional supply relationships—the American links with Ethiopia prior to 1977 afford a good illustration—effectively precluded appeals to Western powers for arms by one party to a dispute. Since Third World countries did not manufacture many of the items that Africans wanted—and were willing to provide even fewer—the Communist states offered the main available source of supply.

The ideological factor has been an enhanced sense of affinity with the Communist countries on the part of at least a number of national-liberation movements and states in the area. This heightened sense of identification had its roots in two types of developments.[15] Some national-liberation movements and ruling groups have undergone internal radicalization. Such a process has been fairly typical of the former, especially those in southern Africa. Because white minorities throughout southern Africa have stubbornly resisted the idea of black-majority government, arguments for seizing political power from these minorities by force and then using that power to deprive them of their privileged economic and social positions have had mounting appeal, and the advocates of such an approach have assumed influential roles within the liberation movements. This commitment to far-reaching transformations of their countries has provided them with a certain feeling of commonality with the Communist states. In other cases, radical elements have overturned rulers of a more conservative bent. The most dramatic illustration is Ethiopia, but it is by no means the only one. Countries like the Congo, Benin, and Madagascar have experienced upheavals of a similar nature.

Although these conditions on the African side afford a partial explanation of the growth of Communist arms transfers to the region, the appearance of new openings in the area does not alone account for the behavior of the Communist states. A variety of motivations have caused the Communist states to move to exploit these openings.[16] The list includes:

1. *A wish to establish a local presence.* The precise reasons for wanting to have such a presence have differed from one Communist country to another. For the USSR, for example, presences in as many individual African states as possible serve to reinforce its claims to global-power status, for they confirm Moscow's reach. While China has forsworn all intentions of becoming a superpower, it does have pretensions to be a global actor, and the existence of a Chinese presence in any sub-Saharan African country gives substance to these pretensions. In the case of Yugoslavia, presences in those states in the area that belong to the nonaligned movement strengthen Belgrade's international position as a practitioner of nonalignment. Such presences perform much the same function for Romania, despite its formal adherence to the Warsaw Pact. For the German Democratic Republic (GDR), a presence in any country of the region enhances its legitimacy as a German state distinct from the Federal Republic. With respect to the East European states in general, presences in countries with raw materials and minerals of use to East European economies help to ensure access to those raw materials and minerals.

2. *A desire for political influence in a given country or with a given national liberation movement.* This desire has had both positive and negative aspects. Sometimes it has merely entailed an intention to enlarge one's own influence, but not infrequently it has involved a wish to curb the influence of another actor as well.

Here again, the ultimate goals have not been the same for every Communist state. The Soviet Union, for its part, has invariably wanted to bolster its assertions that it is a global force to be reckoned with; at the same time, it has often hoped to reduce the influence of the West, particularly the United States, and China. Since the late 1960s, China has focused on curtailing Soviet influence, but it has also been interested in validating its perceived status as the chief mentor of the Third World. Yugoslavia has been concerned to build up clout in sub-Saharan Africa and other areas of the Third World to help it resist any pressures the USSR might try to bring to bear on it. Romania has had similar ends in mind. As for the other East European states, and especially the GDR, they have concluded that an ability to affect events in sub-Saharan Africa and elsewhere in the Third World increases their potential usefulness to the USSR and thereby gives them a degree of leverage on Moscow's policies toward them.[17]

3. *A hope to obtain access to facilities of military use.* In the case of the USSR, requests for such access have at times coincided with or followed the promise of arms. For instance, Moscow in the early 1970s agreed to ship major new supplies of weapons and equipment to Somalia for a quid pro quo. Specifically, Mogadishu consented to the setting up of a Soviet naval complex at Berbera and to Soviet use of certain Somali airfields to reconnoiter the Indian Ocean. In 1975–1976, the USSR and its Cuban and East European allies provided the military means for the Movimento Popular para Libertação de Angola (MPLA) to install itself in power in Angola. Then, in October 1976, Soviet and Angolan leaders signed a treaty of friendship and cooperation that called for "cooperation in the military sphere" on the basis of unpublished "agreements which are being concluded between them."[18] This "cooperation" has included Soviet access to Luanda airfields for purposes of conducting reconnaissance flights over the sea-lanes of the Atlantic Ocean, and visits of Soviet military vessels to Angolan ports. Events moved in a similar fashion in the wake of the USSR's massive arms transfers to Ethiopia in 1977–1978 during the warfare between Ethiopia and Somalia in the Ogaden. Moscow received permission from Addis Ababa to establish facilities on one of the Dahlak Islands off Massawa to provide upkeep for Soviet naval vessels operating in and near the Red Sea.

4. *A wish to earn hard currency.* During recent years, the economies of the USSR, China, and the East European states have all fallen on hard times, and these countries have attempted to solve a lot of their economic problems through imports, especially from the West. Since they have found it hard to come up with the kinds of goods that the West has wanted to buy, they have experienced severe balance-of-payment difficulties. In this context, they have looked with marked interest at the possibilities

of obtaining hard currency through arms sales to Third World countries, especially those that have benefited from rising oil prices. The Soviet Union has been particularly attracted to such a method of raising hard currency, for it not only ranks as the leading manufacturer of conventional arms in the world but also has long evinced a reluctance to discard obsolescent weapons and equipment. Indeed, one estimate places Soviet military deliveries for hard currency at about 65 percent of total Soviet military deliveries to the Third World in 1971–1980.[19]

The relative weight of these considerations in the calculations of individual Communist states, however, has differed. As regards the USSR, a combination of a desire for a local presence and a wish to have a say in local affairs appears to have provided the major impetus for arms transfers to sub-Saharan Africa over the years, but the importance of these two factors has grown substantially since the early 1970s because of Moscow's increased emphasis on military instrumentalities to pursue its goal of winning recognition as a global power. During the 1950s and 1960s, Soviet leaders had looked upon economic means as the USSR's primary tool for achieving this end in the Third World. While military instrumentalities had always had a role, they had not been dominant. The reversal that took place in the 1970s can best be illustrated with respect to sub-Saharan Africa by one set of statistical comparisons. In 1956–1964, the value of Soviet arms transfers to the area ran about half that of the economic assistance that Moscow extended to it. The two were about equal in 1965–1974 (with the value of economic aid offered totaling 96 percent of that of arms transfers), but the value of economic credits proffered in 1975–1979 constituted only 28 percent of that of arms transfers.[20] A hope of gaining access to facilities of utility to Soviet military forces has certainly had a place in Moscow's decisions about arms transfers to sub-Saharan Africa, but that place seems to have been quite secondary. Certainly, the USSR has over a period of years continued to furnish arms to a number of African states that have not given it access to such facilities. Although a desire to earn hard currency has provided a key push to Soviet arms transfers to Third World countries in general since the early 1970s, it has not played a very significant role with regard to those in sub-Saharan Africa. Nigeria has been the prime target for cash sales; however, the value of these sales ($80 million in 1975–1979) has not begun to approach the value of the weapons and equipment that the USSR has supplied to its two leading clients in the region, Angola and Ethiopia ($410 million and $1,300 million, respectively, in 1975–1979).[21]

In the case of China, a wish to establish a local presence and a desire for local influence appear to have constituted the sole reasons for its arms transfers to sub-Saharan Africa. As far as is known, Beijing has not requested access to facilities of use to its armed forces from any of the countries to which it has supplied weapons and equipment. Nor has it expended visible effort to market arms to states in the area with the ability to pay for them—for example, Nigeria. In light of China's limited capabilities to provide arms, moreover, Beijing has relied primarily on other means to create a presence and gain influence. Its economic-aid commitments to states in the region, for instance, totaled $1,973 million in 1970–1979, while its arms transfers in 1964–1978 amounted to just $191 million.[22]

For all the East European countries as well, the motivations behind their arms transfers to sub-Saharan Africa have been essentially a desire for a local presence and a hope to obtain a voice in local affairs. None has evidently sought access to facilities of utility to its own military from recipients of its arms, and none has appeared to strive to drum up sales in states capable of paying cash for arms—at least since the increase in oil prices gave these states significant cash resources. The thrust of the motivations of Yugoslavia and Romania, however, has tended to differ somewhat from those of the remaining East European countries. Both have wanted to set up presences and exert influence in sub-Saharan Africa to demonstrate and help sustain their independent positions in the global arena. The other East European states, in contrast, have been largely concerned about employing presences and influence to enhance their standings with the USSR.

Import of Transfers

The critical issue regarding the growing flow of Communist arms to sub-Saharan Africa, of course, is exactly how it should be interpreted. Its meaning can be assessed in several ways.

One involves some gross statistical comparisons. During 1974–1978, the arms transfers to states in the region from the Communist countries for which data are available—that is, the USSR, China, Czechoslovakia, and Poland—reached $3,065 million. Those of the United States and its major NATO allies—notably France, Great Britain, Italy, the Federal Republic of Germany (FRG), and Canada—totaled only $1,345 million, including $397 million to South Africa and Rhodesia.[23] For purposes of comparability, the sum for China should obviously be excluded from the Communist figure, in light of Beijing's quarrels with Moscow. However, the country data at hand cover fewer of the key states among the USSR's Warsaw Pact allies than they do of the key states among the NATO allies of the United States. Moreover, the Soviet Union and its allies have furnished a sizable, but unknown, amount of weapons and equipment to national-liberation movements in sub-Saharan Africa, while the NATO countries apparently have provided none. A reasonable adjustment to correct for these skewing factors would probably bring the Communist total back to roughly the $3,065-million level. On that assumption, then, the arms transfers of the USSR and its allies to the overall area in recent years would seem to have run about twice those of the United States and its allies, and deliveries to black-African elements, more than three times as much.

A quantitative look at recipients of arms in sub-Saharan Africa, though, modifies the picture to a fair degree. During 1974–1978, the four Communist countries for which data are obtainable sent weapons and equipment to twenty-two black African states in the region and to national-liberation movements in two other countries (Rhodesia and Namibia). But in the cases of three of the African states, China was the sole Communist supplier, so the Soviet Union and its allies provided arms to nineteen states plus national-liberation movements in two countries. The United States and its major NATO allies shipped weapons and equipment to twenty-three black African states and to South Africa and Rhodesia during the same years. Of this total, eleven black African states and South Africa and Rhodesia acquired no arms from any Communist country, and three other black African states got arms only from China. Thus, direct competition between members of the Warsaw Pact and NATO appears to have taken place only in nine instances.

In sum, the USSR and its allies have in recent years tended to furnish arms to black African elements that do not obtain arms from the United States and its Western allies, and they have also concentrated their attention on fewer countries than the NATO allies have. Indeed, two black African states—Angola and Ethiopia—accounted for more than half of the weapons and equipment, in value terms, that the Warsaw Pact countries delivered to the area in 1974–1978.[24]

Another approach to gauging the import of the rising Communist arms transfers entails analysis of a more qualitative kind. As already mentioned, twenty-two black African states and national-liberation movements in two additional countries received Communist weapons and equipment in 1974–1978. Five of these—Cape Verde, Equatorial Guinea, Gambia, Guinea, and Guinea-Bissau—got arms solely from Communist sources, and thirteen others—Angola, Benin, Chad, the Congo, Ethiopia, Madagascar, Mali, Mozambique, Somalia, Tanzania, and Uganda, plus liberation movements in Rhodesia (Zimbabwe) and Namibia—obtained them primarily from such sources. The USSR was either the only or the principal supplier in all cases except Gambia, which acquired its weapons and equipment from China.[25]

It is difficult to see, however, that these seventeen entities most dependent on Soviet arms shipments all qualify as inherently significant.

In strategic terms, several of them lack even a potential to furnish ports of call for the Soviet navy. By no stretch of the imagination, furthermore, is it possible to discern attributes that might prove of particular military utility to the USSR for more than about two-thirds of them, and these in some cases relate to scenarios that are rather far-fetched in the near term. Ethiopia and Somalia might provide territory for the launching of efforts to control traffic into and out of the Red Sea or to disrupt the sea-lanes through which oil from the Persian Gulf travels on its way to the United States and Western Europe. Tanzania, Mozambique, and Madagascar also might serve in the latter respect—although less effectively, since they are farther down the east coast of the continent. In the west, Cape Verde, Guinea-Bissau, and Guinea might afford facilities from which the Soviet Union could deploy naval forces in the North Atlantic or carry out reconnaissance of the Western sea-lanes there, and Angola, the Congo, and a black-ruled Namibia might do the same vis-à-vis the South Atlantic.

From a political and economic standpoint, the number of conceivably important entities is even smaller. Angola and Mozambique constitute two key front-line states in the black struggle against white-minority governments in southern Africa. Moreover, Angola has sufficient mineral resources and economic potential to render it of future consequence in the broader context of sub-Saharan African politics. Of the remainder, only Ethiopia, Tanzania, and a black-controlled Zimbabwe come near to passing muster on either political or economic grounds. The first does so because of the size of its population and territory; the second, in light of the magnitude of its population and the personality of President Julius Nyerere; the third on the strength of its economic potential.

A final perspective for appraising the implications of the mounting Communist deliveries of weapons and equipment derives from the apparent motivations of the suppliers. Specifically, it employs the degree of fulfillment of goals as the criterion for evaluation. Here presence, political influence, and access to facilities of military value are the relevant considerations, for, as noted earlier, the earning of hard currency has seemed to figure only marginally in the reasons that the Communist states have furnished arms to sub-Saharan Africa.

As African desires for weapons and equipment have heightened, arms transfers have become increasingly effective for creating presence. By and large, however, that effectiveness has been directly proportional to the amount of weapons and equipment supplied. The massive Soviet arms shipments to Angola and Ethiopia, for instance, have made the leaders of these states far more conscious of the USSR than the small Chinese deliveries to Somalia and Mozambique have rendered the rulers of these countries sensitive to China.[26] In short, the main beneficiary of arms transfers in terms of presence has been the Soviet Union, in view of the extent of its deliveries to the region.

The matter of political influence is a lot more complicated than that of presence. Where African entities have received large quantities of Communist arms and have seen an overwhelming need to keep such arms flowing, Communist arms transfers have had some impact on their policies, at least those involving questions of peripheral interest to them. The votes of the governments of Angola, Mozambique, and Ethiopia against the U.N. resolution in January 1980 condemning the Soviet invasion of Afghanistan provide a classic illustration. But even in such cases, there have been decided limits to how far these entities have been willing to bend. If the desires of a Communist arms supplier have run counter to their own deeply held convictions about their interests, they have not hesitated to follow their own inclinations. Somalia, for example, in 1977 rejected out of hand Soviet proposals to resolve its dispute with Ethiopia over the Ogaden within the framework of a Marxist federation of the two countries, even though Mogadishu was totally dependent on Moscow for weapons and equipment at that time.[27] Furthermore, African entities that have felt themselves confronted with a continuing, overriding need for Communist arms have tended to be the exception, not the rule. Most currently sovereign African countries, for instance, have never experienced this sense of urgency or have done so only temporarily. Under such circumstances, Communist arms transfers have had relatively little effect on policies. Political influence, if it has come at all, has stemmed largely from other instrumentalities like economic aid and trade, and all the Communist states have in practice employed such tools sparingly.[28]

As for access to facilities of military value—essentially a Soviet motivation—the record of accomplishments can only be termed mixed. During the 1970s, Moscow's armed forces did win permission from the governments of Somalia, Angola, and Ethiopia to use the local facilities described earlier. They also gained regular access to port facilities in Conakry, Guinea, for the Soviet West African Patrol and to air fields elsewhere in the country from which naval aircraft could conduct aerial reconnaissance of Atlantic sea-lanes and U.S. carrier transits along them. Yet before the close of the decade, Mogadishu had deprived the USSR of the use of all Somali facilities, and Guinea had ended Soviet reconnaissance flights from its airfields.[29] Moreover, Moscow has failed to chalk up new advances in this sphere over subsequent years.

Prospects

The last issue that deserves attention concerns the future. Will Communist arms transfers to sub-Saharan Africa remain at present levels and perhaps even increase, or will they decline?

Some signs point to the possibility of a decrease in demand for arms on the African side in the years ahead. For example, the emergence of a black African government in Zimbabwe committed to a reconciliation of the races has had a substantial impact on the situation in southern Africa, and a political settlement in Namibia could ease tensions there still further.

Nevertheless, the thorny problem of South Africa will not go away easily, and conflict in that troubled country may well worsen before it subsides. In the rest of sub-Saharan Africa, too, internal and interstate strife promises to continue to be fairly high—even where real economic progress is taking place. Most African states still lack institutional frameworks for channeling political conflict in peaceful directions, and the OAU, despite the positive role that it has played in trying to resolve the turmoil in Chad, is at best a marginally effective means of handling conflict anywhere on the continent. Thus, the Communist states will, in all likelihood, have plenty of openings to furnish new arms to the region in the 1980s.

Will the Communist countries endeavor to exploit these opportunities? In the case of China, there are good reasons for serious doubt. Because of its limited ability to supply arms, Beijing had already nearly opted out of competition with the USSR in this realm by the late 1970s, and the emphasis of the post-Mao leadership on military as well as economic modernization of China suggests that there will probably be few resources available to reverse this posture, even if the will to do so exists. The Soviet Union is quite another matter. As the main producer of conventional arms in the world, it has the capacity to deliver large quantities of weapons and equipment to other countries. In addition, Moscow in the 1970s decided that military means, and especially arms transfers, constitute the most efficacious tools for pursuing its ends in sub-Saharan Africa, and it has not suffered enough in the way of setbacks in moving toward these goals in ensuing years to render a change of mind on this subject likely in the foreseeable future. Hence, the USSR will probably be diligently looking for arms clients. In this event, so too will the East European states, although largely to advance their own special interests vis-à-vis Moscow.

Since the Soviet Union and the East European countries have accounted for the great bulk of Communist deliveries of arms to sub-Saharan Africa in recent years, the outlook for any reduction of the flow, then, appears fairly dim. At most, it will in all likelihood stay at the level that it had reached by the early 1980s.

Notes

1. See M.J.V. Bell, *Military Assistance to Independent African States,* Adelphi Papers, no. 15 (London: International Institute for Stra-

tegic Studies, December 1964), p. 11; Captain E. Hinterhoof, "The Soviet Military Aid and Its Implications," *Fifteen Nations* (February–March 1962): 79–87.

2. Calculated by the author on the basis of data in U.S. Central Intelligence Agency, *Communist Aid Activities in Non-Communist Less Developed Countries, 1979 and 1954–79*, ER 80-10318U (Washington, D.C., October 1980), pp. 14, 38, and 40; U.S. Arms Control and Disarmament Agency, *World Military Expenditures and Arms Transfers 1969–1978* (Washington, D.C., December 1980), pp. 161–162.

3. U.S. Central Intelligence Agency, *Communist Aid*, p. 14.

4. Ibid.

5. Calculated by the author on the basis of data in U.S. Central Intelligence Agency, *Communist Aid*.

6. Ibid., especially p. 15.

7. Ibid., p. 14.

8. Both commitments and deliveries calculated by the author on the basis of data in U.S. Central Intelligence Agency, *Communist Aid* p. 40; U.S. Arms Control and Disarmament Agency, *World Military Expenditures and Arms Trade 1963–1973* (Washington, D.C.: U.S. Government Printing Office, 1975), pp. 67–68; U.S. Arms Control and Disarmament Agency, *World Military 1969–1978*, pp. 161–162.

9. Both pledges and transfers calculated by the author on the basis of data in U.S. Central Intelligence Agency, *Communist Aid* p. 38; U.S. Arms Control and Disarmament Agency, *World Military 1963–1973*, pp. 67–68; U.S. Arms Control and Disarmament Agency, *World Military 1969–1978*, pp. 161–162. The figure for pledges, it should be pointed out, does not cover the commitments of Yugoslavia, for information on the extent of these is lacking.

10. Compiled by the author from information in U.S. Arms Control and Disarmament Agency, *World Military 1969–1978*, pp. 161–162. The total of twenty-two recipients in 1974–1978, it should be noted, somewhat understates the number of recipients since Communist arms began to flow to sub-Saharan Africa. Ghana, for example, got arms in the 1960s during the rule of Kwame Nkrumah but disappeared from the list of recipients in the 1970s.

11. For further discussion of Zimbabwe and Namibia, with sources, see David E. Albright, "The Communist States and Southern Africa," in *Southern Africa: International Issues and Responses*, Gwendolyn Carter and Patrick O'Meara, eds., (Bloomington, Ind.: Indiana University Press, 1982).

12. The statistics in the preceding paragraph were derived by the author from data in U.S. Arms Control and Disarmament Agency, *World Military 1963–1973*, pp. 67–68; U.S. Arms Control and Disarmament

Agency, *World Military 1969–1978,* pp. 161–162. On the question of arms transfers from Czechoslovakia and Poland to national-liberation movements in southern Africa prior to the mid-1970s, see, for instance, Otto Pick, "Czechoslovakia's Presence in Black Africa," *Radio Free Europe Research,* 19 March 1979; Roman Stefanowski, "Poland's Presence in Black Africa," *Radio Free Europe Research,* 1 March 1979; William F. Robinson, "Eastern Europe's Presence in Black Africa," *Radio Free Europe Research,* 21 June 1979.

13. For more detailed treatment of this topic, see Colin Legum, "African Outlooks toward the USSR," in *Communism in Africa,* David E. Albright, ed., (Bloomington, Ind.: Indiana University Press, 1980), pp. 7–34; I. William Zartman, "Coming Political Problems in Black Africa," in *Africa and the United States: Vital Interests,* Jennifer Seymour Whittaker, ed., (New York: New York University Press 1978), pp. 87–119.

14. For more extended discussion of this trend and the factors contributing to it, see Legum, "African Outlooks toward the USSR," especially pp. 12–24; Colin Legum, " 'National Liberation' in Southern Africa," *Problems of Communism,* 24 (January–February 1975); pp. 1–20; and Colin Legum, "The Impact of the Communist States on Africa's Politics," in *The Communist States and Africa,* David E. Albright and Jiri Valenta, eds., (Bloomington, Ind.: Indiana University Press, forthcoming).

15. It is important to observe here, however, that neither kind has as yet produced a political entity that analysts in at least the vast majority of Communist states regard as a "true" Marxist-Leninist one. For further exploration of this issue, see David E. Albright, "Moscow's African Policy of the 1970s," in *Communism in Africa,* particularly pp. 42–45; David E. Albright, "The Soviet Role in Africa from Moscow's Perspective," in *The Communist States and Africa;* Bruce Larkin, "China and Africa: Politics and Constraints," in *The Communist States and Africa;* Melvin Croan, "East Germany and Africa," in *The Communist States and Africa;* Michael J. Sodaro, "The GDR and the Third World: Supplicant and Surrogate," in *Eastern Europe and the Third World: East vs. South,* Michael Radu, ed., (New York: Praeger, 1981), especially pp. 109–111; Trond Gilberg, "Romania, Yugoslavia, and Africa: 'Nonalignment and Progressivism,' " in *The Communist States and Africa.*

16. See the ensuing contributions in this section. For treatment of these motivations in the context of the overall policies of the Communist countries toward sub-Saharan Africa, see Albright, "Moscow's African Policy of the 1970s," "The Soviet Role in Africa from Moscow's Perspective," and "The Communist States and Southern Africa"; Larkin, "China and Africa: Politics and Constraints"; George T. Yu, "Sino-

Soviet Rivalry in Africa,'' in *Communism in Africa,* pp. 168–188; Croan, "East Germany and Africa"; Gilberg, "Romania, Yugoslavia, and Africa: 'Nonalignment and Progressivism.' ''

17. To be sure, the pattern of the arms transfers of these East European countries to sub-Saharan Africa has conformed fairly closely to that of the arms transfers of the USSR, but it would be a mistake to suggest that East European leaders have entered into arms agreements with African states and national liberation movements against their will and with no thoughts of self-interest. Such interpretations vastly oversimplify a complex situation.

18. The text of the treaty is in *Pravda,* 9 October 1976.

19. See Wharton Econometric Forecasting Associates, "Soviet Exports of Arms to Developing Countries," *Centrally Planned Economies Current Analysis,* 22 January 1982.

20. Calculated by the author from information in U.S. Central Intelligence Agency, *Communist Aid Activities in Non-Communist Less Developed Countries, 1979 and 1954–79,* pp. 14 and 39; U.S. Arms Control and Disarmament Agency, *World Military Expenditures and Arms Transfers 1965–74* (Washington, D.C.: U.S. Government Printing Office, 1976), p. 75. Detailed breakdowns on Soviet deliveries of economic assistance are not available to compare with Soviet deliveries of arms.

For elaboration of Moscow's changing views on the means to employ to implement its policy toward the African continent as a whole, see Albright, "The Soviet Role in Africa from Moscow's Perspective."

21. For the totals, see U.S. Arms Control and Disarmament Agency, *World Military 1969–1978,* pp. 161–162.

22. Both economic aid commitments and arms transfers calculated by the author from data in Yu, pp. 170–171; U.S. Central Intelligence Agency, *Communist Aid Activities in Non-Communist Less Developed Countries 1978,* ER 79-10412U (Washington, D.C., September 1979), pp. 7–8; U.S. Central Intelligence Agency, *Communist Aid,* pp. 18–19; U.S. Arms Control and Disarmament Agency, *World Military 1963–1973,* pp. 67–68; U.S. Arms Control and Disarmament Agency, *World Military 1969–1978,* pp. 161–162. There are no detailed breakdowns in unclassified sources on Chinese deliveries of economic assistance to compare with Chinese deliveries of arms.

23. Calculated by the author on the basis of data in U.S. Arms Control and Disarmament Agency, *World Military 1969–1978,* pp. 161–162.

The USSR delivered $2,880 million worth of weapons and equipment to black African states; China, $110 million; Czechoslovakia, $45 million; Poland, $30 million.

France topped the list of individual Western suppliers with $355 million to black African states, $380 million to South Africa, and $5 million to Rhodesia. It was followed by the United States with $165 million to black African states and $20 million to South Africa; Italy, with $158 million to black African states and $7 million to South Africa; Great Britain, with $130 million to black African states; the FRG, with $95 million to black African states; and Canada, with $45 million to black African states and $5 million to South Africa.

24. All figures on African states calculated by the author on the basis of information in *World Military 1969–1978*. On Communist arms transfers to the national liberation movements in the area, see Albright, "The Communist States and Southern Africa."

25. This discussion relies on data in U.S. Arms Control and Disarmament Agency, *World Military 1969–1978*, pp. 161–162, and, in the case of the liberation movements, on a wide number of reports in the Western press.

26. On this general point, see Legum, "African Outlooks toward the USSR," and Legum, "The Impact of the Communist States on Africa's Political Development."

27. For further analysis of the Somali case, see David E. Albright, "The Horn of Africa and the Arab-Israeli Conflict," in *World Politics and the Arab-Israeli Conflict*, Robert O. Freedman, ed., (Elmsford, N.Y.: Pergamon, 1979), pp. 147–191.

28. For general discussion of this question, see Legum, "The Impact of the Communist States on Africa's Political Development." For a brief overview of Communist economic assistance to sub-Saharan Africa, see U.S. Central Intelligence Agency, *Communist Aid 1979 and 1954–79*, pp. 38–40. Figures for Communist trade with the region across time may be found in the same document, pp. 24–25.

29. For details and sources, see Albright, "Moscow's African Policy of the 1970s," pp. 50–52.

3 Soviet Arms Transfers in the 1980s: Declining Influence in Sub-Saharan Africa

Edward J. Laurance

There is little doubt that the decade of the 1970s saw the Soviet Union emerge as the principal supplier of arms to sub-Saharan Africa. There is almost total agreement on the nature and specifics of this effort. Soviet support of the former Portuguese colonies of Angola and Mozambique was massive, as was its support of Ethiopia in its war with Somalia. Its arms-for-bases behavior in Guinea, Mali, Congo, Equatorial Guinea, Benin and Guinea-Bissau is generally known to have been important not only in the context of the Angolan civil war, but also in support of the Rhodesian insurgency forces. And finally, arms-aid programs with Zambia and Tanzania were helpful in forging a relationship with the so-called front-line states in the fight against Rhodesia and South Africa.

However, the observer surveying the scene in the summer of 1982 sees a totally different picture. As only one example, a systematic look at western coverage will produce very little on Soviet arms transfers to sub-Saharan Africa. This was hardly the case in 1979–1980. Those holding the view that the Soviets have not let up in their effort to gain influence in Africa through arms have to look a little harder these days. As an example, the South African raid on Namibia's South-West African People's Organization (SWAPO) in September 1981 produced this comment from Evans and Nowak: "The death of two Russians in the SWAPO raid is evidence that Moscow seeks to transform black-African guerrilla actions into a conventional war capability against South African-controlled Namibia and eventually South Africa itself."[1]

There was no shortage of analyses, in the 1979–1981 time period, that concluded that the Soviets would continue to supply arms as they had in the past.[2] Yet, the supply of SWAPO, and several other small-scale efforts to established clients, is a far cry from the surge of the 1970s, which produced a significant amount of analysis and commentary that can only be described as anti-Soviet and alarmist. This chapter will attempt to explain what has happened to significantly reduce Soviet arms transfers and to most likely keep them low for the foreseeable future.

This look at Soviet arms transfers is made more interesting because of the anti-Soviet arms-transfer policy of the Reagan administration.[3]

Administration witnesses from the Secretary of State on down made it
clear that the purpose of U.S. arms transfers is to contribute to a global
defense against the Soviet Union. In Africa, the effort to rescind the Clark
amendment limitation on arms transfers to groups such as UNITA
(National Union for the Total Independence of Angola) in Angola is
typical of the effort. Yet, as this chapter will demonstrate, the significantly
diminished Soviet effort does not warrant such a policy focus in Africa.

Briefly, this chapter will summarize the Soviet arms-transfer pattern
of the 1970s and explain it in terms of three dimensions: (1) Soviet
foreign-policy goals; (2) the structure and process that define the Soviet
military-industrial complex; and (3) the African factors that create the
demand for Soviet weapons. This approach yields the conclusion that
Soviet arms transfers in the 1970s appear to have been less related to a
grand strategy and more to an optimum historical period when all three
of the above forces interacted to produce Soviet dominance in arms
transfers to sub-Saharan Africa. Further, events since the achievement
of Zimbabwe's independence in 1980 have served to reinforce the view
that the low profile of the Soviets will hold for the foreseeable future.

Soviet Arms Transfers in Brief

The undeniable ascendance of the Soviet Union as the primary supplier
of conventional arms to sub-Sahara Africa in the 1970s can be readily
documented. First, table 3–1 describes, in dollar terms, the deliveries to
sub-Saharan states by all suppliers. It will be noted that a step-level
increase occurs between 1974 and 1975. Angola, Nigeria, and Uganda
account for most of the increase, corresponding to the massive supplies
to Angola and Mig–21 deals with Uganda and Nigeria. The large jump
in 1976 is due to Angola. The 1977 and 1978 data show an even larger
increase due to Soviet transfers to Ethiopia. Clearly, more arms went into
the region, and most (at least in terms of dollars) are Soviet. Table 3–2
shows Soviet-bloc deliveries by recipient for the five-year period
1974–1978. These Soviet deliveries represent 58 percent of all arms
delivered to sub-Saharan Africa in the period. Smaldone has constructed
tables that demonstrate acquisition styles (tables 3–3 and 3–4).[4] A comparison of his tables with the 1974–1978 period (table 3–5) shows some
interesting shifts. The most noteworthy is the number of sub-Saharan
states with a predominant or solely Soviet connection increased from four
to eleven during this recent decade.

Table 3–6 contains the highlights of Soviet arms transfers to the
region in the decade of the 1970s. These data make it clear that the effort
was concentrated in the years 1975–1979. To complete the description

Table 3-1
Arms Deliveries to Sub-Saharan African States
(millions of constant 1977 dollars)

	1969	1970	1971	1972	1973	1974	1975	1976	1977	1978
Angola						6	133	243	200	176
Benin							5	10	10	9
Cameroon			0	0	0	0	0	5	10	4
Chad			0	0	0	0	0	5	5	0
Congo	0	0	14	0	0	0	11	0	30	0
Equitorial Guinea	0	0	0	14	0	0	11	0	0	9
Ethiopia	16	15	14	14	13	12	33	52	430	1024
Gabon	0	0	0	0	0	0	0	10	10	9
Ghana	0	0	0	0	0	12	11	21	20	37
Guinea	0	0	14	7	13	12	22	10	0	18
Guinea-Bissau							0	0	9	0
Ivory Coast	0	0	7	14	13	0	5	10	10	65
Kenya	0	0	14	0	0	36	11	0	10	46
Madagascar	0	0	0	7	0	0	0	10	5	18
Mali	0	0	0	0	6	0	11	21	30	46
Mauritania	0	0	0	0	0	0	0	21	21	18
Mozambique							33	10	30	111
Nigeria	48	7	7	23	26	24	100	52	10	37
Rwanda	0	0	0	0	0	0	0	5	0	9
Senegal	0	0	0	0	0	0	0	0	10	18
Somalia	16	15	0	0	53	109	77	105	80	158
Rhodesia (Zimbabwe)	0	0	0	28	6	12	5	0	10	0
Sudan	32	61	7	14	13	36	0	5	10	55
Tanzania	8	7	44	26	26	6	11	52	60	55
Togo	0	0	0	0	0	0	11	10	10	9
Uganda	0	0	0	0	13	12	77	31	5	18
Upper Volta	0	0	0	0	0	0	5	0	0	0
Zaire	0	15	29	56	26	60	33	126	20	27
Zambia	1	7	7	28	13	12	22	31	20	55
Total (1968–1977)	121	127	157	231	221	349	627	845	1065	2031

Source: USACDA, *World Military Expenditures and Arms Transfers, 1969–1978* (Washington, D.C.: U.S. Government Printing Office, 1980).

Table 3–2
Soviet-Bloc Arms Deliveries to Sub-Saharan States
(millions of current dollars)

	1974–1978
Angola	440
Benin	20
Burundi	5
Cape Verde	20
Chad	10
Congo	30
Equitorial Guinea	10
Madagascar	20
Mali	100
Mozambique	135
Nigeria	80
Somalia	300
Sudan	30
Tanzania	110
Uganda	120
Zambia	40
Total	2870

Source: USACDA, *World Military Expenditures and Arms Transfers, 1969–1978.*
Washington, D.C.: U.S. Government Printing Office, 1980).

of Soviet arms transfers, some brief comments concerning specific countries follow.

Rhodesian Insurgency

As the fight for Rhodesia escalated, so did the Soviet role in supplying the guerrillas, with particular emphasis on Nkomo's Zimbabwe African People's Union (ZAPU).[5] The Soviets favored ZAPU over Mugabe's Zimbabwe African National Union (ZANU) because of the latter's People's Republic of China (PRC) connection, and a linkage that dated back to the early 1960s. It should be noted that although Soviet transfers to ZAPU were significant (but relatively unsophisticated), some restraint was shown due to absorption and financial problems. The Soviets attempted to alleviate this by sending significant numbers of guerrillas for advanced weapons training to Cuba and the Soviet Union.

The last major Soviet-bloc military effort occurred in the summer of 1979 when Nkomo visited East Germany. One report stated that the East Germans boosted their presence from 1500 to 4500 advisers, to be stationed with both ZAPU and ZANU and to coordinate the final Patriotic Front push to topple the Rhodesian government.[6] Additional equipment, such as SA–7 antiaircraft missiles, artillery, and small arms were also

Table 3–3
African Arms-Acquisition Styles, 1961–1971

Sole Supplier (100%)		Predominant Supplier (50%)		Multiple Supplier (50%)		
West	East	West	East	West	East	Cross-bloc
Central African Republic (Fr.)	Mali (USSR)	Cameroon (Fr.)	Algeria (USSR)[a]	Niger		Ghana
Dahomey (Fr.)		Chad (Fr.)	Congo (USSR)[a]	South Africa		Libya[b]
Gabon (Fr.)		Ethiopia (U.S.)	Egypt (USSR)[a]	Zambia		Morocco[b]
Malawi (U.K.)		Ivory Coast (Fr.)	Guinea (USSR)[a]			Nigeria
Senegal (Fr.)		Kenya (U.K.)	Somalia (USSR)[a]			Sudan
Sierra Leone (U.K.)		Liberia (U.S.)	Tanzania (PRC)[a]			Uganda
Upper Volta (Fr.)		Malagasy Republic (Fr.)				
		Mauritania (Fr.)				
		Togo (Fr.)				
		Tunisia (U.S.)				
		Zaire (U.S.)				

Sources: Joseph P. Smaldone, "Soviet and Chinese Military Aid and Arms Transfers to Africa: A Contextual Analysis," in *Soviet and Chinese Aid to African Nations*, Warren Weinstein and Thomas H. Henrikson, eds. (New York: Praeger, 1980), p. 87. Copyright © 1980 Praeger Publishers. Reprinted by permission. Basic typology derived from Robert E. Harkavy, *The Arms Trade and International Systems* (Cambridge, Mass.: Ballinger, 1975), pp. 7, 104–105, 111–115; however, 50 percent is used here to differentiate predominant- from multiple-supplier relationships, instead of the 60 percent used by Harkavy. Statistics calculated from U.S., Arms Control and Disarmament Agency, *The International Transfer of Conventional Arms: A Report to the Congress*, House Committee on Foreign Affairs, 93d Cong., 2d sess., April 12, 1974, Committee Print, table III, pp. A13–A14.

[a]Despite their predominant Eastern arms connection, these states also maintained cross-bloc ties with Western military suppliers.

[b]Largely dependent on Western-bloc suppliers.

Table 3–4
African Arms-Acquisition Styles, 1967–1976

Sole Supplier (100%)		Predominant Supplier (50%)		Multiple Supplier (50%)		
West	East	West	East	West	East	Cross-bloc
Liberia (U.S.)	Equatorial Guinea (USSR)	Benin (Fr.)[a]	Algeria (USSR)[a]	Ivory Coast		Burundi[b]
	Gambia (PRC)	Central African Empire (Fr.)[a]	Angola (USSR)	Niger		Cameroon[b]
	Guinea-Bissau (USSR)	Ethiopia (U.S.)	Egypt (USSR)[a]	Rhodesia		Chad[b]
		Gabon (Fr.)	Guinea (USSR)	Togo		Congo
		Kenya (U.K.)	Libya (USSR)[a]			Ghana[b]
		Senegal (Fr.)	Mali (USSR)[a]			Madagascar[b]
		So. Afr. (Fr.)	Mozambique (USSR)			Malawi[b]
		Tunisia (U.S.)[a]	Somalia (USSR)[a]			Mauritania[b]
		Upper Volta (Fr.)	Sudan (USSR)[a]			Morocco[b]
			Tanzania (PRC)[a]			Nigeria[b]
			Uganda (USSR)[a]			Rwanda[b]
						Zaire[b]
						Zambia[b]

Note: Ethiopia abruptly shifted to Soviet arms during 1977–1978.

Sources: Joseph P. Smaldone, "Soviet and Chinese Military Aid and Arms Transfers to Africa: A Contextual Analysis," in *Soviet and Chinese Aid to African Nations*, Warren Weinstein and Thomas H. Henrikson, eds. (New York: Praeger, 1980), p. 88. Copyright © 1980 Praeger Publishers. Reprinted by permission. Basic typology derived from Robert E. Harkavy, *The Arms Trade and International Systems* (Cambridge, Mass.: Ballinger, 1975), pp. 7, 104–105, 111–115; however, 50 percent is used here to differentiate predominant- from multiple-supplier relationships, instead of the 60 percent used by Harkavy. Statistics calculated from U.S.. Arms Control and Disarmament Agency, *World Military Expenditures and Arms Transfers 1967–1976*, Publication 98 (Washington, D.C.: July 1978), table VII, pp. 158–59.

[a]Despite their predominant-supplier relationship, these states maintained cross-bloc ties with other military suppliers.

[b]Largely dependent on Western bloc suppliers.

Table 3–5
Sub-Saharan African Arms-Acquisition Styles, 1974–1978

Sole Supplier (100%)		Predominant Supplier (50%)		Multiple Supplier (50%)		
West	East	West	East	West	East	Cross-bloc
Botswana (UK)	Equitorial Guinea (USSR)	Kenya (US)	Angola (USSR)	Ivory Coast	Madagascar	Cameroon 2,3
Liberia (US)	Guinea-Bissau (USSR)	Niger (Fr.)	Congo (USSR)	Malawi		Ghana 2
	Gambia (PRC)	South Africa (Fr.)	Ethiopia (USSR)	Rhodesia		Mauritania 2
		Upper Volta (Fr.)	Guinea (USSR)	Togo		Nigeria 2,4
			Mozambique (USSR)	Gabon		Sudan 2,3,4
			Somalia (USSR)	Senegal		Tanzania 5
			Uganda (USSR)			Zaire 2,3
			Benin (USSR)			Zambia 2,3,4
			Cape Verde (USSR)			Burundi 4
			Chad (USSR)			
			Mali (USSR)			

Source: U.S. Arms Control and Disarmament Agency, *World Military Expenditures and Arms Transfers 1969–1978.* (Washington, D.C.: U.S. Government Printing Office, 1980).

Notes: 1. Designation of USSR as supplier includes supplies from Poland and Czechoslovakia
  2. Largely dependent on western bloc supplies
  3. Cross-bloc with PRC
  4. Cross-bloc with USSR
  5. USSR supplied 61% of Tanzania's arms, the PRC 17%

Table 3–6
Equipment Deliveries to African States

Country	Years	Equipment
Angola	1975–1980	85 T34 Tanks
		150 T54 Tanks
		50 PT–76 Tanks
		150 BTR–50/–60/–152 APC
		ZSU–23–4 SP AA Guns
		SA–6/–7 SAM
		20 Mig–21 MF fighters
		18 Mig–17F fighters
		100 BM–21 122mm MRL
		Sagger Anti-Tank Missiles
Mozambique	1976–1980	300 T–34, 50 PT–76 Tanks
		50 BRDM–1/–2 Armored Cars
		200 BTR–40/–152 APC
		BM–21 122 mm MRL
		Sagger Anti Tank Missiles
		30 SA–3/–7 SAM
		35 Mig–17/–21
Ethiopia	1977–1980	150 T34, 600 T54/–55 Tanks
		40 BMP–1 APCs
		500 BTR–40/–60/–152 APC
		BM–21 122mm MRL
		Sagger Anti-Tank Missiles
		ZSU–23–4 SP AA Guns
		SA–2/–3/–7 SAM
		1 OSA Missile Boat
		17 Mig–17, 50 Mig–21, 20 Mig–23 Fighters
		16 Mi–24 Armed Helicopters
Madagascar	1978–1980	PT–76 Tanks
		ZPU–4 14.5mm AA guns
		4 Mig–17, 8 Mig–21 FL Fighters
Nigeria	1977–1979	65 T–55 Tanks
		30 ZSU–23–4 SP AA Guns
		6 Mig–17, 12 Mig–21 MF Fighters
Tanzania	1977–1980	50 BTR–40/–152 APC
		10 BM–21 122mm MRL
		SA–3/–6/–7 SAM
		11 Mig–21, 10 Mig–19, 3 Mig–17
Zambia	1979–1980	60 T54/–55 Tanks
		50 BRDM–1/–2 Scout Cars
		30 BM–21 122mm MRL
		SA–3/–7
		12 Mig–19, 16 Mig–21
Congo	1975–1980	66 TR 50/–60/–152 APC
		9 Mig–15, 1 Mig–17 Fighter
Guinea	1970–1980	30 T34/–54 Tanks
		20 PT76 Tanks
		40 BTR–40/–152 APC
		8 Mig–17 Fighters
		4 Il–14
Mali	1976–1980	37 T–34 Tanks
		30 BTR–40 APC
		10 BTR–152 APC
		SA–3 SAM
		5 Mig–17

Table 3–6 continued

Country	Years	Equipment
Guinea-Bissáu	1976–1980	T–34 Tanks BTR–40/–152 APCs SA–7 SAM

Source: *The Military Balance 1981–1982* (London: International Institute for Strategic Studies, 1981).

included as part of the package. Research of *The London Times Index* reveals that the last mention of the Soviets involvement in Rhodesia was a July 30, 1979 dispatch reporting that the USSR was holding back on arms deliveries to the Patriotic Front because of disunity among factions.[7]

In 1976, President Machel's call for help to defend his nation against Rhodesian raids was answered by several Communist countries, including the Soviet Union. To meet his internal-security needs, Machel increasingly turned to the Soviet bloc to aid in the fight against two resistance groups that have been backed by South Africa.[8] The conflict continued despite the settlement of the Rhodesian conflict, although Mugabe of Zimbabwe may begin to replace the Soviet bloc in this struggle.[9]

Tanzania

Starting in 1974, Tanzania shifted its dependence for military supplies from the PRC to the USSR.[10] While Tanzania played a major role as an avenue of transit in the Rhodesian conflict, its major use of weapons occurred in the 1979 invasion of Uganda. Most of the weapons employed were Chinese, and there was no known Soviet advisory role. In 1980 Tanzania purchased some tanks, artillery, and aircraft, thereby showing a desire to maintain links with the Soviets as arms suppliers.

Zambia

Prior to the fall of 1978, Kaunda appeared to be holding off the transfer of Soviet arms into his country.[11] But the Rhodesian air strikes of October 19 and November 2 resulted in an immediate call for help. The British responded,[12] but by December Kaunda said that "up to now the West hasn't actually given us anything real. I know that the East is ready to help."[13] The help came in a $85.4-million arms deal announced in Lusaka on February 7, 1980. The transfer included sixteen Mig–21 aircraft, and unspecified numbers of tanks, armored cars, and APCs [armored personnel carriers].[14] Iraq formed the bulk of the training contingent,[15] and the equipment was sold on hard commercial terms. Apparently, Soviet negotiators demanded a sizeable downpayment, perhaps as high as 20 percent. Zambia's neighbors, Mozambique and Angola, have been receiving Soviet military assistance on much more favorable terms.[16]

Ethiopia

The Soviet arms transfers to Ethiopia in 1977–1978 are well documented. The initial bloc of supplies was delivered by the largest air-resupply mission in Soviet history, utilizing 15 percent of Soviet aircraft capacity. The relatively high level of Ethiopian training, in addition to crash training in the USSR, allowed this quick supply of weapons to be used in a relatively short period of time, but not without a significant influx of Cubans to operate the equipment. Arms supplies dropped off in late 1978 and 1979 as the Ethiopian Dergue sought to absorb the equipment, consolidate their military gains and concentrate on critical economic problems.[17] In a highly publicized trip to Moscow in November 1980, Mengistu asked for and eventually received more than twenty MI–24 helicopter gunships for use in Eritrea.[18]

Guinea

Soviet arms transfers to this long-standing client have dropped in the past several years. "The President is peeved at Moscow for not living up to its commitment to equip, train and resupply Guinea's armed forces. These were promised as payment for use of Guinean facilities (oil storage, airfield and naval) to support Moscow's growing military involvement in Southern Africa. Conakry has received less than $40 million of the $1.4 billion in Soviet arms that have poured into tropical Africa in the past five years."[19] In the past few years Guinea has received but a few armored vehicles and some patrol boats.

Cape Verde

The Soviets sent about fifty military advisers to Cape Verde in 1978, along with thirty tanks and armored cars. A 1000-ton Soviet landing craft also visited the islands with two deep-sea patrol boats.[20]

Determinants of Soviet Arms Transfers

We now turn to an examination of the factors that interact to produce the foreign-policy outcome of interest—Soviet arms transfers. For analytical purposes, we will begin by concentrating solely on how factors indigenous to the Soviet Union effect arms transfers in general.

Foreign-Policy Objectives

Listed below is a composite of often-cited Soviet foreign-policy objectives that are served by arms transfers.[21]

1. Establish presence, gain a voice in affairs of recipient country.
2. Undermine or neutralize Western influence in developing world, particularly as it relates to the supply of raw materials.
3. Extend the Soviet defense perimeter and capability to project military power.
4. Enhance internal security of allies and clients
5. Support insurgencies and wars of national liberation consistent with Soviet ideology.
6. Encourage domestic communist movements, particularly those developing in the general direction of the Soviet model.
7. Promote Soviet leadership in the Communist world while preempting or reducing Chinese influence.
8. Improve balance of payments.

Structural Factors

In addition to the above objectives designed to focus Soviet behavior, there are a series of structural factors indigenous to the Soviet Union that impact on the ability to accomplish such objectives.

Large Production/Stockpiles of Conventional Weapons. The Soviet Union is the largest producer of conventional arms in the world. Compared to the United States, they produce six times as many tanks, eight times as many artillery pieces, three times as many APCs, and twice as many combat aircraft per year. The Soviets also are reluctant to discard obsolete weaponry.[22] "In most cases exports are the optimum solution of the problem of the enormous weapons surplus. . . . this export is cheap and carried out without procrastination."[23]

To the above explanation must be added the effect of a planned economy. "The rhythm of Soviet arms exports and the chronology of the Soviet five-year plans are very probably interconnected," concludes a recent study.[24] It can be presumed that unless foreign-policy considerations intervene, arms supplies go first to the Soviet armed forces, then to allied countries, and last to others. With a six year cycle starting in the first year of a five-year plan, exports to the third world would thus surge upwards in the second year of each five-year plan (except the first). This timing is actually the most common case."[25]

Military-Oriented Economy. The major cause of the first factor is an economy geared mainly to the satisfaction of military goals and doctrine. As one example, "every modernization of the tank units of the Soviet Army leads to the formulation of a surplus of several thousand units."[26] This surplus is also caused "by the creation of a huge productive capacity in industry, adapted notably for the satisfaction of the army's needs. A large part of the machine pool of these industries is narrowly specialized and its adjustments to civilian production would require major expenditure and is, more often than not, impossible."[27] The excessive productive capacity and surplus stocks mean that no additional productive factors are required for their export, especially when compared with civilian goods. These factors combine and prompt many observers of Soviet economics to report that weapons are the only commodity in which the Soviets are internationally competitive. As a final note, the above evidence leads us to conclude that the Soviets are not as competent in economic sectors, such as agriculture, that eventually become high priority for most developing countries. "There is no question that the Soviet Union has a decided comparative advantage in the production of arms. The military industry is by far the most efficient manufacturing industry in the Soviet Union; it may even be more efficient than some of the Soviet raw material extracting industries."[28]

Growing Hard-Currency Debt. The Soviets have borrowed heavily (more than $40 billion) in order to purchase badly needed machinery, technology, and food. A major source of hard currency has become weapons sales.[29] "The Middle East with its huge hard currency income is the only region in the world in which it is potentially possible to turn soft-currency goods, like arms, into hard currency."[30] The days are past when the Soviet gave away first-line military equipment, as even politically important countries such as Ethiopia, Zambia, and Mozambique well know.

Growth of Soviet Navy. The Soviet Navy has significantly increased its capability for the global projection of power, to influence local conflict and counter western power.[31] Although their objective is to minimize dependence on foreign facilities, this overall growth, and the expense of support ships, drive them to seek on-shore facilities whenever possible. This includes maintaining access to important airfields for use in surveillance of Western naval activity. MccGwire's work reveals that the USSR decision to opt for a "blue-water" navy as opposed to one of coastal defense predates their recent interest in African facilities[32] (for example, Guinea, Angola, Somalia, and so forth). McConnell and Dismukes show that although the decision was made early on, it took eight–twelve years for the first naval hardware to be produced for the new mission of naval diplomacy. By 1970, the capabilities were such that facilities in Africa became a genuine need.[33] According to the Soviet naval leader, Gorshkov, the new forward-deployed Soviet Navy even has a role to play in "defending the 'national liberation movement,' a phrase representing whatever the Soviet Union regards as positive change in areas like Africa . . . the Soviet Navy must establish a (permanent) 'presence' in these regions and on a scale grand enough to avoid empty bluffing."[34] Haselkorn's most recent analysis concludes that "the modification in Soviet military doctrine to include an 'external function' for the Soviet Armed Forces apparently occurred in the early 1970s."[35] As for the capabilities required to carry out this new doctrine, he cites recent trends in naval construction as an important component. In short, the Soviet Navy has become a crucial element in Soviet foreign policy.

Need for Supply Lines to Support Clients Logistically. Distinct from the foreign-policy goal of supporting wars of national liberation with weapons is the fact that the Soviets must establish supply routes requiring landing sites for aircraft and communications facilities. For example, countries such as Mali and Equatorial Guinea were used in the Angolan operation.

Highly Centralized Logistics Procedures. This well-publicized aspect of the Soviet economic system impacts on arms transfers in two ways. First, Soviet advisors accompanying the equipment can be very inflexible, especially when it comes to spare parts. Whereas the United States plugs a client into its computerized logistics system, the Soviets are more likely to keep a minimal amount of spares in-country and make a special request for each part needed. Second, the Soviets rarely establish major maintenance facilities in client states. Each faulty engine must be shipped back to the USSR. While the effect of this phenomenon may be superior control over the client (who understandably is not happy with this process), the point here is that it is as much a function of the Soviet system and structure as it is foreign-policy manipulation.

Demand for Operational Testing. The capabilities for projection of power, in terms of both airlift and naval forces, having been created, it seems logical that pressure would be created to use it. This structural factor finds its best expression in Allison's organizational-process model.[36] As an example, the Soviet counterpart to the head of the U.S. Military Airlift Command (and other organizations with resupply functions) would welcome and support the efforts of his colleagues to supply massive amounts of equipment, as was done in Ethiopia and Angola.

Presence of Allies Willing or Required to Support Arms Transfers. Put simply, the Soviets have Warsaw Pact nations and Cuba, which for various reasons have performed vital roles in the transfer of arms to developing countries.

Experience in Internal Security and Population Control. The Soviets, East Europeans, and Cubans have developed control of their people, both psychologically and physically, to a fine art. Their obvious lack of concern about how the world views such practices significantly reduces the barriers for its export.

The "Ugly Russian." There is no shortage of evidence that even in so-called progressive developing countries that the Soviets assist, their reputation is one of arrogance, heavy-handedness, and condescension.

> In its relations with Somalia Moscow displayed the same arrogance and insensitivity for which it earlier had to pay so dearly in Egypt and Sudan. While the Kremlin constantly declares that its relations with developing countries are based on reciprocity and mutual respect, in practice Soviet officials appear to be dictatorial and patronizing. . . . This heavy-handedness and neo-colonial arrogance of Soviet diplomacy can prevent the Kremlin from enjoying the friendship of even those African states that are allied with Moscow.[37]

This structural factor is related to the factor of the presence of allies in that it appears that Soviet awareness of the reaction to their arrogant style has them using East Germans whenever possible.[38] The main point to be made in putting forth this factor is that the combination of Russian culture and Soviet ideology produces a government official who has little respect for the attributes, skills, or culture of his counterparts in the developing world.

Factors Determining Demand for Arms Imports in Sub-Saharan Africa

A Soviet Union, with the foreign-policy objectives, capabilities, and structure outlined in the preceding pages, does not operate in a vacuum. Goals must be accomplished in specific environments. It will be argued in this section that there is a common set of factors indigenous to sub-Saharan Africa that significantly influences Soviet arms transfers to the region. In economic terms, these factors combine to create the demand for arms imports to the region.

Centralized, Authoritarian Governments

Colin Legum observes that "in the post-independence period, nationalist forces of liberation, with very few exceptions, ceased to be mass popular movements. Most of the movements came under the control of particular power groups concerned with preserving their dominant positions in highly centralized governments."[39] Arms transferred to such governments can be directly linked to the donor, with either positive or negative implications. One must be careful, however, to distinguish between patron-client and one-party regimes with a certain level of legitimacy (for example, Obote's Uganda, Zambia) and those that rely on coercion (Amin's Uganda, Equatorial Guinea, Central African Empire). The effects of the arms-transfer effort will vary significantly with the type of authoritarian government, but in either case the impact is much more direct, especially when compared to a pluralistic regime fraught with interservice and political rivalries.

Racial Conflict

The struggle for independence from white colonial powers dominated conflict on the continent in the 1970s. The sudden collapse of the Portuguese empire, and the rise to power of new black governments, saw the emphasis shift to the conflicts in Zimbabwe, Namibia, and South Africa. There are no indications that the black-African states will let up in their struggle to topple the remaining white power on the continent, or that they will forego the option of using arms to do it.

Intrastate Conflict

Sub-Saharan Africa is dominated by unstable political structures characterized by frequent coups and cabinet shuffles. "Of the [Organization of African Unity] OAU's 29 founding fathers, two-thirds were deposed. In the 1960s, some 127 coups were staged; 37 succeeded. Nigeria's planned transfer to civilian rule may usher in a bright future, but the recent slayings of three past Ghanian heads of state . . . portrays the bleaker side of the current African era.''[40] In the 1970s, the settlement of the anti-Portuguese and anti-Rhodesian struggles saw an increase in intrastate conflict as the anticolonial factions fought for power. This type of conflict increasingly requires and, in fact utilizes, a far larger volume of arms and advisors than was previously the case (for example, Zaire, UNITA in Angola, Chad, and so forth).

Interstate Conflict

The conditions for interstate conflict remain well into the postindependence era, and may be worsening. ''The enormous borders, totaling some 28,750 miles, were ludicrously drawn up by Europeans in 1885. The boundaries make no economic, cultural or strategic sense. For instance, Morocco, Algeria, Libya, Somalia, Uganda, Malawi, Lesotho, and others have laid claim to a healthy chunk of their neighbors' territory, and few lines have peacefully been withdrawn.''[41] The recent Ethiopian-Somali and Ugandan-Tanzanian conflicts stand out as a unique and new type of event on the continent. Crocker makes the point that ''geopolitical concerns have been aroused by the discovery of raw material deposits and by the heightened vulnerability of many national economies to transport dependency on neighboring states as transport requirements grow.''[42] Bienen's 1980 piece concludes that ''African states have become more differentiated by wealth, power and military capability. More, not less, conflict can be expected between them.''[43]

Economic Underdevelopment

Despite the conflicts outlined above, and the power-security orientation of the elites, economic problems dominate the masses and the concerns of all but the most ruthless governments. The 1979 Organization of African Unions (OAU) Summit endorsed a report which concluded that ''Africa is unable to point to any significant growth rate over the two decades since independence. Africa's GNP [Gross National Product] accounts for only 2.7% of the world product; its per capita income ($365) is the world's lowest. Various U.N. reports declare that parts of Africa are un-developing: 12 states had a GNP lower in 1975 than in 1970.''[44] While it is obvious that the ingrained conflict requires both security and development, it seems that once the crucial armed struggles subside in intensity, attention is quickly turned to solving the overwhelming economic problems. This certainly appears to be the case in Angola, Ethiopia, Mozambique, Zambia, and newly independent Zimbabwe.[45] The extraordinary OAU summit held in Nigeria in 1980 to map out African economic strategy appears to be another indicator of the growing importance of this factor.

Low Levels of Military Effort

Sub-Saharan Africa has traditionally been an area that is basically un-dermilitarized. This is especially true in regard to the more sophisticated equipment such as tanks, fighter aircraft, missiles, and warships. This has several implications for arms transfers into the area. First, demands will be for less than first-line equipment from suppliers. Second, the potential for reactive purchases increases since it is increasingly likely that advanced systems being transferred will be the first of that type in a region. Third, it severely complicates the ability of the supplier to put a competent fighting force in the hands of the recipient without extensive training (and the consequent delays) or the use of surrogates to operate the equipment.

Zone of Air and Naval Transit between Other Regions

Despite the potential importance of strategic materials on the African continent, its most significant current strategic attribute is its location.[46] The build up of U.S. naval forces in the Indian Ocean in relation to Persian Gulf contingencies has seen Kenya and Somalia the object of United States attention in regard to base rights and facilities. Soviet interest in the potential disruption and denial of vital sea-lanes to the west requires their presence in a variety of locations along these routes. One must be careful not to characterize the entire continent as strategically important, since much of it is not.

Presence of Raw Materials Vital to Arms-Supplying Nations

The importance of sub-Saharan Africa's raw materials to the United States and the Western industrial states is well documented. Also, much of the Soviet activity is explained in terms of both obtaining access to materials needed by the Soviets and denying the same to the United States and West Europe.[47]

Anticolonial Ideologies

All but two African Countries—Liberia and Ethiopia—were colonized, all by Western arms suppliers. They became independent in a post–World-War-II era in which the Soviet Union actively employed anticolonialism as a major foreign-policy theme. A variant of this factor would be the presence of Western, capitalist-economic interests throughout the continent.

Metropole Linkages

Many African states either retained the ties with their former colonizers (for instance, Kenya) or have sought to improve relations after a hiatus following independence. France has recently made this linkage a more visible component of its foreign policy.[48] The Portuguese comeback is even more remarkable.[49] This clearly impacts on arms-transfer patterns in that the two major suppliers (the United States and USSR) historically stayed clear of Africa. The metropole linkages definitely limit potential recipients for those two suppliers, particularly in the long term.

Attitude toward Intervention and Imperialism

This factor cuts both ways in Africa. Many would say that, based on the 1970s, one can conclude only that Africans accept foreign intervention as a fact of life. "The norm of nonintervention by outsiders, certainly never upheld perfectly, has broken down completely."[50] "The Soviet Union's position has been strengthened by the African willingness to accept foreign intervention against white regimes in Southern Africa."[51]

On the other hand, African countries both individually and through the OAU clearly state that, while they appreciate the military assistance in the short term, they expect the supplier to bow out as quickly as possible.[52]

Lack of African Unity

The inability of the Organization of African Unity (or any of the several regional groupings) to resolve disputes has resulted in these nations increasingly enlisting the support of major extracontinental powers.[53] A related factor is the effort to create a Pan-African defense force. In the last half of the 1970s there was increased interest in such a force, leading to the OAU Defense Commission's adoption of guidelines for such a force in April 1979. However, at the July 1979 OAU summit, the Foreign Ministers Council expressed its "political determination" to establish the force, but sent it back to the Defense Commission for further study.[54]

Sanctity of Borders

Although the recent Ugandan-Tanzanian conflict strained the credibility of this principle,[55] the sanctity of colonially dictated borders is one of the areas of agreement among OAU members. This clearly effects arms supplies in that the supplier backing a client who violates the principle risks the wrath of Africans in general. The United States was reluctant to back a Somali invasion of the Ogaden, which was universally condemned while the Soviets reaped the benefits of backing an Enthiopia whose border objectives had the support of the OAU.[56]

The Interaction of Supply and Demand—1975 to 1980

Up to this point, we have established that during the last half of the 1970s there was a significant upsurge in Soviet arms transfers to sub-Saharan Africa. It is a major proposition of this chapter that this upsurge was due, in the main, to the historical convergence of long-standing Soviet objectives, recently gained capabilities, and a set of African environmental factors, all of which combined to foster, if not promote, the Soviet behavior. These factors, briefly described in the preceding pages, can be usefully combined in the form of table 3–7 to more clearly explain Soviet arms transfers. A plus mark indicates that the Soviet and African factors were reinforcing and worked together to foster Soviet arms transfers, as opposed to those of other suppliers. A minus mark indicates that these two factors worked against the probability that Soviet arms would be transferred.

The first observation to make is that the plus marks outnumber the minus by a significant margin. The Soviets appear to be on the mark in citing the "correlation of forces" that shifted in their favor. Additional insights are gained by examining some of the specific interactions. In one of the more clearcut examples, it can be seen that the objective of projecting power was reinforced by Africa's strategic location, the conflicts that drew this power to the continent, and the lack of African unity, which did not prevent and perhaps required, outside intervention. The fact that the continent was undermilitarized also means that such projection of power was unopposed. Once on the continent, the Soviets were in a much better position to promote and administer the transfer of arms to African states. Working against this projection of power were the metropole linkages maintained by many African states and the ingrained fear of outside intervention.

The Soviet objective of supporting wars of national liberation is obviously reinforced by the continent's history of colonialism and racial conflict. Where the colonial issue has disappeared, as in the case of some reestablished metropole linkages, one would not expect to see Soviet arms transfers employed using this foreign-policy rationale. If the foreign-policy goal was to improve balance of payments, Africa represented a poor target, given the low level of economic development. Encouraging communist movements fashioned after the Soviet model were intensified by the high levels of intrastate conflict, as well as by the undermilitarization that created the need for outside military assistance. The role of centralized governments in fostering the achievement of this objective is not so clear. It may in fact have worked against the transfer of arms (for instance, the Soviet's failed attempt to overthrow Numeiri in Sudan). Note also that the objective of undermining the People's Republic of China received no significant boost because of African environmental factors. The accomplishment of this objective hinged on factors more related to PRC capabilities than the African environment.

As for Soviet structural factors, the Soviet advantage in the African environment is readily apparent. The large stockpile of conventional weapons produced by their military-oriented economy was tailor-made for an undermilitarized continent that increasingly experienced interstate and large-scale intrastate conflicts in the 1970s. The growth of the Soviet navy preordained the search for facilities in a continent that has traditionally been a zone of air and naval transit between other regions. The demand created for operational testing, given the rise in Soviet power-projection capabilities, was increasingly satisfied, thanks to the high levels of conflict and the lack of African military force. The availability of the Cubans and East Europeans to act as surrogate advisors and operators of Soviet hardware obviously enhanced the prospects for Soviet transfers if a country was engaged in conflict, poor, and lacking equipment and qualified military personnel. The only Soviet structural factor that systematically worked against arms transfers was the arrogant, cynical, and heavy-handed style of the Soviet advisors. This minus was balanced to a significant degree by the presence of Cubans and East Germans more adept at operating in the African environment.

The column under the African environmental factors shows that the metropole linkages and fear of intervention tend to work against Soviet arms transfers. Economic underdevelopment is a mixed blessing for the Soviets, enhancing their objective of presence, while doing little for their hard-currency-debt situation.

There is no doubt that an analysis of this matrix that would include not only the selection of factors, but also the assignment of pluses and minuses to individual cells, is open to legitimate disagreement. However, the 1975–1980 period appears to present a valid explanation for the increase in Soviet arms transfers to sub-Saharan Africa. This is not to say that there are not competing and complementary explanations for the Soviet behavior. One school of thought maintains that a global strategic imbalance between the United States and USSR has encouraged Soviet adventurism, of which arms transfers to sub-Saharan Africa is a significant component.[57] Others focus on the ideological aspects of Soviet behavior.[58] Not to be neglected is the explanation of the upsurge in arms transfers in terms of internal Soviet politics,[59] and weakness or inaction on the part of the United States.[60] All of these approaches to the question undoubtedly improve one's understanding of the issue. However, the major advantage of the systemic approach is the disaggregation of the behavior into its component causes, allowing the analyst to accomplish the most important objective, predicting future trends by examining the changing nature of each individual supply-and demand-factor. It is to this task we now turn.

Soviet Arms Transfers in the 1980s

Soviet arms transfers to sub-Saharan Africa in the 1980s have slowed to a mere trickle compared to the 1975–1980 period. The 1980 package for Zambia appears to be the last big sale, although clients such as Ethiopia, Tanzania, Guinea, and Mozambique continue to purchase what can be categorized as replacement-level packages of equipment. *The Military Balance* lists no Soviet arms agreements for the July 1980–June 1981 period. The recent South African raids into Namibia made it clear that SWAPO uses Soviet equipment, but hardly on the order of the arms sent to ZAPU in the Rhodesian conflict. Just as the supply and demand factors produced an explanation for Soviet arms transfers in the 1970s, they also provide an explanation for a lack of transfers in the 1980s.

The Soviet Factors

If we look only at the Soviet side of the equation, we find that most of the objectives and capabilities point to a continued arms-transfer effort

Table 3–7
Interaction of Soviet and African Factors

	African Environmental Factors												
	Centralized Governments	Racial Conflict	Intrastate Conflict	Interstate Conflict	Economic Underdevelopment	Under-Militarized	Strategic Location	Raw Materials	Anticolonial Ideologies	Metropole Linkages	Fear of Intervention	Lack of African Unity	Sanctity of Borders
Soviet Foreign-Policy Objectives													
Presence			+		+	+	+		++				
Undermine West		+				++	+	+		−		+	
Project power			+	+		+				−	−		
Enhance internal security of clients	+	+	+			+			++				
Support wars of national liberation			+			++			++	−			
Encourage Communist movements	−					+				−			
Undermine PRC											−		
Improve balance of payments					−								
Soviet Structural Factors													
Large production/surplus conventional weapons			++	++	++	++							
Military-oriented economy			++	++	++	++							
Hard-currency debt					−	++							
Growth of navy						++	++						
Need for supply lines to support clients	+	+	+		+	++	+						
Centralized logistics	++	++			+	++	−						
Demand for operational testing			++	++		++	+				−	++	
Cuban/East-European surrogates			++	++	+	++	++			−	−	++	−
Expertise/experience with internal security	+									−	−		
Ugly Russian		−			−				−		−	+	

in sub-Saharan Africa. If anything, the foreign-policy objectives should get even more emphasis. For example, the growing relationship between the United States and the PRC seems to require a renewed effort to undermine the latter in the developing countries. The balance of payments problem will worsen in the 1980s, and her new-found confidence in projecting power is unlikely to diminish. As to structural factors, nothing seems likely to change. In fact, Hutchings has put forth a theory of Soviet arms transfers based on the five-year-planning cycle that predicts that "in the early 1980s, when the cycle is due to enter another period of upswing, Soviet arms delivers to the Third World in general are likely to rise again."[61] The internal bureaucratic pressure for operational testing will increase, and the attitudes and behavior that I have chosen to characterize as the "ugly Russian" certainly will remain part of the Soviet style.[62] The rise in the U.S. defense budget and the creation of a rapid-deployment force insures that large numbers of conventional weapons will continue to be produced by the Soviets as a response. The Soviet's penchant for centralized logistics procedures, resulting in poor service for clients, has the Ethiopian military grumbling in public.[63] About the only factor that is in any doubt as to its durability is the role of the Cubans and East Europeans, although the school of thought that posits increasing independent behavior on the part of these Soviet surrogates is quite speculative at this point.[64]

African Environmental Factors

The key, therefore, to assessing the 1980s is not the Soviet intentions and capabilities, which will remain basically unchanged. Rather, the important indicators to watch will be those indigenous to sub-Saharan Africa, to which we now turn.

Fear of External Intervention

Since its inception the OAU has recognized that a lack of unity has literally invited outside intervention by the major powers.[65] The Angolan situation seemed to spark a renewed interest in this weakness, and it has proceeded to grow ever since. Even though the OAU realized that external aid was needed in the Rhodesian insurgency, channeling the money through the OAU Liberation Committee had a significant impact on the Soviet's ability to shape the outcome. The 1977 OAU summit featured a split regarding how OAU member states should settle disputes, with an increasing number of calls for less interference from outside.[66] In

1978, Numeiri stated that "each invitation for intervention is followed by another for counter-intervention until this armed foreign presence was about to outstrip our capacity to defeat it."[67]

The Libyan invasion of Chad sparked an OAU interest in either a United Nations or an OAU peacekeeping force. An emergency summit meeting of the OAU was held in Nigeria on December 23, 1980, producing a communique that "urged that no foreign troops be stationed in the national territory of Chad except in accordance with the provisions of the Lagos accord of 1979, which speaks only of an OAU peace-keeping force."[68] Nigeria emerged as a force capable of forging African conflict resolution in lieu of unilateral external intervention (for example, from France).[69] President Moi of Kenya visited Nigeria in March of 1981, and the final communique called for an end to big-power rivalry, which was said to be causing instability in Africa.[70] "Getting the OAU strengthened by actually being involved in settling African problems like Chad, is one way of ensuring that superpowers do not unduly penetrate the continent."[71] One final note regarding this increasing emphasis on intervention, it was reported on September 22, 1981, that Guinea-Bissau had refused naval facilities to the Soviet Union in the Geba River Estuary. The Soviets had made similar unsuccessful approaches to Cape Verde.[72]

Movement toward a Pan-African Defense Force

The purpose of the preceding chronicle of events was to demonstrate that the concern for both external intervention and the lack of African unity to deal with it is, in fact, changing. While this concern is by no means unanimous, the trend seems clear. But just as obvious, changing attitudes alone are ineffective in stopping the intervention that is increasingly feared. Albright has correctly pointed out that the lack of OAU ability to either mediate disputes or resist intervention has become patently clear.[73] One of the keys to changing this situation is the formation of a pan-African defense force, an idea whose time may come in the 1980s.

The July 1978 OAU Ministerial Council meeting called for a study of "how to create a Pan-African Force in the light of the dangers threatening the continent and the OAU's efforts at decolonialization." To this end, the defense committee, established by the OAU charter, was to be reactivated to study different aspects of the question.[74] In April 1979, the OAU Defense Commission met and succeeded in adopting general guidelines establishing an OAU defense force, "a dream that had eluded the OAU since the days of Kwane Nkrumah."[75] It should be noted that the force is intended to address two of the three types of conflict that exist on the continent—racial and interstate. OAU official Peter Onu stated:

"The time of paying lip-service to the support of the front-line states is over" and, "The split amongst independent African states has sometimes been settled by force. . . . Africa must find a way in true African tradition to separate the combatants until a peaceful solution is found."[76]

The actual creation of the force received a setback when, at the July, 1979 meeting of the OAU Ministers Council, the plan developed by the Defense Commission was referred back to them for further study. "The feeling was that the OAU Defense Committee which drew up the report on the question should continue its studies with the aid of legal and financial experts."[77] The OAU defense ministers met again in April, 1981 for seven days and could not agree on the text of a protocol for creating an African defense force. They did recommend a series of basic organs for the force, but no new light was shed on questions of command, equipment, and deployment of the force, the major obstacles in the past.[78]

At the regional level considerably more progress has been made. In October, 1979, Zambia, Zaire and Angola signed agreements on security and economic cooperation, and declared that "none of the three countries would be used as launching pads by counter-revolutionaries."[79] In February 1980, the establishment of a defense force was discussed at a meeting of the Defense Committee of the Economic Community of West African States (ECOWAS). The committee consists of Nigeria, Togo, Liberia, Senegal and Ivory Coast. It was reported that "the idea of a regional defense force . . . is in accordance with the recommendations of the OAU Defense Commission guidelines," dating back to a 1971 recommendation to establish a regional defense system.[80] On May 30, 1981, thirteen of sixteen members of ECOWAS finalized and signed a defense pact, agreeing on joint maneuvers, a defense commission, and a defense council.[81]

In July 1981, the West African Economic Commission (Ivory Coast, Upper Volta, Mali, Mauritania, Niger, Senegal, Togo) signed a non-aggression and defense-aid agreement. It was conceived in 1977, at the time of the crusade against Soviet-Cuban influence.[82] Probably the biggest boost toward acceptance of an indigenous pan-African defense force is the developments in Chad. December 1981 saw the inter-African peace-keeping force in Chad taking shape. Troops from Senegal, Zaire, and Nigeria were in place, assisted by France (transported Senegalese troops), Britain (financial help for Nigerians) and the United States (supplies for the Zaire contingent).[83]

One final event provides some evidence that even Soviet clients are tending to look more to an African solution regarding their security. In the aftermath of the South African raid into Angola in September 1981, President dos Santos of Angola and the heads of state of the other front-line states appealed to all OAU members to extend urgent military aid to Angola in its efforts to drive out the racist South African invaders.[84] "One must wonder whether President dos Santos appeal constitutes an implied criticism of the Soviet Union and Cuba."[85]

Decreasing Level of Racial Conflict

Another African environmental factor that is undergoing obvious change is the level of racial conflict. The end of the conflict over Zimbabwe has seen a major decrease in the need for arms and military advisers. Whereas a 1978 headline read "Soviets, Cubans Filling Key Broker Role in Rhodesia," recent headlines read "The Russians' Greatest Reverse in Africa in Years" and "Marxist Tide Ebbs in Southern Africa." One U.S. official, when asked what the Soviets will do now in Zimbabwe, stated that they will "lie in the weeds and hope that Mugabe stumbles."[86] It is interesting to note that shortly after independence, Mugabe traveled to Mozambique and pledged military assistance in helping Machel rid himself of some old enemies.[87] In days past, such a situation was tailor-made for communist assistance.

　　None of this discussion is intended to dismiss the fact that the major white government in sub-Saharan Africa remains strongly entrenched in power. But in the short term, this racial conflict appears destined to be low level for several reasons. The terrain is qualitatively different than Zimbabwe, making a military effort to invade South Africa significantly more difficult. Second, the internal situation in South Africa is more stable than it was in Zimbabwe. Third, there is some evidence that South Africa and key African states are interested in some sort of negotiated settlement regarding Namibia.[88] Fourth, the leader of the insurgent forces in Namibia, Sam Nujoma, has not developed the support in Africa which Mugabe and Nkoma commanded in the last half of the 1970s.[89] All of these indicators point to a significant decline in racial conflict as the decade of the 1980s begins.

Continuing Problems of Economic Underdevelopment

As the racial conflict declines, the countries that triumphed in those conflicts have increasingly turned their attention to economics. Invariably this means a declining role for the Soviet Union. Nigeria has been outspokenly critical of the Soviet Union. "Soviet policy therefore is based on a short-term perception of Soviet defense needs. Economic aid, which is more open-ended, is generally given only to those countries whose socialism is closely linked to the Soviet prototype. Since in the longer run all African countries are primarily interested in furthering their economic development, Soviet policy tends to fall flat on its face sooner or later. . . . This has been the pattern in Sudan, Egypt and Somalia, with Angola and Mozambique soon, it seems, to follow. Guinea is another country which has decided to mend its fences with the West."[90] In Mozambique, Machel is consciously wooing Western investment, and has revived the private sector. "There is now an acceptance, albeit reluctant, in the ruling party's Central Committee that Western technology, enterprise and wealth is the only way Mozambique can achieve its development aims."[91] A similar pattern has occurred in Angola.[92] In a most significant event, dos Santos offered to negotiate with the United States in regard to ending the conflict with UNITA and restoring relations with the United States. The official Angolan news agency chose to give only two excerpts from the speech; one contained the offer, and the other quoted him as praising Ameican businessmen.[93] *The London Times* stated that "although potentially one of the richest countries in Africa, Angola is not being given a chance to develop its wealth because it has to spend most of its oil revenues on importing arms, as well as the food that is not being grown because of the guerrilla war being waged by UNITA guerrillas."[94]

When the Soviets moved in to assist Ethiopia, a Western diplomat in Ethiopia commented that "the Soviets have not done very well when it comes to economic assistance to African countries, so this is a test case."[95] From all accounts, things are not going well economically, and the Soviet Union will have an increasingly difficult time shifting the blame.[96]

In sum, it seems highly probable that, as economic problems increase in intensity, the Soviet role will decline for two reasons. First, they are not as equipped as other nations to aid in solving the problems. Second, their demand for hard currency will prevent any bargains on weapons, except in a case of extreme political importance. Ethiopia, for example, did not get its Soviet weapons free of charge, a fact that adds to her already significant economic woes. Zambia is another country forced to pay a high price for Soviet arms. Since the United States long ago stopped giving away arms, the inability to pay for arms may bring a general decline in such purchases.

Metropole Linkages

There is a growing amount of evidence that the metropole linkages, which were previously cited as a deterrent to Soviet arms transfers, are growing and will increase as an important force on the continent. The French and

Portuguese have already been cited. Portugual's African policy consists
of three levels of interaction: (1) Bilateral socioeconomic relations with
each of its five former colonies; (2) encouraging linkages among the five;
and (3) furtherance of the broader Eurafrican connection as viewed from
the perspectives of the EEC and NATO.[97] The point here is that the
renewed Portuguese presence competes directly with the Soviet Union.
This is especially true in Guinea-Bissau where "Portugal has the Russians
to the sidelines in the fishing industry and where Portuguese doctors,
teachers and technicians are proving an effective counterbalance to the
Soviet and Cuban presence in the area."[98] As for French influence, the
People's Republic of the Congo, "generally characterized as one of Africa's more radical Marxist-Leninist states, has remained in the franc
zone nearly 20 years after independence and has come full circle to the
pragmatic operating principle that French economic cooperation and coun-
selling are more dependable than those of the Soviet Union."[99]

The year 1979 saw the reappearance of another metropole linkage,
Spain and its former colony Equatorial Guinea. The latter had had a
ruthless dictatorship supported by the Soviet Union. When a coup occurred in 1979, Spain was quick to respond with tons of food, medicine,
doctors, police and military assistance, all valued at over $23 million.
Meanwhile, the Soviets have lost their fishing rights and the use of the
port of Luba, which is generally believed to have served as a staging port
for the Angolan operation.[100]

It should be noted that this resurgence of metropole linkages is much
more than symbolic or socioeconomic. All of the former colonizers are
significant producers of military hardware which they must continue to
export to support indigenous production for their own forces.[101]

Undermilitarization

In regard to the undermilitarization of the continent, one would have to
conclude that the situation in the 1980s is quite different from what it
was in 1970. As the first part of the chapter indicated, arms transferred
into sub-Saharan Africa increased significantly in both quantity and quality. Several developments would point to a leveling off of such transfers.
First, as already mentioned, they cost money. Given the decline in racial
conflict which was so overriding that money (and debt) was no object,
states will be less likely to purchase new arms. Second, any large purchase
of arms takes time to absorb. Third, there appears to be a decline in
military governments and the accompanying pressure for high defense
budgets. Fourth, some of the biggest doses of arms have not resolved the
conflicts as intended by purchasers. Angola continues to experience armed

conflict and, despite very high casualties, the Eritreans have not been defeated by Ethiopia.

Regional Factors Promoting a Continuing Soviet Presence

While the above analysis tends to support the conclusion that Soviet arms transfers have declined and will remain at a low level, this decline might be even lower were it not for the following events and circumstances.

Increasingly Militant Foreign Policy of South Africa

There is no shortage of commentary and analysis that make two succinct points. First, generally coinciding with the election of Ronald Reagan, the South Africans began to talk and eventually act tough toward Angola and Mozambique. Second, such a policy almost insures that Soviet and Cuban advisors stay around until some sort of successful conclusion of these conflicts. For example, the raid into Mozambique in January 1981 brought an instant Soviet response in the form of Soviet-ship visits and increased military assistance.[102]

Continuing Conflict

In addition to the South African related conflicts, other indigenous conflicts involving Soviet-arms recipients seemed destined to continue. The Eritrean conflict is still boiling, with little hope for enough of a solution to allow some demilitarization of the situation, and, hence, less reliance on the Soviets. In addition, there are continuing efforts on the part of the disparate Eritrean groups to unite,[103] and the OAU efforts to resolve the conflict have been useless.[104]

Zambia offers an example of how a strictly internal conflict can insure Soviet, and in this case, East German presence. Kaunda finds himself struggling to suppress coups from a labor movement with help from his East German police apparatus. It is a prime example of what Singleton refers to when he cites the Soviets as "working against, not with, the forces of history, hence the present Soviet efforts to maintain a strong internal presence in countries of socialist orientation and to facilitate the evolution of communist organizations out of what are essentially military dictatorships."[105] Problems such as those of Kaunda also exist in Ethiopia, Mozambique, Angola, and several other arms clients of the Soviet Union.

It remains to be seen how long such presence remains a positive factor on the Soviet balance sheet.

U.S. Foreign Policy

An administration that comes into office with a vociferous anti-Soviet policy should expect to see a hardening of the Soviet position worldwide. Sub-Saharan Africa is no exception. To the extent that U.S. arms transfers to the region increase, it creates a convenient rationale for continued Soviet transfers. There is some evidence that the Reagan election saw a general cooling of the pro-Western economic trends in several countries.[106] And finally, the closer U.S.-South African connection has not gone without notice in Africa. The June 1981 OAU summit had a stronger anti-United States tone than normal. The United States veto of the U.N. vote condemming South Africa for its September raid into Angola drew a uniformly hostile reaction from black African states and gave the Soviet Union much-needed fuel for its effort to sustain its presence and influence in the region.

The 1970s: A Balance Sheet

Overall, the preceding analysis shows a changing set of systemic factors that forecast a decline in Soviet arms transfers to sub-Sahara Africa. Any objective Soviet decision maker should see it that way. Albright has pointed out that the level of Soviet involvement will be based partially on "what payoffs Moscow believes it has derived from its past activities and may gain from altering the intensity of them."[107] Before the conclusion of this forecast of Soviet arms transfers for the 1980s, here is a brief assessment of the payoffs from their efforts in the 1970s. On the plus side, they succeeded in gaining access to enough facilities to accomplish their major foreign-policy objectives in the region.[108] The Soviets appear to always have more than enough clients to take losses in stride. Ethiopia has replaced Somalia. As Guinea got piqued over Soviet behavior, we saw renewed efforts in Mali and Cape Verde. The Soviets had some form of base rights or access in Benin, Guinea, Congo, Angola, Mozambique, Ethiopia, and Mali. As one recent analysis notes, "the issue is not only whether the Soviets can manage to make permanent geopolitical and ideological gains in Africa . . . but how much damage is done in the meantime."[109] Also on the plus side is their bringing to power the Movimento Popular para Libertaçao de Angola (MPLA) in Angola, and the number of states professing to be Marxist-Leninist. They have clearly gained on the PRC, but this may have had more to do with declining Chinese capabilities than a preference for Soviet assistance. The Ethiopian venture allowed for a major operational test of new capabilities for the projection of power, and the successful use of Cubans and East Europeans seems to have decreased the normally negative reactions to the Soviet style of advice and assistance.

But a rational Soviet decision maker would have to conclude that Soviet arms resulted in an equal amount of negative payoffs, which should provide a sober backdrop for the rest of the 1980s. In the 1970s, the Soviets were asked to remove or diminish their military presence in the following countries: Sudan, Somalia, Equatorial Guinea, Nigeria, Guinea, Chad and Uganda. In addition, the Soviets no longer are the sole supplier of arms to any sub-Saharan state. While the number of bases they secured for use in the 1970s was adequate, they were obviously disappointed when Mozambique, Guinea-Bissau and Cape Verde specifically denied them naval-base rights. In the short term, the switch from supplying Somalia to arming Ethiopia appeared to pay off. The naval bases in Somalia were easily replaced by the Aden facilities and those constructed in Dahlak Island. And Soviet-Ethiopian relations reached a peak when the Ethiopians regained the Ugaden from Somalia with massive help from Soviets and Cubans. However, the Ethiopians have been unable to defeat the Eritrean insurgents and "there has been criticism of the patronizing attitude of the Russian advisors and grumbling about the spare supply of spare parts and ammunition."[110] Arms do not seem to have overcome the problem of a Marxist-Leninist military force attempting to defeat a genuine national-liberation struggle.

The Outlook for the 1980s

In his piece, "The Natural Ally: Soviet Policy In Southern Africa," Singleton provides the most succinct argument for a continuing Soviet effort in sub-Saharan Africa, despite the evidence that regional factors have been working against its success since the late 1970s. "Southern Africa *is* important to Soviet policy basically because it is the last area in Asia and Africa where Leninism makes sense and the Soviets really are the natural ally."[111] The United States-South African relationship insures that this role will continue, but, there is little else to sustain the Soviet hope that they can make further gains.

The pragmatic, nonideological Soviet planner, looking at the sub-Sahara in the 1980s will find little to support the zeal of his ideological colleagues who foster the natural-ally image.

He should see a declining level of racial conflict, which for two decades has provided an entree into the region. Intrastate conflict and political instability will continue to characterize the region, but no special advantage accrues to the Soviets here. It would be hard to forecast interstate conflicts, but the Soviets are prepared to help any socialist states that ask. The states of the region will increase their attention to solving economic problems, and as their socialist client in Mozambique has so well demonstrated, the Soviet record is not appreciated. The militarization by the Soviets of many sub-Saharan states in the 1970s will insure continued presence in the 1980s, but impatience with Soviet training methods and a cumbersome supply system (as in Nigeria) will see such presence decline. In addition, absorption problems and lack of money will naturally slow arms purchases. The African anticolonial ideologies that fit so nicely with Marxist-Leninist concepts for the past twenty years have significantly declined in importance with the conclusion of the Zimbabwe conflict. Metropole linkages are increasing, as are the level of African unity, the fear of external intervention, and the movement toward pan-African defense forces.

Have Soviet arms transfers brought influence? Clearly they have led to presence, but this has only been transformed into influence in a selective and transient way. Soviet influence is maximal when conflict is high and the Soviets are the primary arms suppliers. Conflict has subsided the Africans have begun to diversify their arms purchases, and by the end of the decade of the 1980s, the Soviets may find themselves in a significantly lower position in the hierarchy of arms suppliers to sub-Saharan Africa.

Notes

1. Rowland Evans and Robert Novak, "Moscow's Designs on Africa," *The Washington Post,* 18 September 1981, p. 29.

2. Joseph P. Smaldone, "Soviet and Chinese Military Aid and Arms Transfers to Africa: A Contextual Analysis," in *Soviet and Chinese Aid to African Nations,* Warren Weinstein and Thomas H. Henriksen, eds., (New York: Praeger Publishers, 1980), p. 110; David E. Albright, "Moscow's African Policy of the 1970s," in *Communism in Africa,* David E. Albright, ed., (Bloomington, Ind.: Indiana University Press, 1980); also see, David E. Albright, "Overview of Communist Arms Transfers to Sub-Saharan Africa," this volume.

3. Anthony H. Cordesman, "Facing the New Soviet Threat: U.S. and Soviet Competition in Arms Exports and Military Assistance," *Armed Forces Journal International* (August 1981):65–68, 70–72; Michael R.

Gordon, "Competition With the Soviet Union Drives Reagan's Arms Sales Policy," *National Journal,* 16 May 1981, pp. 869–873.

4. Smaldone, *Soviet and Chinese,* pp. 87–88.

5. International Institute for Strategic Studies, *Strategic Survey 1978* (London: 1978), p. 48, 92; Richard Deutch, "The African Arms Race," *Africa Report* (March–April 1979), p. 48; William Beecher, "Soviet Aid to Rhodesia Guerrillas," *The Boston Globe,* 29 October 1978, p. 69.

6. Norman Kirkham, "E. Germans to Lead Rhodesian Guerrillas," *London Times,* 1 July 1979, p. 1.

7. *The London Times,* 30 July 1979, p. 4c.

8. John Darnton, "Mozambique, with Cuban Help, Is Shoring Up Its Internal Security," *The New York Times,* 24 June 1979.

9. "Voice of Free Africa: Criticizes Zimbabwe's Mugabe," *FBIS-Sub-Saharan Africa,* 30 May 1980.

10. U.S. Central Intelligence Agency, *Communist Aid to Less Developed Countries of the Free World,* 1976, ER 77–10296 (Washington, D.C.: August 1977), p. 19.

11. Kaunda's reaction to the Soviet/Cuban intervention in Angola was to refer to "the tiger and his cubs stalking in the continent." See Colin Legum, "African Outlooks Toward the USSR," in *Communism in Africa,* David E. Albright, ed., p. 22.

12. Alexander MacLeod, "Britain Steps Up Aid to Zambia," *Christian Science Monitor,* 1 November 1978, p. 5.

13. "Zambia: Kaunda in Soviet Arms Proposals," *Strategic African Affairs,* (22 December 1976):2.

14. "Zambia's MIGs," *African Index* (10 February 1980), p. 5; "Zambia To Get Jets, Weapons From Soviet," *The Baltimore Sun,* 5 February 1980, p. 2.

15. Sol Sanders, "Russia's Mastermind For Southern Africa Strategy," *Business Week* (17 March 1980).

16. Ibid.

17. CIA, *Communist Aid to Less Developed Countries of the Free World, 1977,* p. 17; "New Ministries Established to Aid Socialist Development," in *FBIS Daily Report: Sub Sahara Africa VIII,* 18 May 1979, p. B1; *Strategic Survey 1978,* p. 98.

18. "The Horn: Rumblings In Every Camp," *Africa Confidential,* 22, no. 25 (February 1981).

19. CIA, *Communist Aid to Less Developed Countries of the Free World, 1977,* p. 21

20. Norman Kirkman, "Russian Base in Atlantic," *London Sunday Telegraph* 18 June 1978, p. 1, transcribed in *FBIS Daily Report: Western Europe VII,* 119 (20 June 1978), p. Q1.

21. Smaldone, *Soviet and Chinese*, pp. 3–4; Also see, David Albright, "Soviet Policy," *Problems of Communism* (January–February 1978), pp. 28–35; U.S. Congress, House, Committee on International Relations, *The Soviet Union in the Third World: A Watershed in Great Power Policy?* Report by the Congressional Research Service, 95th Cong., 1st Sess., 1977; George E. Hudson, *Soviet-Black African Military Relations: A Proposition and Framework About Soviet Military Intentions and Behavior*. Paper presented at the Annual Meeting of the Midwest Political Science Association, Chicago, April 1978; Chester Crocker, *Motivations For External Military Assistance to African States: A Policy Perspective;* Paper presented to the eighteenth Annual Meeting of the African Studies Association, October 1975.

22. Donald Rumsfeld, Secretary of Defense. *Annual Defense Department Report FY 1978* (Washington, D.C.: Government Printing Office), p. 11

23. Michael Checinski, "Structural Causes of Soviet Arms Exports," *Osteuropa Wirtschaft* (Munich, September 1977), p. 178.

24. Raymond Hutchings, "Soviet Arms Exports to the Third World: A Pattern and Its Implications," *The World Today* (October 1978), p. 387.

25. Ibid, p. 384.

26. Checinski, "Structural Causes."

27. Ibid.

28. Gur Ofer, "Soviet Military Aid to the Middle East—An Economic Balance Sheet," in *Soviet Economic Prospects For the 1970s*, U.S. Congress, Joint Economic Committee (Washington, D.C.: U.S. Government Printing Office, 1973), p. 236.

29. The CIA reports that "Moscow's hard currency surpluses with the LDCs reached $800 million in 1976 and an estimated $1.2 billion in 1977, due mainly to hard currency payments for military hardware totalling between $1.5 billion and $2.0 billion in each of the two years." *Changing Patterns in Soviet-LDC Trade, 1976–77*, CIA Publication ER 78–10326, May 1978, p. 2.

30. Ofer, "Soviet Military," p. 236.

31. Drew Middleton, "Soviet May Be Seeking Base in Seychelles," *The New York Times*, 23 June 1980, p. 17; Michael T. Kaufman, "Ports and Oil Spur Naval Buildups By U.S. and Soviet," *The New York Times*, 20 April 1981, p. 1; "Soviet Reported Seeking Bases in East Africa," *The Baltimore Sun*, 14 March 1981, p. 2.

32. Michael MccGwire, "The Evolution of Soviet Naval Policy: 1970–74," in *Soviet Naval Policy Constraints and Objectives*, Michael MccGwire et al., eds., (New York: Praeger Publishers, 1975), pp. 505–546.

33. James M. McConnell and Bradford Dismukes, "Soviet Diplomacy of Force in the Third World," *Problems of Communism*, (January–February 1979).

34. Cited in Robert Legvold, "The Soviet Union's Strategic Stake in Africa," in *Africa and the United States: Vital Interests*, Jennifer S. Whitaker, ed., (New York: New York University Press, 1978), p. 160.

35. Avigdor Haselkorn, "The 'External Function' of Soviet Armed Forces," *Naval War College Review* (January–February 1980), pp. 35–45.

36. Graham Allison, *The Essence of Decision* (Boston: Little, Brown & Company, 1971).

37. Dimitri Simes, "Imperial Globalism in the Making: Soviet Involvement in the Horn of Africa," *Washington Review* (May 1978), p. 38.

38. "The East German 'Afrika Korps,' as it is dubbed in the west, enjoys Russian backing because its members are meticulously trained. Russians themselves have had only limited success because of their overbearing ways." *Africa Research Bulletin* (September 1979), p. 5423A.

39. Colin Legum, "The African Environment," *Problems of Communism*, (January–February 1978), p. 6.

40. Kenneth L. Adelman, "Africa's Security Needs," *The Wall Street Journal*, 9 August 1979, p. 20.

41. Ibid.

42. Michael A. Samuels et al., *Implications of Soviet and Cuban Activities in Africa For U.S. Policy* (Washington, D.C.: Center for Strategic and International Studies, 1979), p. 20.

43. Henry Bienen, "Perspectives on Soviet Intervention in Africa," *Political Science Quarterly*, 95 (Spring 1980), p. 37.

44. Adelman, "Africa's Security."

45. "PMAC Chairman Mengistu Addresses May Day Rally," *FBIS Report: Sub Saharan Africa VIII*, 12 May 1979, p. B1; "Neto's May Day Speech Stresses Need to Improve Worker's Lot," *FBIS Report: Sub Saharan Africa VIII*, June 1979, p. E1; "Angola: The Awkward Hiatus," *Africa Confidential* (13 February 1980), pp. 5–6; Cord Meyer, "Darkness at Noon in Ethiopa," *The Washington Star*, 5 April 1980; Mozambique's Hybrid Marxism," *African Index* (6 April 1980), pp. 17–18; "Mozambique: Pragmatism," *Africa Confidential* (16 January 1980); Gary Thatcher, "The Russian's Greatest Reverse In Years," *The Christian Science Monitor*, 22 April 1980; "Congo: What Kind of Marxism?" *Africa Confidential*, (16 January 1980), pp. 5–7.

46. Geoffrey Kemp, "The New Strategic Map," *Survival* (March/April 1977), pp. 50–59.

47. Donald E. Fink, "Availability of Strategic Materials Debated,"

Aviation Week and Space Technology (5 May 1980), pp. 42–46; "Strategic Stockpiles: Who's Hoarding What?" *The Economist* (24 May 1980), pp. 87–88; Peter Vanneman and Martin James, "The Soviet Intervention in Angola: Intentions and Implications," *Strategic Review* (Summer 1976), p. 95.

48. *Africa Research Bulletin*, 15 January 1978, p. 4776; Russell W. Howe, "The Daring French Draw Admiration," *The Baltimore Sun*, 7 October 1979; "The Ubiquitous French," *African Index* (10 February 1980), pp. 5–7.

49. "The Luanda Summit," *African Index* (1–15 June 1979), pp. 37–38; "Mozambique Finds a New Friend in Portugal," *The New York Times*, 27 December 1981, p. 19.

50. Bienen, "Perspectives on Soviet Intervention," p. 36.

51. Christopher Stevens, "The Soviet Role In Africa," in John Seiler, ed., *Southern Africa Since the Portuguese Coup* (Boulder, Colo.: Westview Press, 1980), p. 52.

52. "Recalling a Warning" *Africa Currents*, 12/13 (Winter 1978/1979):25–26; "Condemn All External Interventions Without Reservation," *Africa Currents*, 12/13 (Autumn/Winter 1978/1979):8–9; David Lamb, "Mozambique is Zealously Marxist But No Soviet Satellite," *The Washington Post*, 19 August 1978; Richard R. Leger, "Africa Is Fed Up with Interfence of Foreign Powers," *The Wall Street Journal*, 28 July 1978, p. 8.

53. Legum, "The African Environment," p. 7.

54. "Defence Force Study," *Africa Research Bulletin* (1–31 July 1979), p. 5327.

55. For insights into African reaction to this conflict, see the OAU debate in *Africa Research Bulletin* (1–31 July 1979), pp. 5328–5329.

56. Chester A. Crocker, "The African Setting," *The Washington Review*, (May 1978), pp. 12–19.

57. David E. Albright, *Communism in Africa*, p. 227–232; Michael J. Dean, "The Soviet Assessment of the 'Correlation of World Forces:' Implications for American Foreign Policy." *Orbis* (Fall 1976), pp. 625–636.

58. David E. Albright, *Communism in Africa*, pp. 221–223.

59. Jiri Valenta, "Soviet Decision-Making on the Intervention in Angola," in Albright, *Communism in Africa*, pp. 93–117.

60. "For the origin of American influence on Soviet African policy has been essentially the opposite of that of Soviet influence on U.S. African policy. While the latter has resulted from unprecedently strident action, the former for the most part stemmed from inaction." W. Scott Thompson," The African American Nexus in Soviet Strategy," in Albright, *Communism in Africa*, p. 189.

61. Hutchings, "Soviet Arms Exports," p. 389.

62. For a recent example, see Pranay B. Gupte, "Ethiopians' Links to Soviet Strained," *The New York Times*, 19 December 1981.

63. Ibid. "Moscow is also said to be insisting that heavy military and technical equipment purchased by Ethiopia be transported back to the Soviet Union when major repairs are necessary, and it wants the Ethiopians to pay the transportation costs."

64. A.M. Kapcia, "Cuba's African Involvement: A New Perspective," *Survey*, (Spring 1979), pp. 142–159; Melvin Croan, "A New Afrika Corps?," *The Washington Quarterly* (Winter 1980), pp. 21–37.

65. *Africa Research Bulletin* (1–31 May 1976), p. 4015C.

66. *Africa Research Bulletin* (1–31 July 1977), pp. 4486C, 4487A; *Africa Research Bulletin* (1–31 January 1978), p. 4699B.

67. *Africa Research Bulletin* (1–31 July 1978), p. 4911C.

68. *Africa Research Bulletin* (1–31 December 1980), p. 5907.

69. *Africa Research Bulletin* (1–28 February 1981), pp. 5965–5967.

70. *Africa Research Bulletin* (1–31 March 1981), p. 5986.

71. Ibid., p. 5986C.

72. *Africa Research Bulletin* (1–30 September 1981), p. 6196B.

73. David E. Albright, *Communism in Africa*, p. 220.

74. *Africa Research Bulletin* (1–31 July 1978), p. 4911B.

75. *Africa Research Bulletin* (1–30 April 1979), p. 5218B.

76. Ibid., p. 5218A.

77. *Africa Research Bulletin* (1–31 July 1979), p. 5327A.

78. *Africa Research Bulletin* (1–30 April 1981), p. 6011.

79. *The Daily Telegraph*, 16 October 1979.

80. *Africa Research Bulletin* (1–29 February 1980), p. 5568B.

81. *Africa Research Bulletin* (1–30 June 1981), pp. 6071–6072.

82. *Africa Research Bulletin* (1–31 July 1981), pp. 6102–6103.

83. *Africa Research Bulletin* (1–31 December 1981), p. 6275.

84. *Africa Research Bulletin* (1–30 September 1981), p. 6194.

85. Raymond R. Copson, "Ethiopia, Angola, and Mozambique: Reaction to the Soviet Tie." (Unpublished paper presented to annual meeting of the African Studies Association, Bloomington, Indiana, October 1981), p. 15.

86. Gary Thatcher, "The Russian's Greatest Reverse In Africa In Years." *The Christian Science Monitor*, 22 April 1980.

87. "The Zimbabwean Prime Minister has . . . officially declared that he was sending troops to the border in order to aid the Communist Samora Machel to put an end to the armed rebellion against Machelism." "Voice of Free Africa Criticizes Zimbabwe's Mugabe," *FBIS-Sub Sahara Africa*, 30 May 1960.

88. Graham Hovey, "Rhodesian Settlement Raising U.S. Hopes For Namibia," *The New York Times*, 26 December 1979.

89. Michael Clough, *Where Is South Africa Headed?—A Conference Report*. Mt. Kisco, New York: Seven Springs Center, 1980.

90. *Daily Times* (Nigeria), 11 January 1979.

91. "Mozambique's Hybrid Marxism," *African Index* (6 April 1980), pp. 17–18.

92. "Angola: The Awkward Hiatus," *Africa Confidential* (13 February 1980), pp. 5–6.

93. *Africa Research Bulletin* (1–31 December 1981), p. 6292.

94. Ibid.

95. David B. Ottaway, "Ethiopia Looks to Communist Allies For Economic Aid," *The Washington Post*, 19 March 1979, p. A–18.

96. Dan Connell, "Visit With Rebels Shows Ethiopia Failure," *The Washington Star*, 4 August 1979; Daniel Southerland, "Soviet Setbacks on Horn of Africa," *The Christian Science Monitor*, 6 August 1979; Cord Meyer, "Darkness At Noon In Ethiopia," *The Washington Star*, 5 April 1980; "New Famine in Ethiopia," *San Francisco Chronicle*, 9 May 1980; Gupte, "Ethiopians' Links."

97. "The Luanda Summit," *African Index* (1–15 June 1979), pp. 37–38.

98. Ibid.

99. "Congo: What Kind of Marxism?" *Africa Confidential* (16 January 1980), 5–7.

100. David Lamb, "Soviets Lose Base In Equatorial Guinea," *The Los Angeles Times* (28 January 1980), p. 4; "A Soviet Departure," *African Index* (18–31 December 1979), p. 88.

101. For the example of France, see Edward Kolodziej, "Determinants of French Arms Sales: Security Implications," in Patrick McGowan and Charles Kegley, eds., *Threats, Weapons and Foreign Policy* (Beverly Hills, Calif.: Sage, 1980), pp. 137–175

102. *Africa Research Bulletin* (1–28 February 1981), p. 5957.

103. *Africa Research Bulletin* (1–31 March 1981), p. 5993.

104. *Africa Research Bulletin* (1–30 June 1981), p. 6070.

105. Seth Singleton, "Soviet Policy and Socialist Expansion in Asia and Africa," *Armed Forces and Society*, 6 (Spring 1980):346.

106. Copson, "Ethiopia, Angola, and Mozambique," p. 14.

107. Albright, *Communism in Africa*, p. 235.

108. Ibid., p. 50.

109. Simes, "Imperial Globalism," p. 35.

110. "Ethiopia: Nationalism Versus Ideology," *Africa Confidential* (16 January 1980), p. 5,

111. Seth Singleton, "The Natural Ally: Soviet Policy In Southern

Africa: in *Political Change in Southern Africa: Implications For United States Policy,* ed. Michael Clough (Berkeley, Calif.: Institute of International Studies, 1982).

4

Military Relations between Eastern Europe and Africa

Roger E. Kanet

The Evolution of East European Relations with Africa: Economic and Political Dimensions

To a substantial degree the policies of the East European countries—with the partial exception of those of Romania—have followed closely the policies of the Soviet Union throughout the Third World ever since the 1950s. The political leaders of Eastern Europe share a common view with the Soviets concerning the significance of the developing world in the struggle with the capitalist West. This aspect of East European interest can probably best be seen in the upsurge of contacts with and support for revolutionary movements and regimes in sub Saharan Africa during the 1970s. Along with the Soviet Union and Cuba, several of the East European countries have played an important role in providing military and economic support to Angola, Mozambique, and Ethiopia, among others. In the Middle East, the East Europeans, with the notable exception of Romania have followed the Soviet lead in providing support of various types to the more radical of the Arab governments in their struggle with Israel. In recent years, for example, periodic East European propaganda campaigns against the Egyptian-Israeli negotiations and treaty have been modeled almost precisely on Soviet statements.

In Africa the movement toward independence in the late 1950s and early 1960s afforded the communist states the opportunity to develop relations in a region that had been virtually inaccessible to them in earlier years. In one of the first studies dealing with East European and Soviet involvement in the Third World, Jan Wszelaki argued that, "It is the East-Central European countries which have opened the Afro-Asian non-communist markets to the Soviet bloc's economic offensive, the political implications of which have so alarmed the West. . . ,"[1] In 1956, for example, East European trade with the countries of sub-Saharan Africa was more than four times greater than that of the USSR, and in 1958 it was still more than twice as large. By 1960 and 1961, Ghana, Guinea, and Mali were the recipients of credits from several of the East European states, and technicians and advisors from the USSR and Eastern Europe were at work in a number of African countries. Guinea, whose first years

79

of independence were especially difficult because of the complete rupture of relations with France, was a major target of this assistance. By 1960, one could find technicians from all of the Communist states in Guinea. Among other things, they acted as advisors to Guinean government administrators, and Czechoslovakia was involved in reorganizing and training the military.[2] Officials from the Communist states were delivering lectures in the schools in Guinea and instructors from the World Federation of Trade Unions taught at the Workers University in Conakry.[3]

The initial interest of Eastern Europe in developments in Africa, as well as in the Third World more broadly, paralleled closely the interests of the USSR. The struggle for independence and the conflicts of interest that arose between certain African states and the former European colonial powers the opportunity for the Soviets and their allies to gain a presence in an area of potential importance in the long-term struggle with the capitalist West. Ghana, Guinea, and Mali were the most significant links in what the European Communist states hoped would be the beginnings of a socialist-oriented Africa that would lay the foundations for eventual entrance into the socialist community as full-fledged Marxist-Leninist states allied to the Warsaw Treaty Organization. However, in some cases, other factors motivated the East European leaders, as well. For the East Germans the search for diplomatic recognition and international legitimacy was an important factor that influenced the attempt to develop political contacts with the newly established states. In a number of cases, the late 1950s witnessed the resumption of trading patterns that had been terminated by World War II and the Cold War.[4] On the whole, however, East European policy in Africa in this early period seems to have been motivated far more by the collective goals of the European socialist community—that is, by Soviet goals—than by the specific interests of the six individual East European states themselves. For the Soviet Union and its European allies, Africa represented a great new potential for the expansion of the world revolution, in spite of the fact that African societies lacked both a proletariat and an industrial base.

In the mid-1950s Soviet and East European ideological pronouncements on the developing world, including sub-Saharan Africa, changed significantly. The most important reformulation was the development of the theory of peaceful coexistence and the role of the developing nations as a part of a worldwide "peace zone." The failure of most Third World states to support Communist positions in international affairs, however, led to a refinement of communist theory as it related to the developing world. In 1960 the concept of "the state of national democracy" was introduced as a means of differentiating among Third World states and of paving the way for the gradual development of the necessary prerequisites for socialism in societies in which the proletariat was extremely weak.[5] Most important for the present discussion is the fact that Soviet and East European leadership saw events in the developing world as an integral part of the struggle with Western "imperialism." Support for national-liberation movements was viewed as an essential element of the competition with the capitalist West.[6] In the first stage of the revolutionary process local nationalists, even bourgeois nationalists, committed to the establishment of politically independent states, play a progressive role and, therefore, are worthy of support from the Communist states. The second stage of the struggle for liberation, which emphasizes the acquisition of economic independence, requires active participation of the most progressive forces in developing societies—that is, those committed to the creation of the foundations for scientific socialism.[7] The only means by which the developing countries can successfully achieve full economic development is by emulating the experience of the communist states, according to the present view of the Communist leaders of Eastern Europe. As a result, the members of the (CMEA) have emphasized support for the expansion of those areas of the economy in Third World states that strengthen the noncapitalist aspects of the economy—that is, nationalization of industry, investment in the state-controlled sectors of the economy, and so forth. The most important indicator of progress, however, is the foreign-policy orientation of the individual developing country. Support for positions taken by the Soviet Union and its allies is critical to the successful development of Third World states whose interests coincide objectively, in the view of the communists, with those of the socialist community.[8]

In sum, the ideological-political position of the European-communist states toward the developing world has been related primarily to the competition between capitalism and communism. Political and ideological support—as well as various forms of military assistance—have been granted overwhelmingly to those Third World states viewed as hostile to the West or likely to establish the foundations for future socialist development. This has become especially evident in Africa during the last decade, where the more radical states—for instance, Angola, Benin, Ethiopia, and Mozambique—have become the major recipients of European communist support.

An important aspect of European-communist interest in Africa has related to the geopolitical significance of portions of the continent and of the Soviet Union's attempts to expand its position of influence in world affairs. Angola, Ethiopia, and other African states—as well as developing countries in the Middle East and elsewhere—have afforded the Soviet Union the opportunity to obtain bases of operations from which to expand its military and political activities in the conflict with the West.[9] As we shall see below, the East European states have played an important role in providing support for the development of such bases of operation which are aimed at strengthening the geopolitical position of the Soviet Union and the Warsaw Pact vis-à-vis the West.

In addition to the general ideological-political interests that motivate the policies of the East European states in Africa, one must also take into account the specific political and economic interests of the individual East European states in Africa and in the developing world more generally. The German Democratic Republic (GDR), for example, has been especially concerned with establishing and strengthening its position as a recognized sovereign state independent from the Federal Republic. While this motive clearly played a more important role prior to East German recognition by the West in the early 1970s, it continues to influence GDR policies in Africa where, after Cuba, it has become the most active Communist supporter of recent Soviet activities. In addition, for the past decade and a half, Romania has deviated from Soviet policy on a variety of issues related to the Third World as part of its position as a developing country and in the attempt to expand its political and economic ties with other developing countries.[10]

While political and ideological concerns have played a dominant role in Soviet and East European interest in sub-Saharan Africa during the past two decades, there is evidence of increasing interest in the economic potential of the continent. Africa—and the Third World more broadly— is seen as a potential market for the industrial exports of the European-Communist states and as a source for the raw materials required for the continued growth of their economies. However, to date, there has been little coordination in the economic policies of the CMEA-member countries,[11] and Africa does not yet rank as an important region for the commercial activities of the communist countries. In recent years trade with sub-Saharan Africa has comprised only about 0.5 percent of total trade for the six East European countries combined, and only Hungary conducts more than one percent of its total trade with sub-Saharan Africa.[12] In absolute terms, trade with sub-Saharan Africa increased by almost 7.5 times during the period 1960–1977, from approximately $86 million to almost $650 million—still a very small amount when compared with African trade with the West. In 1977, for example, trade between Nigeria and Great Britain alone amounted to more than one billion pounds sterling—more than three times as much as East European trade with all of sub-Saharan Africa.

The East European states now maintain diplomatic relations with virtually all of the members of the Organization for African Unity (OAU). The GDR, for example, has relations with forty-seven of the fifty OAU members and has resident ambassadors in twenty-one of these countries.[13] An important aspect of East European policy toward Africa for the last quarter of a century has been the political and diplomatic support provided to the Africans in their struggle with the colonial powers for independence and, more recently, in their disputes with the industrial West over such issues as terms of trade, economic assistance, and the general conditions of the international economic system. During the early 1960s, the CMEA-member states made major efforts, as we have already noted, to establish diplomatic relations with the newly independent African states. For the most part, however, these efforts succeeded in only a few states whose political orientation was decidedly anti-Western—particularly in Ghana, Guinea, and Mali—although some efforts were also made in Nigeria and the Sudan. By the late 1960s, the European communist states seemed to have abandoned their attempts to make a significant political breakthrough in relations with sub-Saharan Africa. Friendly regimes in Ghana and Mali had been overthrown and few other African states had indicated major interest in a significant expansion of political or economic ties with either the USSR or its East European allies. The GDR, for example, in spite of strenuous attempts to obtain diplomatic recognition by means of offers of economic and technical assistance, was unable to overcome West German influence policy in Africa.

The changes in the international political environment in the 1970s—in particular, the change in the relative power positions of the United States and the USSR— and the changing political situation in Africa itself, with the rise of vigorous revolutionary movements in the remaining colonial areas, provided the European Communist states with new opportunities for political involvement in Africa. Since approximately 1972 or 1973 most of the East European states have initiated a much more active policy toward Africa that has included numerous high-level state and party visits, treaties of friendship and cooperation, the development of interparty relations, and economic and military cooperation.

One indicator of the political importance that has been assigned to the development of diplomatic contacts with Africa—and with the Third World as a whole—has been the significant rise in the number of East European state and party delegations that have traveled to Africa in recent years, and the number of return visits that have been made by African leaders. The most spectacular of these high-level visits have probably been the trips to Africa undertaken by East German and Romanian leaders.[14]

In addition to the development of formal state-to-state relations, several of the East European Communist parties have begun to establish close relations with revolutionary parties in Africa. By the 1960s, such relationships had already begun to develop, and representatives from ruling parties in Ghana, Guinea, and Mali participated in the congresses of the Soviet and East European communist parties. A clear purpose of the establishment of such ties with African revolutionary parties is to strengthen the possibility of influencing the policy orientation of those parties. Virtually all of the East European Communist parties have signed agreements with African parties that provide for ''bilateral exchanges of visits, experience, and documents, study tours by the African parties to Eastern Europe to examine the work of Central Committee agitprop, mass organization, ideological, and foreign affairs departments, and courses of study of the training of African party cadres.''[15]

Overall, the decade of the 1970s witnessed a significant increase in East European political activity throughout Africa. The collapse of the Portuguese colonial empire and the radicalization of a number of other African states, plus the expanded role of the Soviet Union and its East European allies in world politics in the 1970s have provided an environment favorable to increased political activity on the part of the communist states. With the major exception of Romania, the European CMEA members have focused on the development of long-term relationships with African states committed to some form of Marxist-Leninist socialism. Their experiences with radical allies in the 1960s has convinced the European communist leaders that stable relationships must be built on a confluence of interests on both sides and that an important element of such a coincidence is the existence in Africa of strong socialist-party organizations. However, as we shall see in the next section, political support continues to be tied to military-security support in the development of East European relations with Africa. Military and security assistance to regimes faced with either internal or external hostility remains a primary method employed by the European Communist states in establishing or maintaining a presence.

Military Relations between Eastern Europe and Africa

During the 1970s several East European states, in addition to the Soviet Union and Cuba, became involved on a large scale in providing various forms of military support to African governments and revolutionary movements. In one respect this is not a new policy, since East European states have been providing military equipment and training to Third World states ever since the mid-1950s, when Czechoslovakia acted as an intermediary for the Soviet Union in the first major arms sale to Egypt.[16] During the period 1955–1979, East European states signed agreements for the delivery to developing countries of military equipment valued at almost $4.3 billion and actually delivered equipment worth $3.4 billion (see table 4–1). Until the 1970s, however, very little of the equipment was designated for sub-Saharan Africa. In the 1970s Angola and Ethiopia,

Table 4–1
Soviet and East European Military Relations with Developing Countries, 1955–1979
(millions of current U.S. dollars)

	Agreements		Deliveries	
	USSR	Eastern Europe	USSR	Eastern Europe
Total	47,340	4,285	35,340	3,405
1955–1969	5,875	935	5,060	840
1970	1,150	50	995	75
1971	1,590	120	865	125
1972	1,690	155	1,215	75
1973	2,890	130	3,135	130
1974	5,735	635	2,225	210
1975	3,325	635	2,040	285
1976	5,550	345	3,085	330
1977	8,715	475	4,705	345
1978	2,465	555	5,400	470
1979	8,365	250	6,615	525

Source: Central Intelligence Agency, National Foreign Assessment Center, *Communist Aid Activities in Non-Communist Less Developed Countries, 1979 and 1954–79: A Research Paper*. ER 80–10318U, October 1980, p. 13.

along with a number of other African states, became important recipients of various forms of military assistance, including increasingly sophisticated military equipment and the training necessary to use the equipment. Although Czechoslovakia was the most active of the East European states in supplying armaments to Third World states in the 1950s and 1960s, the GDR has apparently replaced Czechoslovakia during the past decade as the most important East European supplier of military support to developing countries. Most of this support, however, has come in the form of military and security training rather than in the supply of military hardware. It is precisely in Africa that the GDR has focused its assistance program, and it has been estimated that the GDR had 2,720 military advisers in Africa in early 1980, including 650 in Libya and Algeria.[17] In the case of East German military assistance, as well as that of other East European states' military involvement in Africa, there is clear evidence of cooperation with the Soviet Union.

While military assistance and military sales have made up an increasingly important part of Soviet relations with developing countries, they have remained relatively less important for Eastern Europe as a whole.[18] Soviet deliveries of military equipment and services to all Third World countries rose from an average of less than $400 million annually in the 1960s, to almost $3,900-million-per-year after 1972; deliveries from Eastern Europe increased from about $60 million annually to slightly more than $325 million during the same period. Deliveries of military equipment to Africa for both Czechoslovakia and Poland—the only two countries for which detailed data on deliveries are available—make up twenty-eight and fifty-two percent respectively of their deliveries to all developing countries for the period 1964–1978 (see table 4–2). In 1979 new agreements between East European and African countries for the delivery of military equipment actually dropped to $250 million, the lowest amount since 1975, while new Soviet commitments totaled more than $8 billion.

An important aspect of East European military relations with Third World countries has been the training of troops, both in Eastern Europe

Table 4–2
Czechoslovak, Polish, and Soviet Deliveries of Arms to Africa, 1964–1978
(millions of current U.S. dollars)

Recipient	Czechoslovakia	Poland	USSR
World	3,995	2,545	42,780
Developing Countries	1,115	460	31,695
Africa	285	240	8,020
Algeria	—	—	1,480
Angola	10	10	410
Benin	—	—	20
Burundi	—	—	5
Cape Verde	—	—	20
Chad	—	—	10
Congo	—	—	40
Equatorial Guinea	—	—	10
Ethiopia	30	10	1,300
Ghana	5	—	5
Guinea	—	—	70
Guinea-Bissau	—	—	10
Libya	180	220	3,525
Madagascar	20	—	20
Mali	—	—	105
Morocco	25	—	25
Mozambique	5	—	130
Nigeria	5	—	110
Somalia	—	—	370
Sudan	negl.	—	95
Tanzania	—	—	110
Tunisia	5	—	—
Uganda	—	—	120
Zambia	—	—	40

Sources: United States Arms Control and Disarmament Agency, *World Military Expenditures and Arms Trade, 1963–1973*. Washington: U.S. ACDA, 1975, pp. 67–68; idem, *World Military Expenditures and Arms Transfers, 1969–1978*. Washington: U.S. ACDA, 1980, pp. 161–162.

Notes: (1) Components may not add because of rounding. (2) These data include only military hardware and do not agree with the data in table 4–1, which also include training and other services.

and in the Third World. During the period 1955–1979 more than 6,000 military personnel from the Third World, including almost 1,800 from Africa, were trained in Eastern Europe (see table 4–3). In addition, the number of Soviet and East European military technicians seconded to the countries of the Third World has risen substantially during the past decade. For Africa, including North Africa, the figure has risen from about 2,600 in 1975 to 6,800 four years later[19] (see table 4–4).

Although all of the East European states have been involved militarily in Africa, the German Democratic Republic has been by far the most active in recent years. Most important has been the GDR's training of military and security personnel, both in Africa itself and in the GDR. The GDR's military involvement seems to have begun in 1973 when it first signed a military-and security-training agreement for Somalia, An-

Table 4–3

Military Personnel from African Countries Trained in the USSR and Eastern Europe, 1955–1979

	USSR	Eastern Europe
Total from all Developing Countries	45,585	6,345
Africa	14,420	1,760
North Africa	3,580	555
Algeria	2,195	200
Libya	1,310	285
Other	75	70
Sub-Saharan Africa	10,840	1,205
Angola	55	5
Benin	30	—
Burundi	75	—
Congo	505	85
Equa. Guinea	200	—
Ethiopia	1,290	500
Ghana	180	—
Guinea	885	60
Guinea-Bissau	100	—
Mali	360	10
Mozambique	400	30
Nigeria	790	35
Somalia	2,395	160
Sudan	330	20
Tanzania	1,970	10
Zambia	190	—
Other	1,085	290

Source: Central Intelligence Agency, National Foreign Assessment Center, *Communist Aid Activities in Non-Communist Less Developed Countries, 1979 and 1954–79: A Research Paper*. ER 80–10318U, October 1979. p. 16.

Note: Data refer to the estimated number of persons departing for training. Numbers are rounded to the nearest five.

Table 4–4
Communist Military Technicians in Africa, 1979 and 1980

	1979		1980			
	USSR and Eastern Europe	Cuba	USSR and Eastern Europe	USSR	Eastern Europe	Cuba
Total, All Developing Countries	15,865	34,315				
Africa	6,825		5,750 (10,180)[b]	2,950	1,480	29–30,000
North Africa	2,835		3,000			
Algeria	1,015	15	—			
Libya	1,820	15	3,000			
Sub-Saharan Africa	3,990	33,045	2,750	2,950	1,480	29–30,000
Angola	1,400	19,000	(1,850)[b]	850	1,000[a]	18,000
Benin	—	—	12,000			
Congo	—	—	200[a]			
Equa. Guinea	40	200	(100)[b]	100		
Ethiopia	1,250	13,000	(2,180)[b]	2,000	180[a]	11–12,000
Guinea	85	50	200[a]			
Guinea-Bissau	60	50	600			
Mali	—	—	—			
Madagascar	180	—	(300)[b]		300	
Mozambique	525	215	550			
Other	450	530	—			

Sources: The estimates for 1979 are taken from Central Intelligence Agency, National Foreign Assessment Center, *Communist Aid Activities in Non-Communist Less Developed Countries, 1979 and 1954–79: A Research Paper*. ER 80–10318U, October 1980, p. 15. Estimates for 1980 are from *The Economist*, 19 September 1981.

[a]East Europeans consist of East Germans only.
[b]Includes data listed separately for the USSR and Eastern Europe.

gola, Mozambique, and Ethiopia, among others.[20] Possibly one of the most important aspects of the GDR's activities in Africa has been the training of elite "palace guards" and domestic-security police in countries such as Mozambique and Ethiopia.[21] This emphasis has been influenced by the experience of the 1960s when "progressive" African leaders such as Nkrumah of Ghana were unable to resist domestic opposition successfully. The presence of well-trained and loyal security forces is now viewed by the Soviets and their allies as essential to stabilize the existence of "progressive" Marxist-Leninist governments in various African countries.

East European military assistance to radical African states—and to national-liberation movements in the southern portion of the continent—has been of secondary importance to that of the USSR or of Cuba; however, in certain countries it has been important. This assistance is motivated primarily by East European support for the global strategic interests of the Warsaw Pact— that is, the Soviet Union—and it is important, therefore, to analyze the major motives of Soviet arms transfer in Africa. In particular, the Soviets and their allies have used the provision of military support as an important instrument in the attempt to undermine Western influence and strategic interests in regions of concern for the Soviet Union. Closely related to the desire to weaken Western dominance in the Third World has been the goal of establishing and extending the presence of the Warsaw Pact states themselves. In almost all cases where Soviet and East European military equipment has been supplied to a developing country, military technicians have arrived along with the equipment, in order to instruct the local military in its use. The major example of the growing role of the Soviets and, to a much lesser extent, their East European allies occurred in Egypt prior to the expulsion of approximately 21,000 Soviet military advisors by President Sadat in summer 1972.

Other, more recent, examples of large-scale Soviet-East European presence in the Third World—in part, in connection with military support to those states—have occurred in Angola, Somalia (until 1977), Ethiopia, and—at a totally different level—Afghanistan since before the Soviet invasion of that country in late 1979. In all of these cases the provision of military equipment and technical support has been one of the means employed by the Soviets in gaining a presence and in attempting to influence the course of political developments in the recipient country.

Related to the Soviet desire to strengthen its global role is the continuing military competition with the United States—and with the People's Republic of China. Over the course of the past fifteen years, or so, Soviet policy in the Third World has been based, in part, on the desire to expand the capability of projecting power abroad in support of Soviet state interests. These projection capabilities depend upon two separate but interrelated developments. First, there was the need for the Soviets to produce the military equipment necessary to exert military power in regions beyond the territory under the control of the Soviet army. Throughout the 1960s and 1970s the Soviets proceeded with a construction program that has now given them a large and modern ocean-going navy and long-distance-transport aircraft.[22] The second requirement was the gaining of access to military facilities throughout the Third World at which to refuel, repair, and refurbish the newly developed military capabilities.

The evidence points to the acquisition of military facilities in areas of strategic interest to the USSR as one of the primary motivating factors for Soviet policy in the Third World—and, indirectly, for the policy of the Soviet Union's allies. The USSR has employed both the distribution of economic assistance and, more importantly in recent years, the transfer of military equipment as part of an overall policy of competition with the West for the acquisition and maintenance of strategic access. During the course of the past decade the Soviets have been especially successful in creating a network of such facilities throughout the Indian Ocean area, the Middle East, and various parts of Africa, that now permit them to influence events far from Soviet territory. It must also be noted that the development of the Soviet network of military facilities has depended on the support that the Soviets have been willing to provide to host countries, either in local conflicts or in conflicts with the West.

Among the most important developments that have enabled the Soviets and their East European allies both to export military equipment and to acquire basing facilities has been the Arab-Israeli conflict. By the early 1970s the Soviets had established a major set of facilities in Egypt—later to be lost. Similarly, they were also able to gain access to various types of military facilities in Syria and Iraq, although they have never exercised the type of control of these that they maintained in Egypt prior to their expulsion in 1972.

In Africa the conflict between Somalia and Ethiopia has afforded the European communists a dual opportunity—first, the acquisition of large-scale military facilities in Somalia; later, after their decision to opt for support for the new revolutionary regime in Addis Ababa and the loss of the Somali facilities, the acquisition of military facilities in Ethiopia.

The civil war in Angola in 1975 and, more recently, the war between Somalia and Ethiopia in the Horn of Africa have indicated both the extent of existing Soviet military facilities and their importance to the Soviet Union in supporting its allies and clients throughout the Third World. Without access to air facilities in Algeria, Benin, Congo, Guinea, and elsewhere in West Africa, the rapid and large-scale shipment of Soviet military equipment and Cuban troops essential for the MPLA's (Popular Movement for the Liberation of Angola) victory would have been impossible.[23] More recently, Soviet access to facilities in Iraq, South Yemen, and Libya were indispensable for the movement of massive amounts of Soviet military equipment and large numbers of Cuban troops to help the new friends of the USSR in Ethiopia.

We have already noted the apparent connection between Soviet and East European arms transfers and the acquisition of military facilities. All of the countries that have provided the Soviets with facilities over which they exercised substantial control have been major recipients of Warsaw Pact military equipment and most of them have also received substantial economic aid—at least relative to the total population of the country. In addition, all of the countries that have provided at least limited access to air and naval facilities have also received military supplies from the Soviet Union and Eastern Europe—although in some cases the amounts have been quite limited. It should be noted, however, that not all major recipients of Communist military support have provided the Soviet Union with major military facilities.

A final point must also be emphasized concerning the weakness of the Soviet-East European position in many of the countries in which they have acquired access to military facilities. Both Egypt and Somalia expelled the Soviets when their own goals and those of the Soviet Union clashed. During the 1976 civil war in Lebanon, Syria restricted Soviet access to naval facilities in that country in order to show its displeasure with Soviet opposition to Syrian intervention against the PLO and the Lebanese leftists.[24] The Soviets have apparently been quite aware of the tenuous nature of their military presence in the developing countries and have generally followed a policy of establishing parallel, or backup, facilities. For example, throughout the late 1960s and early 1970s they simultaneously courted North Yemen, South Yemen, Somalia, and Egypt. When Somalia expelled the Soviets as a result of the latter's military support for Ethiopia in 1977, the Soviets were still able to use the facilities in Aden, South Yemen. In West Africa as well, the Soviets seem to have developed a parallel set of facilities in Benin, Guinea-Bissau, Equatorial Guinea, Congo, and Mali.[25]

To date, Soviet military capabilities in the Third World have been employed for a variety of purposes. First, they have been used to support allies or client states against a regional opponent—for example, the Arabs versus Israel, and Ethiopia versus Somalia—or to support one faction in a domestic civil war, as in Angola. The Soviets and their East European allies have also provided substantial military assistance to revolutionary movements committed to the overthrow of colonial regimes—as at present in southern Africa. Finally, their overseeing of military capabilities has provided the Soviets with the opportunity to monitor the activities of Western civil and military shipping in the major shipping lanes from the oil-rich Persian Gulf region through the Indian Ocean and South Atlantic to Europe and North America.[26]

As we have seen, in much of Africa the East European countries have worked closely with the Soviets, and their activities can be viewed as an integral part of overall Soviet military policy.[27] Yet, other concerns apparently also play a role in East European military relations with the countries of Africa, and of the Third World more broadly. For Czechoslovakia, for example, the sale of military equipment to some Third World states, such as Libya, has become an important source of hard currency. Ever since the rise in OPEC oil prices and the resulting availability of large amounts of hard currency in a number of countries, the Soviets and East Europeans have been receiving hard currency for some of the weapons shipped to the Third World.[28]

For other East European countries—especially the GDR and Romania—military involvement in Africa has provided a means of achieving political goals. The East Germans have been especially concerned with competing for influence and prestige with the Federal Republic. For Romania, arms aid is a means of strengthening its position as a friend of the Third World and of bolstering its semiautonomous position in international affairs. For all of the East European governments military assistance to Africa represents one important method of supporting revolutionary activity in the Third World.[29]

Eastern Europe and Sub-Saharan Africa: An Assessment and Projection

During the past decade Africa has become a primary target of European Communist political and military activity. Although the Soviet Union and Cuba have been the most visible of the communist actors on the continent, the smaller East European members of the Warsaw Pact have also played an important role. To a substantial degree, David Albright was correct when he stated that East European activities in Africa have been ancillary to the involvement of the Soviet Union.[30] This assessment is especially apt concerning East European military involvement. However, it tends to overlook several important aspects of East European involvement in Africa. First of all, it ignores the degree to which all of the East European states—Romania and the German Democratic Republic in particular— have expanded their involvement in sub-Saharan Africa during the course of the past decade. In addition, it fails to recognize the factors beyond socialist solidarity with the USSR that motivate East European involvement in Africa. For Romania, for example, the development of political and economic ties with Africa has become an integral aspect of the overall attempt to play a role in international politics that is at least partially autonomous from that of the USSR. Continuing efforts by the leadership of the GDR to strengthen its international and domestic position vis-a-vis West Germany have had a strong motivating force on the development of relations with sub-Saharan Africa. Moreover, the concern with the creation of stable, long-term economic relations with developing countries as markets for East European industrial exports and as sources of raw materials have also had an impact on East European policy in Africa.

The countries of Eastern Europe have become active participants in African politics during the past decade and their involvement in the affairs of the continent is likely to expand in the future. In concluding this discussion of East European relations with Africa, I would like to restate several points that I have noted above. First of all, in the military and political realm there has been a substantial degree of policy coordination by the Warsaw Pact states in Africa. In this area the East European states and the Soviet Union have been interested in supporting ideologically compatible allies, in searching for strategic benefits, and in building the foundations for future political influence on the continent. The change in the relative military positions of the United States and the USSR during the past decade and the deterioration of the U.S. ability to act effectively after the debacles of Vietnam and Watergate provided the Soviets and their allies with an international environment conducive to more assertive policies. In addition, the collapse of the remnants of the European colonial empire, in conjunction with the radicalization of a number of African states, have provided opportunities for Soviet and East European political and economic involvement in Africa that did not exist in the 1960s.

It is likely that the Soviets and their European allies will continue to attempt to take advantage of political and military instability in Africa, in order to strengthen the strategic position of the Warsaw Pact in Africa. The success of this policy, however, will depend upon a number of factors over which the European Communist states themselves have little control. Most important is the fact that the success of the Communist states in establishing and maintaining a position of influence in Africa depends upon local developments. As the WTO members have learned, the overthrow of an Nkrumah, the death of a Nasser, the seizure of power by a Mengistu, and related events, have had a major impact on the success or failure of their policies. So long as the interests of those African leaders whom the Communists have befriended continue to coincide with the interests of the Warsaw Pact states, cordial relations are likely to persist. When, however, interests diverge—as they have in Egypt, the Sudan, and Somalia—the communist states are likely to find it difficult to maintain their position. Closely related to this is the fact that changes in regime in an African country may bring to power individuals with goals divergent from those of the European Communist states. An interesting recent example has been the electoral victory of Robert Mugabe in Zimbabwe. All of the European communist states except Romania had backed the losing faction of Joshua Nkomo, while Romania had maintained relations with both nationalist parties. Only Romania was represented at the Zimbabwe independence ceremonies by a high-ranking delegation; other East European states were not even invited to the celebrations.[31]

Another important factor that must be taken into account is the continuing ability of those East European states that have become actively involved in Africa to bear the cost of such involvement. Both the GDR and Romania suffer serious balance-of-payments deficits in their trade with the West. In addition, domestic economic growth throughout Eastern Europe has dropped off significantly in recent years. The question arises of the ability and willingness of these two countries, and of other East European states, to continue to invest in expensive economic and military assistance programs in Africa.

However, so long as political unrest exists in Africa—and the prospects for the peaceful resolution of problems in South Africa and Namibia do not appear bright—the Soviets and their allies will continue to be afforded the opportunity for involvement. Without a significant change in attitudes in Moscow—and in some of the East European capitals—attempts will be made to take advantage of such unrest and to build on the existing positions that have been established in Angola, Ethiopia, and elsewhere.

In the economic realm, East European activity remains extremely limited and uncoordinated. Sub-Saharan Africa has not been important to Eastern Europe, either as a market for exports or as a source of imports, although Romania has attempted to expand its economic cooperation with a number of African states during recent years. Moreover, there exist serious limits on the prospects for a significant growth in East European economic relations with sub-Saharan Africa. First of all, most of the African states lack the exports required by the East European states. The oil-producing countries of the Middle East and North Africa will continue to dominate East European trade with Third World countries. Besides the fact that these countries have the petroleum needed by Eastern Europe, they also have currency with which to pay for imports of industrial products from Eastern Europe. Economic relations with most of sub-Saharan Africa can be developed almost exclusively on the basis of cooperative economic arrangements that will involve substantial East

European commitments of capital to Africa. Given the economic problems that beset most East European states, it is questionable whether major long-term commitments of such assistance are likely.

Although the East European states clearly have an interest in expanding their economic relations with sub-Saharan Africa, it is most probably that political and security interests will continue to dominate East European involvement in Africa—in particular for the two countries that are most actively involved in African affairs, Romania and the GDR.

Notes

1. Jan Wszelaki, *Communist Economic Strategy: The Role of East-Central Europe* (Washington, D.C.: National Planning Association, 1959), p. 91.

2. Rolf Italiaander, *The New Leaders of Africa* (Englewood Cliffs, N.J.: Prentice Hall, 1961), p. 282.

3. Fritz Schatten, *Communism in Africa* (New York: Praeger, 1966), p. 134.

4 For a discussion of these issues see Robert and Elizabeth Bass, "Eastern Europe," in *Africa and the Communist World*, Zbigniew Brzezinski, ed. (Stanford, Calif.: Stanford University Press, 1964), pp. 84–89.

5 For a discussion of the development of these concepts see Roger E. Kanet, "Soviet Attitudes Toward Developing Nations since Stalin," in *The Soviet Union and the Developing Nations*, Roger E. Kanet, ed. (Baltimore, Md.: The Johns Hopkins University Press, 1974), pp. 35ff. For an examination of the Czechoslovak ideological position on the Third World, which agreed totally with that of the USSR, see Robert F. Lamberg, *Prag und die Dritte Welt* (Hanover: Verlag für Literatur und Zeitgeschehen, 1966), pp. 28ff. For the East German interpretation see Wolfgang Sprote and Gerhard Hahn, *DDR-Wirtschaftshilfe contra Bonner Neokolonialsmus: Studien uber die wirtschaftliche und wissenschaftlich-technische Unterstützung der Nationalistaaten durch die DDR unde die staatsmonopolistische Forderung der neokolonialistischen Politik des westdeutschen Monopolkapitals* (Berlin: Staatsverlag der DDR, 1965), especially pp. 5–65.

6. See, for example, Lothar Rathmann and Hartmut Schilling, "Problem des nichtkapitalistischen Weges der Völker Asiens and Afrikas in der gegenwärtigen Etappe der nationalen Befreiungsbewegung," in *Nichtkapitalistischer Entwicklungsweg: Aktuelle Probleme in Theorie und Praxis. Protokoll einer Konferenz des Zentralen Rates fur Asien-, Afrika-*

und Lateinamerikawissenschaften in der DDR, die in Verbindung mit der Sektion Afrika- und Nahostwissenschaften der Karl-Marx Universität Leipzig vom 20. bis 22. Mai 1971 in Leipzig veranstaltet wurde (Berlin: 1973), second edition, p. 16. See also, Miroslav Mika, "Vychova k socialistickemu internacionalismu," *Noya Mysl,* no. 6 (1963), as translated in Lamberg, *Prag und die Dritte Welt,* pp. 33–35.

7. See, for example, Marian Paczyński, "Nowy Międzynarodowy lad ekonomiczny (Refleksje na tle IV Swiatowej Konferencji Handlu i Rozwoju)," *Ekonomista,* no. 1 (1977): 128–132.

8. See V. Berezin, *Cooperation Between CMEA and Developing Countries* (Moscow: Novosti, 1976), p. 5.

9. For a brief discussion of these points see Roger E. Kanet and William Morris (pseudonym for Boris Ipatov), "Die Sowjetunion in Afrika: Eine neue Phase sowjetischer Afrikapolitik?" *Osteuropa,* 28 (1978): 978–985. See also, Walter F. Hahn and Alvin J. Cottrell, *Soviet Shadow over Africa* (Coral Gables, Fla.: Center for Advanced International Studies, University of Miami, 1976), and Ian Greig, *The Communist Challenge to Africa: An Analysis of Contemporary Soviet, Cuban and Chinese Politics* (Richmond, U.K.: Foreign Affairs Publishing Co., 1977).

10. See Trond Gilberg, "Romania, Yugoslavia, and Africa: 'Nonalignment and Progressivism,' " unpublished paper, prepared for the Conference on Socialist States in Africa, Monterey, California, 26–28 July 1979; Michael Radu, "Romania and the Third World: The Dilemmas of a 'Free Rider,' " in *Eastern Europe and the Third World: East vs. South,* Michael Radu ed. (New York: Praeger, 1981), pp. 235–272; and Dumitru Tanasa, "Romania and the Nonaligned Movement," *Revue roumaine d'etudes internationales,* 13 (1979): 363–370.

11. At a conference of Africanists from the European communist states held in late 1976, it was argued that economic relations of the CMEA states with Africa were developing erratically because of a lack of common principles, strategies, and programs. *Kulpolitika,* no. 1 (1977): 132; cited in Aurel Bereznai, "Hungary's Presence in Black Africa," *Radio Free Europe Research,* RAD Background Report, no. 75 (Hungary), 2 April 1970, p. 10.

12. Data are taken from the official statistical yearbooks of the East European states. For a discussion of East European economic relations with Africa, see Roger E. Kanet, "Eastern Europe and Sub-Saharan Africa," in *The Communist States and Sub-Saharan Africa,* ed. Thomas H. Henriksen, ed. (Stanford, Calif.: Hoover Institution Press, 1981).

13. See "Honeckers Afrika-Korps: Hilfstruppe für Moskaus Machtstrategie," *Der Spiegel,* 35, no. 10 (3 March 1980): 43.

14. For East Germany, see Johannes Kuppe, "Investitionen, die sich

Lohnten: Zur Reise Honeckers Nach Afrika," *Deutschland Archiv,* 7 (1979), pp. 347–352; "Honeckers Afrika-Korps," pp. 42–43; and Klaus Willerding, "Zur Afrikapolitik der DDR," *Deutsche Aussenpolitik,* 24, no. 8 (1979): 9–11. For Romania, see Gilberg, "Romania, Yugoslavia, and Africa," p. 46.

15. William F. Robinson, "Eastern Europe's Presence in Black Africa," *Radio Free Europe Research,* RAD Background Report, no. 142 (Eastern Europe), 21 June 1979, p. 4. For a discussion of East German relations with African parties and the role of the GDR in training African cadres see Bernard von Plate, "Aspekte der SED-Parteibeziehungen in Afrika und der arabischen Region," *Deutschland Archiv,* 7 (1979): 132–149.

16. For a recent authoritative discussion of the Soviet-Czechoslovak arms shipment to Egypt in 1955 see Mohammed Heikal, *The Sphinx and the Commissar: The Rise and Fall of Soviet Influence in the Middle East,* (New York: Harper and Row, 1979), pp. 57–60.

17.. "Honeckers Afrika-Korps," p. 43. In early 1979 another estimate placed the number of East German military and police advisers working in Africa and the Middle East at between 3,000 and 4,500. See Elizabeth Pond, "E. Germany's Quiet African Role," *The Christian Science Monitor,* 22 February 1979. According to CIA estimates, only 1,300 military technicians from all of Eastern Europe were working in developing countries in 1978. See Central Intelligence Agency, *Communist Aid to Non-Communist Less Developed Countries 1978: A Research Paper,* ER 79–10401U, September 1979, pp. 3–4.

18. To date the only examination of East European military relations with the Third World is "Revolutionary Agents and Weapons Merchants: East European Arms Transfers to the Third World," by Trond Gilberg. It is scheduled for publication in *Communist Military Aid Programs,* edited by Daniel Papp and John Copper. (Boulder, Colo.: Westview Press, 1982).

19. Central Intelligence Agency, *Communist Aid to Less Developed Countries of the Free World, 1975.* ER 76–10372U, July 1976, p. 4 and *idem, Communist Aid Activities in 1979,* p. 15. According to figures published in *The Economist,* 19 September 1981, the number of Soviet and East European military technicians working in Africa in 1980 came to almost 10,200.

20. See "Honeckers Afrika-Korps," pp. 43ff. Jiri Valenta and Shannon butler (in "East German Security Policies in Africa," pp. 153–155) have provided strong evidence to support the argument that East German military advisors played a major role in training the rebels who invaded Shaba Province of Zaire in May 1978. An interesting Polish *samizdat* article has outlined in some detail the military activities of the GDR in

Africa. Portions of the article from the *KSS KOR* journal have been translated in Robinson, ''Eastern Europe's Presence'' pp. 9–10.

21. Robinson, ''Eastern Europe's Presence,'' p. 7.

22. For a discussion of the growth of Soviet conventional military capabilities see C.G. Jacobsen, *Soviet Strategic Initiatives: Challenge and Response* (New York: Praeger, 1979), pp. 51–72. See also, William J. Durch, Michael D. Davidchik, and Abram N. Shulsky, ''Other Soviet Interventionary Forces—Military Transport Aviation and Airborne Troops,'' in *Soviet Naval Diplomacy,* Bradford Dismukes and James McConnell, eds., (New York: Pergamon Press, 1979), pp. 336–351; and Part IV: ''Projection Capability,'' in *Soviet Naval Influence: Domestic and Foreign Dimensions,* Michael MccGwire and John McDonnell, eds., (New York: Praeger, 1977), pp. 239–320.

23. For a discussion of the importance of these facilities see Hahn and Cottrell, *Soviet Shadow Over Africa,* especially pp. 60ff.

24. ''Syria-USSR: Soviets Asked to Leave Syrian Naval Port,'' *Defense and Foreign Affairs Daily,* 14 January 1977, cited in Robert Harkavy, ''The New Geopolitics: Arms Transfers and the Major Powers' Competition for Overseas Bases,'' in *Arms Transfers in the Modern World,* Stephanie G. Neuman and Robert E. Harkavy, eds., (New York: Praeger, 1979), p. 137.

25. See Nimrod Novik, *On the Shores of Bab Al-Mandab: Soviet Diplomacy and Regional Dynamics* (Philadelphia, Pa.: Foreign Policy Research Institute, 1979); ''New Soviet Role in Africa Alleged,'' *The New York Times,* 10 December 1975, p. 11.

26. For an excellent analysis of the Soviet use of military forces in the developing world see James M. McConnell, ''The 'Rules of the Game': A Theory on the Practice of Superpower Naval Diplomacy,'' in *Soviet Naval Diplomacy,* Dismukes and McConnell, eds., pp. 240–280. For a much more comprehensive study of the Soviet use of military force for political purposes see Stephen S. Kaplan, et al., *Diplomacy of Power: Soviet Armed Forces as a Political Instrument* (Washington, D.C.: Brookings Institution, 1981).

27. According to an agreement signed by Hungary and Mozambique in November 1978, Hungary was to provide military equipment, including tanks and aircraft (most likely acting on behalf of the USSR), as well as military advisors and instructors. *Africa Research Bulletin: Political,* 15, no. 11 (15 December 1978): 5078.

28. For the period 1973–1978, an estimated 43 percent of Soviet military deliveries were paid for in hard currency—$7,390 million of a total of $17,200. This represents approximately one-third of the total hard-currency deficit in Soviet merchandise trade experienced by the Soviet Union during those years. See Paul G. Ericson and Ronald S.

Miller, "Soviet Foreign Economic Behavior: A Balance of Payments Perspective," in *Soviet Economy in a Time of Change*, U.S. Congress, Joint Economic Committee (Washington, D.C.: U.S. Government Printing Office, 1979), II, pp. 212, 214. Unfortunately, comparable date on East European arms transfers are not available.

29. There is evidence, however, that some of the East European governments are reluctant to expand their support to underdeveloped socialist states, such as Vietnam, Afghanistan, Angola, and Mozambique. See Ernst Kux, "Growing Tensions in Eastern Europe," *Problems of Communism*, 29, no. 2, (1980); 34.

30. *Communism in Africa*, David E. Albright, ed. (Bloomington, Ind.: Indiana University Press, 1980), p. 5.

31. The Soviet Union was represented at the independence celebrations, but by a low-ranking delegation. See Radu, "Romania and the Third World," p. 249.

5 Chinese Arms Transfers to Africa

George T. Yu

Arms transfers have become a major instrument of foreign policy of the world's powers, Communist and non-Communist.[1] Although the Soviet Union and the United States were the major suppliers of conventional arms, with 34 percent and 33 percent respectively of the total world arms exports in 1978, other suppliers such as China, France, and the United Kingdom also contributed.[2] The major recipients by region have been the Middle East, Africa, Warsaw Pact nations, and members of NATO, 37 percent, 25 percent, 10 percent, and 9 percent, respectively.[3] Arms transfer has served a number of objectives for the suppliers, including political influence and leverage, direct and indirect economic benefits, security considerations, and other factors. For the recipients, the arms have served equally vital needs, support of political and military elite security and stability, establishment and maintenance of special relationships with external powers, and other considerations. Here it is important for us to emphasize that arms transfer does not take place in a vacuum: A felt need by the recipient, real or perceived, must be present. In short, arms transfers as a foreign-policy instrument will continue to be utilized by the world's powers as long as it is thought to achieve foreign-policy objectives and to serve some needs on the part of the recipients.

This chapter will examine Chinese arms transfers to Africa on three primary levels. First, we will analyze the context of China's arms transfers, namely, China's African policy. Both the stages and the objectives of China's policy will be discussed. Second, Chinese arms transfers to Africa will be examined. Here we will look at the extent and level of Chinese arms exports to Africa. Finally, a case study of Chinese arms transfers to Africa will be presented. China's role as Tanzania's principle arms supplier for almost a decade will be considered. It is our contention that political influence and leverage has been China's major foreign-policy objective in Africa and that arms transfers have served as a useful but marginal foreign-policy instrument.

China's African Policy

The development of China's African policy can be divided into five major periods. Though Chinese Communist elites had long accepted Lenin's

101

thesis that national liberation struggles in colonial areas against the imperialist powers constituted a primary feature of international politics, the People's Republic of China following its establishment in 1949 did not immediately extend its international activities to Africa. In the early 1950s, Chinese foreign policy was chiefly directed at resolving the issues of protecting its eastern and southern flanks against the perceived American threat, and cultivating the friendship of the Asian states to its south and southwest. A firm alliance with the USSR and the Communist world was also instituted. The initial stage of China's relations with Africa, therefore, did not begin until the mid-1950s, following the Bandung Conference of 1955.

The Bandung Conference marked the beginning of a formal Chinese policy toward Africa. First, six African states were represented at Bandung, thereby providing for direct Chinese contact with Africa. Egypt, one of the six African states at the conference, was the first African state to recognize China in 1956. Second, China extended the five principles of peaceful coexistence, first developed as a framework for relations with India and Burma in the early 1950s, to Africa and the rest of what came to be known as the Third World. Indeed, in subsequent relations with Africa, China never failed to include the five principles as the guiding doctrine governing relations with each African state. Finally, by the time of the Bandung Conference the Chinese elite had begun to appreciate the importance of the Third World in combating adversaries and winning international support and recognition. The formal recognition of the provisional government of the Republic of Algeria in 1958, participation in the Cairo-based Afro-Asian People's Solidarity Organization in the 1950s, and the establishment of formal relations with three other African states, Guinea (1959), Morocco (1958) and Sudan (1958), can be seen in this light. By the end of the decade, China's formal presence was clearly in evidence in Africa north of the Sahara; developments south of the Sahara combined with new directions in Chinese foreign policy were to soon greatly intensify China's role in Africa.

The second period in China's African policy, covering the years 1960–1965, was an era of great activity. Two dominant factors explain the high tide of Chinese interest. First, these years constituted a high point in the African decolonialization movement. Between January 1960 and December 1965, twenty-nine African colonies won independence, with sixteen African states gaining independence in 1960 alone. At the height of its offensive (1964–1965), China initiated a major campaign to secure African recognition and support, almost indiscriminately seeking relations with the new African states. No fewer than fifteen new African states entered into formal relations with China during this period. It was during these years that Zhou Enlai and Chen Yi made their grand tour of Africa, intended to further Chinese-African relations and to gather support for a second Bandung-type Afro-Asian conference. The conference was doomed by a coup d'etat in Algeria, site of the proposed meeting; however meanwhile China had succeeded in establishing a presence in the region south of the Sahara, thereby extending its influence to the entire continent.

A second factor that explained heightened Chinese interest in Africa was the Sino-Soviet conflict. Following the open break with the Soviet Union in the early 1960s, China sought to challenge Soviet influence and to subvert Soviet revolutionary credibility. Africa, therefore, became a battlefield in the Sino-Soviet struggle. Chinese activities in Africa during this period, directed toward the subversion of Soviet influence and credibility, took many forms, including the drive to identify the Soviet Union as a European state and the attempt to link the Soviet Union with United States imperialism. In addition, China sought to exclude the Soviet Union, politically and otherwise, from the African continent. One of the most overt examples of attempts to achieve this objective was China's campaign to win African support to exclude Soviet participation at the abortive Afro-Asian conference of 1965.

By the mid-1960s, China's African campaign was well launched, although a number of important African states remained to be won over, including Ethiopia, Nigeria, Zaire, and others. The efforts to win friends and combat adversaries in Africa appeared to have constituted a primary focus of Chinese foreign policy. This is supported by the expenditure of resources directed toward Africa, human, financial, and otherwise. We have already mentioned Zhou Enlai's and Chen Yi's visits to Africa during 1964–1965; it should be also noted that through 1966 Chinese economic-aid commitments to Africa totaled $428 million.[4] These and other measurements of Chinese activities seem to point in the direction of a greater Chinese role in Africa.

The outbreak of the Cultural Revolution in 1966 changed China's African policy. The third period in China's relations with Africa without question was a stage of retreat. Several factors contributed to this new situation. First, China's militant posture did much to antagonize many African states. The radical call for the Third World countryside to surround the Western industrial cities, the support for violent revolutionary change, and the promotion of armed struggle were not well received by the independent African states, who were mainly preoccupied with the problems of nation building and survival. Second, China's appearance of withdrawal from the international arena, symbolized by the recall of all its ambassadors to Africa (except China's emissary to Cairo) and the great reduction its economic assistance, further contributed to its hostile image among the African states. Finally, preoccupied as the country was with domestic developments—the political and social upheavals of the Cultural Revolution, China's budding African policy (and its foreign policy in general) fell victim, in operational terms, to the demands and needs of the moment. Friendly relations with select African states such as Tanzania constituted the excepton rather than the rule during this period. One measurement of China's retreat is the fact that, whereas eighteen African states maintained formal diplomatic internation with China just prior to the Cultural Revolution, only thirteen did so in 1969.

The early 1970s was the fourth period in China's African policy. China reemerged as a major actor on the African continent. While the conclusion of the Cultural Revolution enabled China to once again turn outwards, a primary factor explaining the new international activism was China's deteriorating relationship with the Soviet Union. The Soviet invasion of Czechoslovakia in 1968, the growing military confrontation along the Chinese-Soviet frontier, and the border clashes in 1969 signaled to China that the Soviet Union, rather than the United States, had become the primary adversary, threatening China's security. A consequence of this view was China's renewed drive to secure international recognition and support in Africa, an attempt to internationalize its anti-Soviet policy. China's new views of the world were formally presented as the "theory of the three worlds" in 1974.[5] The world was now divided into three parts: the superpowers, the United States and the USSR; the Second World, comprised of Eastern and Western Europe, Japan, and Oceania; and the Third World, the developing countries of Africa, Asia, and Latin America. The international struggle consisted of the opposition of the Third World (joined by the Second World) against the superpowers, principally the Soviet Union. And China was a member of the developing Third World. China's theory of the three worlds was clearly an attempt at an international-united-front strategy directed against the Soviet Union. In line with this strategy, China sought to cultivate relations with all the African states.

In operational terms, Chinese activities in Africa were intensive during this period. China undertook an almost indiscriminate search for recognition and support among the Africa states, from Equatorial Guinea to Ethiopia. Between January 1970 and December 1972, China established formal diplomatic relations with eleven additional African states and restored relations with four. By early 1973, China had established formal relations with a total of twenty-nine African states. Meanwhile, African leaders invited to visit China included the President of the Mozambique Liberation Front (1971) and the President of Zambia (1974). On the economic front, Chinese economic-aid commitments to Africa totaled almost $3 billion for the 1970–1974 period.[6] There can be no doubt that in both strategical and operational terms, Africa was a primary theater of activitics of Chinese foreign policy in the early 1970s. China had once again become a force in African international politics.

The fifth and final stage to date of Chinese policy toward Africa dates from the mid-1970s on. This period has witnessed both a decline in the Chinese attention level and an attempt to formulate new patterns of relations with Africa. Several considerations explain China's behavior. First, China's stress upon internal development, the "four modernizations", has diverted attention and resources from its international activities. Consider, for example, economic assistance. Whereas Chinese aid commitments to Africa totaled almost $3 billion for the 1970–1974 period, as we have noted, economic aid totaled only $1 billion for the years 1975–1979.[7] China itself experienced serious domestic economic problems beginning in the mid-1970s, which no doubt limited its ability in the foreign-aid arena. Second, by the mid-1970s China's objective of securing the recognition and support of the majority of the African states had been achieved. China had also gained admission to the United Nations and other international organizations. Third, the movement toward reconciliation with the United States, begun in the early 1970s and cumulating in the establishment of formal diplomatic relations in 1979, took up much of China's diplomatic energies, thereby limiting its attention to the Third World. The importance of relations with the United States were both economic, a possible source of assistance for the "four modernizations", and strategic, a potential ally against the Soviet Union. Finally, with the American connection established, in the early 1980s China began to redirect its attention to the Third World. This included a visit by China's Foreign Minister to Africa in 1981, discussions between Chinese and African leaders, and Chinese attempts to formulate a new assistance program stressing technical aid. On a more general plane, China also supported Africa's and the Third World's demands for a new international economic order. In the early 1980s, China appeared to be struggling with how best to reestablish close ties with the Third World; as part of the Third World, Africa was certain to continue as a focus of Chinese foreign policy.

Given the history and stages of China's African policy since the late 1950s, it is clear that the policy has experienced vast changes over time, with specific policy goals at different periods. Nevertheless, three primary objectives can be identified, though to be sure, these have not been stressed equally, nor always sought concurrently, as we have noted. First, international recognition and support has constituted a prime objective. For example, in the late 1950s and early 1960s China sought African support both to enhance its international status and to combat American imperialism; the goal of recognition and support remained constant during the 1960s and 1970s, though Soviet social imperialism replaced the United

States as the principle enemy; and in the 1970s and 1980s China sought support for its theory of the three worlds of uniting with Africa and the Third World to oppose Soviet hegemony to and recognize China as a Third World nation. Second, Africa has served as a battlefield against the superpowers. This has been especially true with regard to combating the Soviet Union. The two high tides of Chinese activism in Africa, the early 1960s and the early 1970s, were both periods of intensive competition with the Soviet Union. Finally, the development of Africa has been viewed as a stage in the world's unfolding revolutionary struggle, and the unfailing support of African liberation movements served the vital function of establishing and maintaining China's revolutionary credibility, China's support of the Mozambique, Zimbabwe and other liberation movements together with strong ties with those African states supporting such movements, for example, Tanzania, gave credence to China's revolutionary posture. We should mention that this objective has been linked to China's attempt to win the status of ideological guide in the context of the Sino-Soviet conflict.

It remains for us to examine how China has sought to achieve its objectives in Africa, focusing on the utilization of one foreign-policy instrument, arms transfer.

Chinese Arms Transfers

China, as other major powers, employs a variety of formal and informal instruments in the conduct of foreign policy. These range from arms transfers, diplomatic interaction, and cultural exchange to economic and technical assistance, radio broadcasts, trade, and other instruments. The decision to utilize one instrument or one set of instruments as opposed to another has been a function both of the value that China assigned to the foreign-policy objective and Chinese capabilities for effective use of a given instrument within a given context. We cannot, of course, ignore the felt need and considered expectation of the recipient; the donor must attempt to employ the correct tool or tools. In the instance of China's African policy, China has used a vast variety of instruments to achieve its goals; not all the instruments have been used with equal effect, nor equally. And China may have been limited in the use of a specific instrument due to limitations of its own capabilities. The use of foreign policy instruments, therefore, is neither automatic in terms of choice, nor free in terms of utilization outside a specific context. China's use of arms transfers as a tool in the conduct of its African policy must be understood in this setting.

In terms of dollar value, known Chinese arms-transfer commitments have been relatively limited. Table 5–1 sets forth Chinese arms transfers to the non-Communist Third World; the table lists the value of Chinese arms transfer during the 1970–1979 period, with the value of Soviet arms transfer for the period also provided for comparison. This is followed by table 5–2, which sets forth Chinese and Soviet arms transfers to African countries for 1967–1976, an intensive period of Chinese activities. Finally, a summary comparison is presented, in table 5–3, of Chinese military and economic assistance to Africa for 1965–1974 and 1974–1978; this is provided to offer a sense of the ratio of economic to military assistance. All three tables are designed to provide both the basic data on Chinese arms transfer to Africa and the situational-environmental context and level of activity. (No doubt our tables would have greater meaning if the periods and the years for all three tables were identical. Unfortunately, this is not now possible, especially for arms-transfer data that match Chinese arms transfers to African countries on an annual basis. Our data, therefore, do not allow us the luxury of comparing common periods and years.)

Let us turn to an examination of the tables. First, it is evident from the data that Chinese arms transfer to Africa has been limited. The data in tables 5–1 and 5–2 suggest that Chinese arms transfers have been minuscule, especially when compared to those of the Soviet Union, whether on a global (Third World) or regional (African) basis. The level of Chinese arms transfers has been also very small when compared to the utilization of another foreign-policy instrument, economic assistance, as indicated in table 5–3. This may suggest a Chinese choice of favoring one foreign-policy tool over another or it may suggest a problem of

Table 5–1

Chinese and Soviet Military Aid to the Non-Communist Third World, 1970–1979

(millions of U.S. dollars)

Year	China	Soviet	Ratio of Chinese to Soviet Aid
1970	65	1,150	.06
1971	80	1,590	.05
1972	80	1,690	.05
1973	25	2,890	.01
1974	90	5,735	.02
1975	40	3,325	.01
1976	145	5,550	.03
1977	75	8,715	.01
1978	135	2,465	.05
1979	140	8,365	.02

Source: U.S. Central Intelligence Agency, National Foreign Assessment Center, *Communist Aid Activities in Non-Communist Less Developed Countries, 1979 and 1954–79*, October 1980, p. 13.

Table 5–2
Chinese and Soviet Arms Transfers to Africa, 1967–1976
(millions of U.S. dollars)

African State	China	USSR
Algeria	—	315
Angola	—	190
Benin	—	1
Burundi	1	—
Cameroon	5	—
Central African Empire	—	1
Chad	—	5
Congo	10	10
Egypt	5	2,365
Equatorial Guinea	—	5
Gambia	1	—
Guinea	5	50
Guinea-Bissau	—	5
Libya	—	1,005
Malagasy	—	1
Malawi	1	—
Mali	1	25
Morocco	—	10
Mozambique	1	15
Nigeria	—	70
Rwanda	1	—
Somalia	—	181
Sudan	5	65
Tanzania	75	30
Tunisia	5	—
Uganda	—	65
Zaire	21	—
Zambia	5	—
Totals	$142	$4,424

Source: U.S. Arms Control and Disarmament Agency, *World Military Expenditures and Arms Transfer 1967–1976*, Washington, D.C., 1978, pp. 158–159.

Chinese capabilities, or both. Whatever the answer, it is clear that, as a general foreign-policy instrument, arms transfers have not been China's strength. However, this has not precluded China's use of military aid as one instrument among several in the conduct of its African policy, nor has it prevented China's use of this tool with considerable effect in a specific context, as we shall presently note. Second, the number of African recipients of Chinese arms were also fewer compared to those of the Soviet Union, fifteen versus twenty-one. However, the number of recipients had increased over the years, no doubt representing China's acknowledgment of the importance of this foreign-policy instrument. For example, during 1973–1976, there were eleven new recipients of Chinese

Table 5–3
Chinese Military and Economic Assistance to Africa, 1965–1974 and 1974–1978
(millions of U.S. dollars)

Period	Military	Economic	Ratio of Economic to Military
1965–1974	81	1,636	.05
1974–1978	160	1,509	.11

Source: U.S. Arms Control and Disarmament Agency, *World Military Expenditures and Arms Transfer 1965–1974*, Washington, D.C. 1976, pp. 74–75; *World Military Expenditures and Arms Transfers 1969–1978*, Washington, D.C., 1980, pp. 160–161; and Joint Economic Committee, Congress of the U.S., *Chinese Economy Post-Mao*, Washington, D.C., 1978, pp. 852–853.

Note: Includes Egypt.

weapons (Burundi, Cameroon, Egypt, Gambia, Malawi, Mali, Mozambique, Rwanda, Sudan, Tunisia, and Zaire); the value of arms transfers to these new recipients totaled about $50 million.

Third, African recipients of Chinese arms received an average of only $10 million worth of military equipment, as against the average of $210 million that recipients of Soviet weapons obtained, as noted in table 5–2. But even the $10 million figure constituted an inflated value of Chinese arms transfer. Eighty percent or twelve of the fifteen recipients received $5 million or less worth of Chinese arms, with six or 50 percent of the 80 percent receiving only $1 million per recipient. This pattern suggests that Chinese arms transfer may serve other than meaningful military value. As one observer has noted, such support may increase China's international recognition, but it "has had little more than a nuisance value from a military standpoint."[8]

Fourth, China has extended a generally higher level of arms transfer, as noted above, in a few instances. The best example was Tanzania during 1967–1976, which received $75 million or 53 percent of China's military assistance to Africa. Another major recipient was Zaire, $21 million. But in both cases, the value of Chinese arms transfer to the two recipients represented a poor comparison to the level of Soviet military aid to some of its principle recipients, Algeria, $315 million; Egypt, $2.3 billion; and Libya, $1 billion.

Finally, Chinese arms transfers have not operated in a vacuum, free of the felt needs of the recipients or without direct competition. During the 1967–1976 period, China improved its position among select recipients by supplying most of their military needs. This is measured by the percentage of arms supplied by China in terms of the total arms import by the recipient. Thus China provided for 33 percent of Cameroon's military needs, 50 percent of the Congo's, 100 percent of Gambia's, 20 percent of Malawi's, and 60 percent of Tanzania's.[9] Whether because of choice or capabilities, China has not always been able to maintain a leading position as a supplier; the felt needs of African states have also been increasing. These needs have not infrequently been meet by the USSR, China's competitor. For example, during 1974–1978 the USSR replaced China as the principle arms supplier to Tanzania, $110 million to $30 million.[10] Soviet arms transfers represented 61 percent of Tanzania's total arms imports for the period, with China now supplying only 17 percent of Tanzania's military needs.

What arms have China supplied Africa? According to the U.S. Arms Control and Disarmament Agency, during 1973–1977 China transfered to Africa a variety of weapon systems, including (1) 110 tanks and self-propelled guns, (2) 140 artillery pieces, (3) 20 naval crafts, (4) 20 supersonic combat aircraft, (5) 5 subsonic combat aircraft, and (6) 10 helicopters, representing about 2 percent of Africa's major weapons imports.[11] On a country basis, China has supplied T-62 tanks to the Congo; MiG-19 and F-6 aircraft to Egypt; Shanghai-class naval craft to Guinea; T-62 tanks, MiG-17 and MiG-19 aircraft, and Shanghai-class naval craft to Tanzania; T-62 tanks and Shanghai-class naval craft to Zaire; and MiG-19 aircraft to Zambia.[12] The above constituted a sample of the known and registered arms transfers,[13] but there also have been reported Chinese arms transfers to African liberation groups, said to have been supplied via third countries. Thus, the Front for the Liberation of Mozambique (FRELIMO) of Mozambique reportedly received Chinese arms in Tanzania during the liberation struggle and the Zimbabwe African National Union (ZANU) of Zimbabwe obtained Chinese weapons in Mozambique, following the latter's independence.[14] China was also reported to have supplied arms to Angola's FNLA's (National Front for the Liberation of Angola) forces via Zaire.[15]

As part of the military assistance program, China has also sent military advisers and instructors to Africa and trained African military personnel in China. Tables 5–4 and 5–5 provide some data on these two programs.

Tanzania: A Case Study in Chinese Arms Transfer

Until 1974, China was the principle arms supplier to Tanzania, providing more than 50 percent of Tanzania's needs. What was the extent of China's arms transfer to Tanzania and what was the specific situational-environmental context in which this transfer took place? An examination of China's arms transfer to Tanzania provides a good case study of both the

Table 5–4
African Military Personnel Trained in China, 1955–1979

African State	Number of Personnel
Cameroon	125
Congo	415
Guinea	360
Mali	50
Mozambique	50
Sierra Leone	150
Somalia	30
Sudan	200
Tanzania	1,025
Togo	55
Zaire	175
Zambia	60
Other	10
Total	2,705

Source: U.S. Central Intelligence Agency, National Foreign Assessment Center, *Communist Aid Activities in Non-Communist Less Developed Countries, 1979 and 1954–1979*, October 1980, p. 16.

Table 5–5
Chinese Military Personnel in Africa, 1977, 1978, and 1979

African State	1977	1978	1979
Equatorial Guinea	100	100	100
Guinea	25	30	—
Mali	—	15	5
Mozambique	100	100	15
Other	350	345	185
Total	575	590	305

Source: U.S. Central Intelligence Agency, National Foreign Assessment Center, *Communist Aid to Less Developed Countries of the Free World, 1977*, November 1978; U.S. Central Intelligence Agency, National Foreign Assessment Center, *Communist Aid Activities in Non-Communist Less Developed Countries 1978*, September 1979; and U.S. Central Intelligence Agency, National Foreign Assessment Center, *Communist Aid Activities in Non-Communist Less Developed Countries, 1979 and 1954–1979*, October 1980.

context, in terms of Tanzania's felt needs, and the Chinese capabilities, measured in terms of the extent and level of the military assistance program.

Chinese-Tanzanian military interaction began in the early 1960s, following Tanzania's independence. Once begun, the military ties experienced a phenomenal growth, with Tanzania becoming the primary African recipient of Chinese arms.[16] This relationship was to last well over a decade. Chinese military assistance was primarily in the form of training and supplies provided by China to Tanzania under existing economic-

and technical-assistance agreements and special agreements covering specific military programs. One of the first programs was the shipment of 6,000 tons of small arms and the dispatch of an eleven-man army military-training mission by China to Tanzania in September 1964.[17] The mission was commanded by a Colonel Huang and consisted of six military instructors and four interpreters. Interestingly, it was reported that the military program was provided by China under terms of its 1964 Economic and Technical Cooperation Agreement with Tanzania.

The Tanzanian army was the first branch of the armed forces to establish military ties with and receive supplies from China. The relationship eventually included Chinese instructors for domestic training of Tanzanian army officers and new recruits, and training in China for specialized personnel, such as tank crews. In addition, China contributed toward the building of Army House at the Migombani military camp on Zanzibar and provided $1.5 million for a barracks complex at the Nachingwea military base in southern-mainland Tanzania. Chinese military hardware provided included small arms, mortars, T-59 medium-weight tanks, and T-62 lightweight tanks.[18] By 1969, most of Tanzania's army supplies were provided by China.[19]

During the middle and late 1960s, China began to provide the military requisites for the Tanzanian navy and air force. It was during President Nyerere's state visit to China in 1968 that additional Chinese military assistance was secured, including jet fighters and training of Tanzanian pilots. Though no announcement was made in 1968, a hint of China's new arms-transfer program was revealed in a report of the President's visit to a Chinese air-force base near Beijing, where he saw an exhibition of flight and met with the pilots. In a report to the Tanzanian National Assembly in 1969, the Minister of Defense announced that work on the establishment of an Tanzanian air force had begun; this was reported completed in 1970. However, in neither instance was the source or the type of jet fighter made public. Not until April 1972 did Tanzania formally announce that China would be providing assistance to the air force; there was no announcement from the supplier, China. The Tanzanian Defense Forces reported that Tanzania expected to receive at least one squadron of Chinese-built MiG jet fighters in late 1973.[20] A Chinese-built military field was reported near Morogoro, some 100 miles west of Dar es Salaam, the capital. According to the London-based International Institute for Strategic Studies, China would supply Tanzania with 12 MiG-17/F-4 aircraft in 1973.[21] *The Military Balance 1979–1980* reported that Tanzania's air-force combat aircraft included three MiG-17/F-4 and nine MiG-19/F-6 Chinese-supplied aircraft.[22]

China had also agreed during President Nyerere's 1968 visit to assist Tanzania in building a navy. An agreement was signed on 21 June 1968 in Beijing, providing for China's assistance in the constructon of a naval base at Dar es Salaam.[23] Work on the base began in January 1970; it was officially opened on 6 December 1971 and was designated Tanzania's naval headquarters.[24] In 1966, China had supplied Tanzania with four 20-ton patrol boats and had trained naval personnel in China.[25] By 1979–1980, the Tanzanian navy had received from China seven Shanghai-class patrol boats, four hydrofoils, four coastal-patrol craft and two LCMs.[26]

The development of China as Tanzania's principle supplier of conventional arms cannot be understood apart from Tanzania's security needs. First, there was the need by the new nation to create a national security force. This must be viewed against the background of the foreign influence on the military-command structure after independence and the army mutiny of 1964. At the time of Tanganyika's independence in 1961, its military consisted of two understrength and ill-equipped battalions; total manpower was about 1,000. The troops were commanded by British officers; there were only three Tanganyikan junior officers in 1961. The new government undertook a program to develop the security forces, and, beginning in 1962, Africanization was also initiated. Despite these and other efforts, overt progress was slow, especially in the command structure. By 1964, while the number of Tanganyikan officers had increased to about thirty, the military continued to be commanded by the British, who manned the army headquarters the key post commands, and the technical services. A number of other problems faced the military, including an unfavorable wage scale—$15 a month for a private. These and other issues came to a head in the army mutiny of January 1964, which brought about drastic changes.

One immediate consequence of the mutiny was the Tanzanian government's decision to construct a new military force; another was to seek military assistance other than British. The formal reconstruction of the military began in March 1964, with the army selected to spearhead the movement. By September a new army of about 2,000 had been recruited. The initial problems were stupendous: there were no officers with any command experience; the army headquarters lacked officers with staff experience; there were not enough commissioned officers nor enough noncommissioned officers; there were no qualified technical personnel; there were insufficient numbers of weapons; and there was no logistical support, including vehicles, equipment, uniforms, and accommodations.

In view of the known lack of human and material resources, it was clear that Tanzania required foreign assistance if it were to construct a national military force. Exclusive dependence upon British aid was no longer acceptable; the mutiny had been led by British-trained troops. Tanzania thus looked to other foreign sources for assistance. A Chinese military-assistance program was begun in September 1964, as we have noted. In addition, Canada, Israel, and West Germany also assisted Tanzania in building up its security forces. Help in the form of training for infantry-officer candidates in India, Pakistan, Russia, the Sudan, the United Arab Republic, and even the United Kingdom was also received. For various reasons the majority of the foreign military-assistance programs were unable to fully meet Tanzania's security needs. Only China provided both training and hardware for all the military services. In fact, by the early 1970s Chinese assistance to Tanzania constituted one of the few foreign-military programs that had remained in continuous operation since 1964. During this period, the Tanzanian military had grown from a 2,000-man army to an 11,000-man multiservice military establishment.

A second factor that contributed to Tanzania's security needs and the development of Chinese-Tanzanian military interaction was Tanzania's propinquity to the southern African region and its active support of African liberation movements. Before Mozambique's independence in 1975, Tanzania perceived a security threat from the militarily superior Portuguese. Tanzania had also been concerned with a threat from South Africa. Tanzania's security concern was increased by its extension of shelter and support to African liberation movements, such as FRELIMO before Mozambique's independence, and Tanzania's active support of the total liberation of Africa from colonialism and white-minority rule, such as its membership in Africa's front-line states. Before 1975, Tanzanian territory had been raided by the Portuguese along the Mozambique border; Tanzania also considered itself well within the range of South African missiles and bombers. It also was worried about possible South African (and earlier Portuguese) retaliatory actions against liberation movement bases in Tanzania, much as Israel had attacked guerrilla bases in Arab countries. These consequences of geography and policy were perceived as requiring the building of a Tanzanian military establishment—thus the growth of China's military-assistance program to Tanzania.

A final factor that contributed to the growth of Chinese-Tanzanian military ties was Tanzania's difficulties in arms procurement. Given Tanzania's determination to create a national security force and its urgently felt security needs, Tanzania was equally determined to acquire a degree of conventional military capability. To this end Tanzania sought to acquire the traditional symbols of military power. However, it found that arms procurement was not always easy. In its search for military assistance, Tanzania concluded a five-year agreement with the Federal Republic of Germany in 1964, whereby Germany would provide help for the creation of an air wing and assist in the formation of a marine-police unit, complete with patrol boats.[27] The military projects were suddenly terminated when Tanzania allowed the German Democratic Republic to establish a consulate general at Dar es Salaam in 1965. The Federal Republic of Germany, adhering to the Halstein Doctrine, which held that the Federal Republic could not have diplomatic relations with any country that recognized the German Democratic Republic, ''unilaterally and without notice, broke [the] five-year training agreement relating to the new air wing, and returned all their technicians overnight.''[28] The marine-police-unit agreement was also terminated. Tanzania's predicament was partially resolved by a Chinese offer to assume responsibility for the marine-police-unit training program and to make a gift of four patrol boats.

Another instance where China assumed a military-assistance program originally undertaken by a different donor, thereby further increasing China's military interaction with Tanzania, was the case of Canada. In 1964, Canada agreed to provide military assistance to Tanzania. This included the training of the Tanzanian army and the taking over the defunct German pilot-training project.[29] In 1967 the Canadian program was reported to be worth $15 million and included a fifty-six-member air-training team, a thirty-three-member army-training team, and provision for eight noncombatant aircraft. For a number of reasons, however, the Canadian military-assistant program did not work out to Tanzania's satisfaction. In a debate in the Tanzanian National Assembly, for example, members questioned whether Canadian assistance was not designed to weaken the Tanzanian military, since both Canada and Portugal were members of NATO.[30] More immediately, Canadian assistance did not provide the military weapons—jet combat fighters, other combat aircraft, and military armaments—that Tanzania regarded as security essentials. For these and other reasons, the Canadian-Tanzanian military-assistance program was not renewed when it ended in early 1970. With Canada's departure, China became the principle military source for Tanzania: the army would be trained by Chinese instructors, China was supplying the naval craft and training for the navy and China was providing the aircraft and training for the air force. China by the 1970s had thus established itself in close military linkage with Tanzania.

China's role as the principle supplier of Tanzania's military needs came to an end in 1974; the Soviet Union replaced China as Tanzania's most important arms source. Among the factors contributing to the change was the ability of the Soviet Union to provide the modern weapons considered necessary by Tanzania to counter Uganda, weapons that China was either unable or unwilling to supply. During the mid-1970s Tanzania was also in need of arms to support the Zimbabwe liberation struggle.

China has not since reestablished its role as Tanzania's principle arms supplier.

Concluding Observations

This inquiry has provided an examination of an instance of arms transfer from a major power to a world region, specifically, Chinese arms transfer to Africa. Three concluding observations can be suggested. First, arms transfers have not been a major tool of Chinese foreign policy toward Africa. As one foreign-policy instrument among a set of instruments, including economic aid and technical assistance, arms transfer has been a useful, but marginal, Chinese foreign-policy tool. During certain periods and toward specific recipients, China has used with profit, political and otherwise, this instrument, meeting the security needs of selected African states and groups. As a whole, the extent and levels of Chinese arms transfers to Africa has been limited by international standards, especially from China's competitor, the Soviet Union. China's limitations as an arms supplier have been due to many reasons, including capability constraints in terms of supply levels and types of weapons, and changing policy choices that gave greater stress to internal-development needs and utilization of new foreign-policy instruments.

Second, Chinese arms transfers can be best understood as a barometer of Chinese foreign policy toward Africa and the politics of Chinese-African interaction. In the first case, China's use of overt arms transfers was most widespread during periods of heightened diplomatic activity, such as during the early 1970s. Arms transfers, together with economic aid and technical assistance and other instruments, constituted the tools utilized to achieve Chinese foreign-policy objectives. The importance of Chinese weapons lay not so much in their military impact as in their political dimensions of winning friends and gaining influence among African nations and groups. In the latter instance, Chinese arms were vital in establishing close relations with certain African nations, for instance, Tanzania. Here again, the role of Chinese arms, while not insignificant over a period of time, must be .nderstood in the context of Chinese-Tanzanian political interaction, China's most successful African linkage through the early 1970s. We must not neglect the huge expenditure of Chinese economic aid ($360 million through 1979) that furthered the relationship. In short, similar to other Chinese foreign-policy instruments, the function of arms transfer was far greater in terms of developing and maintaining friendly political relations than was the military impact upon the African recipients.

Finally, China's past record of limited arms transfers to Africa should neither exclude China's continued use of this foreign-policy instrument nor preclude China's future effective use of this tool in a specific context. China possesses the capabilities of providing some conventional weapons and military training to friendly African states and groups. It is one instrument among a set of foreign-policy instruments and it is likely that China will continue to employ all instruments to achieve foreign policy goals. As the case of Tanzania demonstrated, should the situational-environmental context provide an opportunity, China can supply the basic security needs of an African nation, should China decide to make that policy choice. In sum, China can be expected to continue to utilize arms transfers in relations with African states and groups.

Notes

1. Andrew J. Pierre, *The Global Politics of Arms Sales* (Princeton, N.J.: Princeton University Press, 1982).

2. U.S. Arms Control and Disarmament Agency (USACDA), *World Military Expenditures and Arms Transfer 1969–1978* (Washington, D.C.: Government Printing Office, 1980) p. 9.

3. USACDA, *World Military Expenditures and Arms Transfer 1969–1978*, p. 8.

4. U.S. Department of State, *Communist States and Developing Countries: Aid and Trade in 1974*, Washington, D.C., February 1976.

5. Deng Xiaoping presented China's "theory of the three world" in a major address to the United Nations in April 1974. Earlier, in February 1974, Mao Zedong reportedly first discussed this theory with President Kaunda of Zambia during his state visit to China. Institute of West-Asia and African Studies, Chinese Academy of Social Sciences, *Feizhou gai-kuang* (African Survey) (Beijing, 1981) pp. 347–348. For an official statement on Mao's theory, see editorial department, "Chairman Mao's Theory of the Differentiation of the Three Worlds is a Major Contribution to Marxism-Leninism," *Renmin Ribao*, 1 November 1977.

6. U.S. Central Intelligence Agency, *Communist Aid to Less Developed Countries of the Free World, 1976*, August 1977; U.S. Central Intelligence Agency, *Communist Aid Activities in Non-Communist Less Developed Countries 1978*, September 1979; and U.S. Central Intelligence Agency, *Communist Aid Activities in Non-Communist Less Developed Countries, 1979 and 1954–1979*, October 1980.

7. U.S. Central Intelligence Agency, *Communist Aid Activities, 1979*.

8. Waldemar A. Nielsen, *The Great Powers and Africa* (New York: Praeger, 1969) p. 212, as quoted in Joseph P. Smaldone, "Soviet and

Chinese Military Aid and Arms Transfers to Africa: A Contextual Analysis,'' in Warren Weinstein and Thomas H. Henriksen, eds., *Soviet and Chinese Aid to African Nations*, New York: Praeger, 1980, pp. 76–116.

9. USACDA, *World Military Expenditures 1969–1976*, p. 159.

10. USACDA, *World Military Expenditures 1969–1978*, p. 161.

11. USACDA, *World Military Expenditures 1968–1977*, p. 16!.

12. These examples are taken from The International Institute for Strategic Studies, *The Military Balance 1979–1980*, London, 1979, pp. 48–56, 103–107.

13. International Institute for Strategic Studies, *Military Balance*, and the yearbooks World Armaments and Disarmament published by the Stockholm International Peace Research Institute, Stockholm, Sweden, various years.

14. See for example the account by Michael H. Glantz and Mohamed A. El-Khawas, "On the Liberation African Liberation Movements," in Warren Weinstein, ed., *Chinese and Soviet Aid to Africa* (New York: 1975) pp. 202–221.

15. According to John Stockwell, former chief of the CIA-Angolan Task Force in the 1970s, 112 Chinese military advisers arrived on 29 May 1974 in Zaire to train FNLA forces. See Stockwell, John, *In Search of Enemies* (New York: Norton, 1978) p. 67.

16. This section borrows liberally from my *China's African Policy: A Study of Tanzania* (New York: Praeger, 1975), especially, chapter 5. Unless noted otherwise, all the data is from this source.

17. *Standard* (Dar es Salaam), 1, 10, 16 and 17 September 1964.

18. International Institute for Strategic Studies, *The Military Balance 1972–1973*, London, 1972, p. 40.

19. *Standard*, 2 September 1969.

20. *The Christian Science Monitor*, 26 December 1973.

21. The International Institute for Strategic Studies, *The Military Balance 1973–1974* (London, 1973) p. 42.

22. The International Institute for Strategic Studies, *The Military Balance 1979–1980*, (London, 1970) p. 54.

23. Information Service Division, Ministry of Information and Tourism, *Press Release*, Dar es Salaam, 6 December 1971.

24. Ibid.

25. *Standard*, 5 and 18 November 1966.

26. *The Military Balance 1979–1980*, p. 55.

27. *Standard*, 18 November 1966.

28. Nyerere, Julius K., "Principles and Development," in *Freedom and Socialism*, Dar es Salaam, 1968, p. 190.

29. *Standard*, 6 July 1967.

30. Ibid, 4 July 1967.

Part III
Western Arms and Military Assistance to Africa

6 Western Approaches to Military Assistance to Sub-Saharan Africa: An Overview

Cynthia A. Cannizzo

Western security assistance to sub-Saharan Africa is a tortuous and convoluted phenomenon. Although such a statement could be applied to most security assistance, Africa presents a unique situation in terms of Western assistance for three basic reasons.

First, it is important to note the marginal significance of African security assistance to the West's global pattern. In no case does a Western country's arms trade with sub-Saharan Africa (excluding Rhodesia and South Africa) amount to more than 20 percent of its total arms trade; with the exceptions of France, the Federal Republic of Germany, and Canada, at about 15 percent, the African trade is less than 10 percent of the total.[1] This is not to say 10 or 15 percent is negligible, simply that it is not very impressive when compared to intra-Western trade, to the Middle Eastern, or even to the North African trade. On the assumption that security assistance is an indicator of relative importance to the supplier, Africa is clearly a low priority. And because of this, most Western countries, with the possible exception of France and maybe the United Kingdom, do not have an African policy. Security assistance, therefore, takes place largely on an ad hoc basis without coherent guidelines. African states tend to buy weaponry with regard to their internal situations, but Western states tend to sell weaponry with regard to factors external to African politics and security, such as their own need for exports, need for oil or strategic minerals, and need for access to other parts of the world, especially the Middle East. Due to this policy-less nature of Western assistance, one finds some rather anomolous situations occurring. Western aid has gone to Marxist regimes on occasion, and a fair number of African countries obtain armaments from both Eastern and Western countries. Arming both sides in a serious conflict is also not unknown. There is a marked lack of consistency in applying any kind of human-or political-rights criterion. This is most notorious in the case of French sales to South Africa, but few African states have admirable records on human rights and few suppliers seem to care.

The second important consideration is the market structure in Africa. It is relatively new, really opening up only in the late 1960s with the

121

creation of several new states. The United States is one of the smallest suppliers in the region, rather than the dominant one, as in many other markets. The African market is a buyers' market, with over two dozen suppliers, many of whom are Third World themselves, such as Brazil and India, or Israel and South Africa. A number of factors account for the ability of smaller-supplier countries to obtain a share of this market, including the desire of many of the African states to throw off their colonial heritage, to show Third World solidarity, and the low-cost and high suitability of these suppliers' weaponry to the Africans' own needs. We are also beginning to see the start of indigenous-production capability in some of the larger, more prosperous black African states, such as Kenya and Zaire.

The implications of such a fluid structure are crucially counterposed to some basic reasons for Western transfers. There is a pronounced lack of stability in supplier-recipient relationships, either through an East-West shift, or a deliberate diversification for economic or ideological reasons. Such a situation not only hinders long-range planning and compatibility and training of forces for the recipient, it also clearly reduces the amount of influence a supplier can exert. This, in turn, reinforces the ad hoc nature of Western transfers. Also, any attempts at embargoes are doomed from the start. The buyers' market further suggests that convention arms control is going to have to come from the recipients themselves, since there will always be a supplier if there is a demand. The underlying trends in the market can be seen in table 6–1.

One of the most striking things about this table is that the differences between former French and British colonies are not very great. The Francophone countries were initially more dependent upon France than were the Anglophone ones on the United Kingdom, but both have broken that dependency. The only group to show a highly marked tendency to shift to the Soviet Union are the former Portuguese colonies. The table also indicates the high turnover of main suppliers; that is, there is a lack of stability in supplier-client relationships, and an increasing tendency of African states (with the exception of former British colonies) to buy from several suppliers and from non-major suppliers. The remaining vestiges of the colonial heritage are to be found mainly in the acceptance of foreign troops, either as small garrisons, advisory and training personnel, or interventionary forces. This pattern is strongest for France's former possessions, as discussed in the Kolodziej and Lokulutu chapter of this book.

The third unique aspect of a Western security assistance is a difference in emphasis given to various components of the trade. For example, the

Table 6–1

Changes in Supplier Patterns, 1964–1977, for Sub-Saharan Africa (excluding South Africa and Rhodesia), by Former Colonial Power

	Former Colonial Power (FCP)				
	Britain $N=9$[a]	France $N=15$[b]	Portugal $N=3$[c]	Belgium $N=3$[d]	Others $N=3$[e]
Percent of states with FCP as main supplier[f]					
1963–1974	38	60	xx[g]	0	xx
1974–1977	22	20	0	0	xx
Percent of states changing main supplier between time periods	55	60	xx	33	33
Percent of states with USSR as main supplier					
1963–1974	25	30	xx	0	33
1974–1977	55	20	100	66	66
Average number of suppliers[h]					
1963–1974	5.6	2.1	xx	2.3	2.3
1974–1977	3.6	2.2	3.7	4.0	3.3
Percent of states buying from nonmajors[i]					
1963–1974	75	23	xx	xx	33
1974–1977	80	40	67	33	33

Sources: *World Military Expenditures and Arms Trade, 1963–73; World Military Expenditures and Arms Transfers, 1968–1977.* U.S. Arms Control and Disarmament Agency. Washington, D.C.: U.S. Government Printing Office, 1975 and 1979, respectively.

[a]Includes Botswana, Ghana, Kenya, Malawi, Nigeria, Sudan, Tanzania, Uganda, Zambia. The Gambia, Lesotho, Mauritius, Sierre Leone, and Swaziland are not recorded as purchasing armaments during these time periods.

[b]Includes Benin (Dahomey), Cameroons, the Central Africa Republic, Chad, Congo (B), Gabon, Guinea, Ivory Coast, Madagascar, Mali, Mauritania, Niger, Senegal, Togo, and Upper Volta. For the 1963–1974 period, $N=13$, with Gabon and Madagascar not reported as purchasing armaments.

[c]Includes Angola, Guinea-Bissau, and Mozambique. Cape Verde and Sao Tome not reported as purchasing armaments.

[d]Includes Burundi, Rwanda, and Zaire.

[e]Includes Equitorial Guinea (formerly Spanish), Ethiopia and Liberia (not colonized).

[f]'Main supplier' is defined as the state supplying the most in terms of dollar value, not necessarily the majority.

[g]An 'xx' implies inappropriate or missing data.

[h]The average number of suppliers is an underestimate, as the WME and AT handbook lumps small suppliers together under an 'Others' category and there is no indication of how many countries this is in a particular case. Thus, if a country purchased from other than a major supplier, it was coded as having one additional supplier, even though there may have been more than one.

[i]For the 1963–1974 period, the 'major suppliers' include: US, USSR, France, United Kingdom, Czechoslovakia, PRC, Poland, Canada, and the FRG. For the 1974–1977 period this category includes all of the above and Italy.

use of grant aid and the transfer of second-line or obsolete equipment has been quite pronounced in Africa, although, gradually, these states are acquiring more sophisticated armaments. One also finds a higher percentage of aid and trade go to training and advisement, rather than to direct sales of major equipment. More recently, though, there are signs that the West will transfer sophisticated armaments to states that can pay. The tendency of the West to supply armaments to states that have something to offer in return is also very clear in Africa. In the U.S. case, especially, there is a direct correlation between security assistance on the one hand, and basing/port/overflight rights and strategic resources (oil, minerals) on the other. (The Smaldone chapter draws this parallel quite forcefully.) Thus, Zaire, Kenya, and Nigeria have come to figure rather prominently in Western arms transfers.

Given this background of lack of coherent policy, fluid market structure, and trade-offs for economic and extra-African strategic assets, we can basically expect more of the same in the future. None of the authors in the chapters that follow predict any radical change, but all agree on the continuation and possible acceleration of basic trends. There is likely to be an increased emphasis on economic factors and strategic-resource criteria. Security assistance to Africa will probably continue to reflect its low-priority status, except in instances where the West perceives that its own security can be increased, such as the securing of oil routes against Soviet encroachment. This implies a focusing of attention on the Horn of Africa and in central-northeast states. Since the United States is in the forefront of this move to bolster and protect the Persian Gulf area, the United States is likely to attempt to increase its share of the market. However, internal political factors in the African states themselves will probably limit the extent to which the major Western suppliers can insinuate themselves, and instead, encourage purchases from other Third World countries.

Note

1. U.S. Arms Control and Disarmament Agency, *World Military Expenditures and Arms Transfers, 1968–1977,* ACDA Publication 100 (Washington, D.C.: U.S. Government Printing Office, 1979). See also more recent figures reported in the chapters on France, the United States, and Western Germany.

7

Security Interests and French Arms-Transfer Policy in Sub-Saharan Africa

Edward A. Kolodziej and
Bokanga Lokulutu

This chapter evaluates French arms-transfer policy within the general framework of French security interests in sub-Saharan Africa. Part one sketches the evolution and current structure of France's security ties in sub-Saharan Africa with special attention to Francophone Africa.

Part II outlines the pattern of French arms transfer to sub-Saharan Africa and relates this pattern to developing French security interests in the region and overall French arms-transfer policy. A final section briefly discusses France's prospects in sub-Saharan and Francophone Africa.

The Structure and Evolution of French Security Interests

The Fourth Republic and French Union

Until World War II, French imperial and metropole security interests were viewed as a seamless fabric. Domestic critics of French colonial policy worried that the diffusion of French military capabilities would weaken France's capacity to meet the threat on its eastern border posed by an ascendant Germany. Instead the French empire was invoked to balance German power. Of 700,000 colonial troops who fought in World War II, 160,000 came from black Africa. In his celebrated appeal for assistance from the French people of June 18, 1940, General Charles de Gaulle specifically referred to the existence of the French empire as a major asset in the struggle against German occupation.[1] "Without Empire," declared Gaston Mannerville before the consultative assembly several days after Germany's capitulation, "France would only be a liberated country. Thanks to its Empire, France is a conquering nation."[2]

The empire continued to have a major hold on French strategic thinking throughout the Fourth Republic. The reluctance of postwar regimes to liquidate French colonial and protectorate positions in Southeast Asia, sub-Saharan Africa, and North Africa was conditioned by the view that

The authors would like to thank Jeffrey Starr for his research assistance in the writing of this chapter.

125

French security interests and foreign-policy bargaining power, not to mention French prestige and *grandeur,* depended critically on the preservation of the empire. There was a general recognition, signaled by de Gaulle's Brazzaville speech and the constitution of the Fourth Republic, that France would have to extend greater autonomy to its possessions to maintain its influence and dominance in the developing world. The 1946 constitution created the French Union and provided for representative assemblies to be founded in the overseas territories through the limited suffrage of the indigenous population. The territories were also permitted to elect deputies to the French National Assembly. Several African leaders who were later to lead their countries to independence, including Félix-Houphouët-Boigny of the Ivory Coast and Léopold Senghor of Senegal, served in the National Assembly.

These limited extensions of autonomy had little effect on French security and foreign-policy practices. These remained firmly in the hands of Paris. The empire and the metropole were still conceived of as a unitary grouping in which the security interests of both parts were viewed as inextricably tied. At French prompting, the North Atlantic Treaty was extended to include Algeria. The Cold War provided added justification for French resistance to independence movements. The French argued that local uprisings were provoked by Communist agitation. France was engaged, therefore, in defending the West against Communist expansionism. In meeting these challenges around Europe's periphery, France was supposedly defending European and Atlantic security interests. Drawing on the unhappy experience in Vietnam, French strategists elaborated a theory of revolutionary war in which the Algerian struggle was viewed as the second stage of a Bolshevik effort to encircle the West. The first stage ended with the Communist success in Vietnam.[3] The war in Algeria was stage two. General Paul Ely, chief of staff of French armed forces, raised the possibility of Europe's defeat through a Soviet outflanking move through Africa and the Middle East. Soviet power was seen to be moving along three axes: Europe, the Middle East and Africa, and Southeast Asia. The latter was already lost, leaving two strategic lines of defense in the Middle East and Africa exposed. In the Mediterranean, Soviet pressures were seen to run from Paris to Toulon, Mers el-Kébir and Bizerte in the Middle East, and in Africa from Paris through Dakar and Brazzaville. France's efforts to retain control of its colonies was, therefore, legitimate (because it served to contain Communist and Soviet expansionism, acting in the guise of national independence) and militarily astute (because it prevented the erosion of the West's flank and rear).[4] "This conviction that the security of the nation was at stake on the Mediterranean and African fronts of the European continent," as one observer notes, "was shared not only by the military and conservative politicians, but also by the Socialist Left for whom the Paris-Algiers-Brazzaville axis was central to French security."[5]

The Fifth Republic and the French Community

The French Union and the Fourth Republic that gave it birth were too weak to withstand the strains engendered by demands for independence from the colonies. The Fifth Republic of General Charles de Gaulle, who had been called back to power by the National Assembly to forestall a military takeover, offered the formula of the French Community to contain decolonial pressures and resistance within France to independence. De Gaulle's formula also corresponded to his view of a military defense of metropole and imperial interests. If this strategic perspective remained constant; in Gaullist thinking, the modalities of its realization were always subject to revision, even radical redefinition as the liquidation of the French Empire by the Gaullist regime suggested. Gaullist France did not lose interest in Africa (although its priority in relation to Europe and the Mediterranean inevitably diminished); what did clearly change were the instruments of power and political arrangements by which French interests would be promoted.

Under the new constitution of 1958, the Community included France and the overseas territories and provinces. The latter were given a choice of joining the new grouping or of declaring independence. The constitution offered the overseas areas "new institutions . . . conceived with a view to their democratic evolution."[6] These new institutions included a president of the Community who was also the president of the French Republic. He presided over an executive council composed of the heads of government of the member states and ministers concerned with Community affairs. Also created was a senate whose members were drawn from the local legislative assemblies.

While the Community was in form more liberal than the Union, most important decisions still remained under the control of Paris and these were firmly placed in the hands of the French president. Considering the centralization of power in the office of the president under the Fifth Republic and the dominating political power and style of President Charles de Gaulle, who inspired the constitution of the Fifth Republic, the member states could be said to have been accorded less influence, but more formal authority, over metropole decision making than under the Fourth Republic where political power was more diffuse and decentralized. Questions of foreign and defense policy as well as economic, monetary, and financial affairs were largely left to France and the French president for decision. The Senate and executive council were purely advisory bodies. All Com-

munity legislation was proposed by the president and required no coun-
tersignature. In case of a national emergency with a member state of the
Community, the president of the Community was empowered to decree
a state of emergency on the request of a local head of government. As
one commentator concluded, "Actually, the Community was nothing
more than another version of the French state."[7]

These arrangements were tailored to suit President de Gaulle's notions
of presidential power and French Community. For de Gaulle, threats to
the French Community arose not only from Soviet and Communist expansion, but also from the local pressures for independence that, contrary
to the view expressed by some of his supporters, were quite apart from
internal Communist subversion, such as Islamic stirrings for self-expres-
sion and freedom in North Africa. Threats arose, too, from the designs
of Great Britain and the United States. American use of the United Nations
to advance its interests in the Congo crisis of the early 1960s confirmed
the French president's suspicions. Along with the Soviet Union, the de
Gaulle government refused to pay its share of the support for the world
organization's peacekeeping force for the Congo. According to President
de Gaulle, the U.N. operation under American prompting introduced the
Cold War into central Africa where French influence in Francophone
Africa was directly challenged.[8]

The unitary character of early Fifth Republic defense thinking was
crystallized in the ordinance of January 7, 1959. It affirmed the concept
of a global defense for France and the Community. Since none of the
member states possessed a sizeable military force, the definition of defense policy and security interests was essentially left to the president of
the Community. During the Community's short life, member states
largely fell into step behind the line drawn by Paris. Few openly raised
objections to the Algerian war where elements of Community forces were
serving. Those voiced by the presidents of Mauritania and Mali were
exceptions to the rule of Community discipline, and in any case had little
effect. Similarly, Community members sided with France's explosion of
an atomic device in the Sahara desert at Reggane. At a session of the
executive council of the Community in July, 1959, the group unanimously
rejected the protests of Ghana and Guinea. President Tsiranana of Madagascar declared further that the Community needed the bomb for its
defense.[9]

The Community was unable, however, to withstand rising pressures
for independence. The decision of Sekou Touré's Guinea to reject Community status in 1959 set the stage for other members of the Community
to demand independence. Fifteen new states were eventually fashioned
from the Community. To prevent the balkanization of these states an
entirely new security structure had to be devised. The answer was found

in a set of bilateral and multilateral security treaties with most of the Francophone states. Of the fifteen states formed from the French Union, twelve signed defense accords regulating their security relations.[10] Those not signing such agreements were Guinea, Mali, and Upper Volta. Guinea refused to join the French Community or be subject to external control; Mali denounced its defense accords with Paris on assuming independence; Upper Volta limited French access to its territory. While refusing to enter into a formal treaty with France, Upper Volta did agree to permit, on proper request, overflight, landing, and transit of French military forces over its territory.

These treaty arrangements, which formally recognized the independence of the African states, had little immediate practical impact on their assumption of independent security and foreign-policy powers. French forces in Africa at independence were more than a match for indigenous military elements, whether considered separately or collectively. Under the treaties, France enjoyed important basing and access rights and was given great liberty to define the external and internal conditions of security of the contracting parties and the terms under which it might intervene with military force. The treaties also recognized France's global responsibilities. Some, like those with Senegal and Madagascar, continued to speak of the French Community although this integrated notion of security was never applied either by France or by its former colonies. Attached to most of these treaties were protocols that defined France's responsibilities for maintaining order within the territories of the contracting parties. Only Togo and Dahomey resisted this formal extension to France of a right to intervene. Under these accords, the French army could be called to join the military forces of a local state to preserve internal order. Aid could be indirect (logistical support, supplies) or direct, in the form of military intervention by French forces. Requests for assistance were normally to be made by a head of government, although, as noted above, French officials retained considerable discretion over the timing and conditions of French intervention. Elaborate bilateral and multilateral military consultative and planning bodies were also envisioned by the treaties, but were never really empaneled on a regular basis.[11]

Complementing the defense treaties between France and its former colonies were technical agreements regulating military assistance to African signatories. All of the African states except Guinea signed such agreements. Their aim was to assure France a priority status in the organizaton, instruction, and equipment of national forces. Modest amounts of military equipment, primarily transport and logistics capabilities, were transferred to the newly independent African states under terms of these annexes. All signatories to these military assistance accords except Togo and Mali also signed logistic-support agreements. Six states additionally signed understandings covering foreign policy and strategic-raw-materials cooperation.[12]

These security and foreign-policy arrangements were parts of a series of other economic, financial, cultural, judicial, and postal treaties, protocols, and understandings the overall effect of which was to retain France's predominant position in black Africa while paying tribute to African aspirations for independence.[13] De Gaulle's unitary conception of French-African interests had not changed so much as his views about how they should be promoted. Neither French colonial rule, Union, nor Community would work in an era of rising nationalism within the developing world. France's own example, dramatized by de Gaulle's intransigence during World War II and by the defiance of the Fourth Republic in rejecting the European Defense Community and in constructing a nuclear weapon, implied that what was good for France—its claim to be independent—was also good for its former colonies.

Turning necessity into virtue, de Gaulle facilitated rather than forestalled African independence, once the member states of the Community insisted on it. In acceding so readily to African claims to statehood, the de Gaulle government also paved the way for Algerian independence, which was granted shortly thereafter. De Gaulle portrayed his regime and France as a major power with generous instincts ready to develop a new North-South relationship that contrasted with the imputed hegemonial drives of the superpowers. The Cold War was condemned as unstable and illegitimate. The conflict not ony risked war between Moscow and Washington, but it also threatened to envelop other states, including newly emerging countries in the developing world. Moreover, local disputes, de Gaulle argued, tended to become extensions of the superpower struggle as smaller states sought patrons and big powers pursued clients. The security interests of smaller states were gradually being redefined to suit the interests of the superpowers, whose ability to manage their conflict relations and those of their clients was increasingly doubtful. This latter circumstance undermined the system of independent states composing the international community. The superpowers were therefore infringing on the rights of other states to participate in establishing viable and stable regional- and global-security arrangements affecting their security. According to de Gaulle, only a more diffuse international system, based on a multiplicity of sovereign states, would assure greater stability and preserve the principle of national independence. Local conflicts would not be raised to global proportions; limits to the expansion of the superpowers would be created; and states would regain at least some measure of control over their security interests.[14]

The Secular Decline of French Influence in
Sub-Saharan Africa

Neither this line of Gaullist protest to superpower rule, nor the formal granting of independence, nor the intricate sets of cooperative ties defined by France and its former colonies was able to maintain French power at its former level.

The defense and military-assistance accords of the early 1960s were revised a decade later. Several of the black African states felt uncomfortable with the broad prerogatives accorded to France to intervene in their countries. Others, like Mali, were drawn toward the Socialist bloc. Congo, Benin, and Madagascar also gravitated toward the Soviet Union. Arms, assistance, and foreign military advisors were drawn increasingly from the Soviet Union, East European states (especially East Germany), and Cuba. Chad temporarily joined these ranks in 1980 when Libyan troops intervened militarily on the side of President Goukouni Oueddei in the Chadian civil war after French troops had been withdrawn.

Table 7–1 lists the military technical assistance accords in force in 1977. Included in the sixteen countries are the three former Belgian colonies of Burundi, Rwanda, and Zaire. Of twelve states having initially signed defense accords, only five remained faithful in 1977 (Central African Republic, Gabon, Ivory Coast, Senegal, and Togo). After 1977 military agreements were added with newly independent Djibouti to permit the stationing of France's largest force in Africa and a technical-assistance agreement was signed with Comoros to train its 1,000-man army. While these accords are formally still in force, their practical import is primarily a function of the degree of closeness desired by France and an African state and the competition for allegiance, sought by other states, especially the Soviet Union and its surrogates.

While de Gaulle spoke of a new North-South relation, French priorities shifted elsewhere. The bulk of French attention and resources focused politically on Europe and strategically on the construction of a nuclear strike force. Between 1962 and 1964, 300,000 French troops were withdrawn from North and sub-Saharan Africa. By one estimate, approximately 60,000 of this total were stationed in black Africa and Madagascar. A decade later these forces fell to about 6,400.[15] The strategic importance of former African bases, particularly in Niger and Mali, declined. French forces were concentrated at only four points: in Dakar (Senegal), Abidjan (Ivory Coast), Fort Lamy (later D'jamena in Chad) and Diego Suarez (Madagascar). The latter two bases were subsequently abandoned and Djibouti, the Central African Republic (CAR), and French Indian Ocean territories replaced them.

To compensate for the reduction in force, France proposed to rely

Table 7-1
French Military-Technical-Assistance Agreements

States	Date of Signature
Benin	February 27, 1975
Burundi	October 7, 1969
Cameroon	February 21, 1974
Central African Republic	August 13, 1960
Chad	March 6, 1976
Congo	January 1, 1974
Gabon	August 17, 1960
Ivory Coast	April 24, 1961
Madagascar	June 4, 1973
Mauritania	September 2, 1976
Niger	February 19, 1977
Rwanda	July 18, 1975
Senegal	March 29, 1974
Togo	March 23, 1976
Upper Volta	April 24, 1961
Zaire	May 22, 1974

Defense Agreements in Force in 1977

States	Date of Signature
Central African Republic	August 15, 1960
Gabon	August 17, 1960
Ivory Coast	April 24, 1961
Senegal	March 29, 1974
Togo	July 10, 1963

Source: Ministère de la Coopération. Service de presse et d'information: *La Coopération Français en Afrique Noire, dans l'Océan Indien et a Haiti, Dossier Economique,* Paris, 1978. As cited in Pierre Lellouche and Dominique Moisi, "French Policy in Africa: A Lonely Battle Against Destabilization," *International Security,* 3, no. 4 (Spring 1979): 155 and Jacques Guillemin, *Coopération et Intervention: La Politique Militaire de la France en Afrique Noire Francophone et à Madagascar,* thèse pour le Doctorat d'Etat en Droit (Nice 1979).

on a three-tiered defense structure to cover the African states: local forces to be equipped and trained by France; small contingents of French troops stationed on the African continent; and an intervention force positioned in France for rapid deployment to crisis spots. These air, sea, and ground forces, including parachute units, were to be designed for quick dispatch to trouble spots throughout Africa.

Since independence, however, these layers have been rather indifferently maintained and have become thin and brittle. Table 7-2 outlines French military assistance to sub-Saharan Africa between 1960 and 1980. Until 1978, France's general attitude toward Africa might be largely characterized as one of benign neglect with intermittent surges of interest, during crisis periods, in one or the other of the Francophone states. Real military aid over the eighteen-year period from 1960 to 1978 remained essentially static since prices rather than aid doubled.

Also interesting is the distribution of spending levels. By far the most

Table 7–2
French Military Assistance to Sub-Saharan Africa: 1961–1980
(millions of francs)

Year	Total Assistance	Spending		Training of African Military in France
		Material Assistance	French Personnel	
1961–1963	100	2	—	—
1964	45	3	—	—
1965	124	6	—	—
1966	127	6	—	—
1967	131	9	—	—
1968	135	8	—	—
1969	143	20	—	—
1970	169	47	—	—
1971	181	45	—	—
1972	210	69	—	—
1973	204	58	134	12
1974	230	73	141	16
1975	230	73	137	20
1976	250	78	151	21
1977	262	78	163	21
1978	380	134	204	42
1979	468	210	212	46
1980	578	277	236	65

Sources: Jacques Guillemin, *Coopération et Intervention, La Politique Militaire de la France en Afrique Noire Francophone et à Madagascar*, Thèse pour le Doctorat d'Etat en Droit (Nice, 1979), p. 62, and *Stratégie Afrique, Moyen-Orient*, No. 8, October, 1980, cited in Thomas Jallaud, "La Coopération Militaire, Outil de Contrôle," *Tricontinental* 1 (1981), p. 105.

important expenditure was for the support of French military personnel on training missions with African armies. Material assistance represented less than 30 percent of the total through the 1960s, and hovered around 30 percent until the end of the 1970s. Local armed forces received very little assistance in the way of weapons and training materials, which presumably reduced their effectiveness and usefulness much beyond their borders. The major beneficiaries of French aid were Senegal, Ivory Coast, Cameroon, Gabon, and Chad. For example, in 1974, Chad received three times as much military assistance as any other state.[16] Less favored were Niger, Upper Volta, Togo, and Benin. Other Francophone states (Madagascar, Mauritania, Mali, Congo, CAR) enjoyed varying assistance, depending on the evolution of relations with France. Zaire received most of the assistance given to Belgium's former colonies. Table 7–2 also indicates a sharp departure in military assistance to Africa after 1977. The implications of the shift upward will be discussed later under prospects for France's position in Francophone sub-Saharan Africa.

If French military assistance until recently did not do much to organize and train indigenous military forces, the deployment of French forces in Africa did little to compensate for these weaknesses in French security efforts in sub-Saharan Africa. Table 7–3 summarizes the distribution of foreign military forces in Africa. Since the 1960s, France's military position has receded, compared to that of the Socialist bloc. Soviet, Cuban, and East European troops and advisors are almost three times as many as French forces, which are spread thinly over a larger number of countries. (If the 4,000 French troops on Mayotte and Reunion in the Indian Ocean are excluded from the totals, French troops on the African continent are 7,610 for figures drawn from the *Economist* and Lellouche and Moisi, and 7,795 for the latter only, as revised in table 7–3. The ratio of Soviet bloc to French forces then changes to five to one.) The largest concentrations of Soviet and East European military personnel are found in Angola, Benin, Ethiopia, Libya, Mozambique, and Guinea-Bissau. The former Portuguese colonies have offered a favorable climate for Soviet penetration. Socialist-bloc troops in Angola and Mozambique anchor Soviet influence in southern Africa. With the help of its East European (especially German) and Cuban surrogates, the Soviet Union has also established a major hold on the Horn of Africa. France's contingent in Djibouti is thus exposed. It cannot count on substantial assistance from the United States or Great Britain in any confrontation of these forces. Neither can it maintain sizeable contingents in the region; forces that are present are largely assigned training and aid tasks.

France's third line of African defense, its intervention forces, leave much to be desired as an effective deterrent or defensive force. According to some sources, there are approximately 15,000 men serving in France's

Table 7-3
Foreign-Troop Deployments in North Africa and Sub-Saharan Africa

Country	Russian and East European	French	Cuban	British	United States
Algeria	(1,850)	(80) 90			
Angola	(1,200)		(18,000) 21,000		
Benin[b]					
Botswana				80	
Burundi		30			
Cameroon		(60) 90			
Central African Republic		(1,700)			
Chad[b]					
Congo	(200)	10	300		
Djibouti		(3,700) 4,500			
Egypt					300
Ethiopia	(2,180)	500	(11–12,000) 12,000		
Gabon		500			
The Gambia[c]				85	
Guinea	(200)		200–300		
Guinea-Bissau[d]	(600)		70		
Guinea (Equatorial)	(100)		20 to 30		
Ivory Coast		(120) 500			
Kenya				100	100
Liberia					
Libya	(3,000)	25	100 to 125		
Madagascar	(300)	50	30		
Malawi[e]					
Mauritania		(110) 100			
Mayotte		2,000			
Morocco		(150) 250	300		
Mozambique	(550)				
Niger		60			
Reunion		2,000			
Senegal		(650) 1,300			
Sierra Leone[f]					
Somalia			100 to 125		100

Table 7–3 Continued

Country	Russian and East European	French	Cuban	British	United States
Sudan					300
Tanzania			20 to 30		
Togo		80			
Tunisia		(85) 40			
Uganda^g		20	20 to 30^g		
Upper Volta		70			
Zaire		(100)			
Zambia				60	
Indian Ocean Islands^a		80			
Zimbabwe^i				380	
Total	(10,200)	(11,610) 11,795	(31,340) 34,000–34,500	475	800

Sources: Pierre Lellouche and Dominique Moisi "French Policy in Africa: A Lonely Battle against Destabilization," *International Security*, 3 no. 4 (Spring 1979), 109 and the *Economist* September 19, 1981, p. 44. Figures in parentheses drawn from the *Economist*. Totals in parentheses combine figures from Lellouche and Moisi and those cited for selected states in the *Economist*.

a Iles Glorieuses (10), Tromelin (10), Juan de Nova (50), Bassas de India, Europe (10)

b Lellouche and Moisi list 500 for Benin and 1800 for Chad. The French contingent in Benin has apparently been withdrawn and the force in Chad was called back in 1980.

c 2,700 Senegalese to put down *coup d'etat*.

d Also 100: Morocco

e 100: South Africa

f 2,000: Guinea-Bissau

g 1,000: Tanzania. The Cuban contingent may have been withdrawn.

h 120: China; 350: Belgium

i Also 200: North Korea

forces d'intervention.[17] Elements include a paratroop division stationed in southwest France, naval marines located in Brittany, and a paratroop regiment in Dieuze. Units include the Ninth Marine Infantry Division, the Eleventh Airborne Division, and the Foreign Legion. In June 1979 the French military reportedly created a new airborne group in Albi within the Eleventh Paratroop Division, including 3500 men divided into infantry, artillery, naval units and the motorized Foreign Legion. The emphasis has also shifted from ship to airborne support. However, as with the American Rapid Deployment Force, much remains to be done to make the force an effective instrument for intervention. In the Shaba crises of 1977 and 1978 in Zaire, France had to rely on American logistics capability. Insufficient airborne capacity was available to transport French equipment with troops to the troubled area. Parachutes reportedly had to be left in France and French legionnaires were forced to use parachutes of the Zairian army in making their jumps. Since the end of the Algerian war, conventional and overseas-intervention forces have been starved for funds as French military spending gave priority to nuclear strike forces. These trends shifted slightly in favor of conventional forces for European defense in the middle 1970s. France's *force d'intervention* is still assigned a lower priority than its European or strategic strike forces, despite the generally accepted view that French interests are under heavy strain in Africa.[18]

In their present form, French forces are incapable of long, sustained, or costly operations in Africa. They lack adequate logistics capability, equipment, and material to conduct extensive field operations. Any effort to mount a large-scale intervention would seriously detract from their European and strategic military missions. Unless interventions are quick, punctual, and of short duration, as in Shaba I and II, the French military forces risk overextension. As already noted, they cannot presently count on allied assistance where almost alone they patrol an exposed western salient; nor can they expect compensation in Europe where French forces have not cooperated with NATO since the 1960s.

French Intervention in Africa

Table 7–4 catalogs French intervention in black African states over the past twenty years. In almost every case, French intervention was directed at internal unrest, not overt, exterior aggression. Even in the Shaba I and II incidents the central government was being threatened by Katangese dissidents based in Angola. However, French intervention did not imply the existence of a defense accord with a beleaguered state. French forces operated in Cameroon before the formal implementation of a defense

Table 7–4
French Military Interventions in Sub-Saharan Africa

Year	Countries	Nature of Intervention: Outcome
1960	Cameroon	Repression of the members of the l'Union des Populations du Cameroun
	Congo	Maintaining public order
	Gabon	Settling a local dispute
	Congo	
(1960–1962)	Chad	Maintaining internal order
1961	Cameroon	Repression of the U.P.C.
	Mauritania	Maintaining internal order
1962	Congo	Maintaining internal order
1963	Chad	Maintaining public order
	Niger	Military support to President Hamani Diori in his power struggle against his political opponents.
1964	Gabon	Reestablishing President M'ba in power.
1968	Chad	Maintaining internal order
April 1969	Chad	Suppressing members of the FROLINAT and maintaining order
January 1971[a]		
Sept. 1975[b]		
1977	Zaire	Logistical aid to Zairian National Army
1978	Mauritania	Protection of French Technical Assistants
	Zaire	Protection of French nationals and European technical assistants against Katangese elements.
	Chad	Maintaining internal order
1979	C.A.R.	Overthrow of Bokassa regime

Sources: Déclaration de M.A. Peyrefitte, A.F.P., *Bulletin quotidien de l'Afrique Noire*, no. 316, March 4, 1964; W.A. Nielsen, *The Great Powers and Africa*, (London, 1969); R. Buijtenhuijs. *Le Frolinat et les révoltes populaires au Tchad, 1965–1978*, (Paris: Mouton, 1978).

[a]The official date of French intervention in Chad.

[b]Repatriation of French military expeditionary corps.

treaty. France also had no security agreement with Zaire when it intervened to save the Kinshasa regime from its internal foes and European settlers from being massacred. On the other hand, France did not intervene in the Congo in 1963, when Bishop Philibert Youlou was confronted with an internal revolt, although a defense accord was in place. As Alain Peyrefitte, French Minister of Information, explained, "Our troops began to intervene but President Youlou having himself signed his resignation, our troops stopped their intervention."[19] The de Gaulle government also relied on the absence of a defense treaty with Togo to justify its refusal to intervene following the assassination of President Olympio. In October 1963, Paris also stood by as President Maga of Dahomey was forced to resign under pressure. These examples suggest that having or not having a defense treaty within Francophone Africa is neither a bar to nor a guarantee of French intervention.

France's pragmatic approach characterizes its interventions in the other cases cited in table 7–4. Its support for African leaders appeared motivated by various policy considerations and conjunctural needs. Leon M'ba was apparently restored to power in Gabon to preserve French strategic interests in Gabonese mineral resources, including uranium and oil. Similar economic and strategic objectives appeared at play in Zaire and Mauritania. France's military operations in Mauritania may be seen as an effort to protect French workers and technicians operating mining enterprises in the country and, at the time, to bolster the Moroccan campaign against the Polisario in the western Sahara. The Shaba interventions were conditioned by humanitarian aims as well as concern for Zaire's strategic position and its mineral resources. The overthrow of the Bokassa regime in the Central African Republic, on the other hand, seemed impelled by a desire to reduce French support for a tyrannical regime that had become an embarrassment. The subsequent removal by army officers of Bokassa's successor, President Dacko, with tacit French complicity, suggests that factors other than humanitarian purpose animated France's conscious nonintervention in CAR politics. That the French garrison stationed in the CAR did not move to save President Dacko indicates how tenuous French political support can be. On the other hand, as in the Gabonese case in 1964 and the CAR in 1980, French forces have intervened although local authorities did not ask for assistance.

The French military withdrawal from Chad in May 1980 also raises serious questions about France's long-term staying power as the gendarme of Francophone Africa. The French departure, in tandem with a unanimous resolution of the Organization of African Unity (OAU) calling for withdrawal of foreign troops, unwittingly opened the way for Libyan military intervention on the side of President Goukouni Oueddei in late 1980 at the expense principally of the forces of Hissène Habré. France's rapid withdrawal, if understandable, reversed an over-a-decade-long policy of intervention to settle the Chadian civil war and to bolster France's strategic position and the security of the West African states. As late as May 1978, French troops returned in sizeable numbers to quell further disturbances. Libyan influence in Chad threatens the ring of shaky Francophone regimes around Chad, including Niger, Cameroon, and the CAR. Repercussions of the Libyan penetration into Chad with no effective opposition by France could be felt as far as Gabon and Zaire whose regimes depend on French military support. (Gabon, for example, has five Jaguar aircraft stationed on its territory.) Soviet influence is not far beyond, since approximately 3,000 Russian and East European troops and advisors are stationed in Libya. Although Libya agreed, under OAU pressure, to withdraw its troops from Chad, its influence remains strong and a challenge to reassertion of French presence in the region. French reliance on the OAU to keep Libya at bay through the creation of an OAU peacekeeping force for Chad repairs some of the damage occasioned by French withdrawal, but it also underscores the weakness of the French position in Chad and the eroding credibility of unilateral French security guarantees to its clients in Francophone Africa.

French Arms Transfers to Sub-Saharan Africa

French arms-transfer policy reflects the dilemmas confronting French strategists seeking to maximize French overall military power and regional position in Africa, on the one hand, and, on the other, to strengthen its resource base, in order that France can continue to exert influence on the major African actors that can affect outcomes in areas of its interest. Table 7–5 reflects this dilemma. First, there is concern with economic needs, depicted in France's lucrative arms trade with South Africa despite African condemnation of these ties. Until the Giscard d'Estaing government reluctantly imposed an embargo on arms shipments to South Africa, in 1977, France sent more arms to Pretoria than to the rest of sub-Saharan Africa. At first France tried to maintain the fiction that its sale of sophisticated military aircraft, helicopters, missiles, armored ground equipments, submarines, and naval craft contributed exclusively to South Africa's external security needs, and were not "susceptible to be used for police or repressive action."[20] As early as October 1963 French representatives to the United Nations informed the Security Council that the French government "would take every measure . . . to prevent the sale to the South African government of arms usable for repression."[21] Seven years later, President Georges Pompidou informed President Kenneth Kuanda, representing the OAU, that France would not renew sales of helicopters and light tanks to Pretoria. On August 9, 1975, during a visit to Zaire, President Giscard d'Estaing narrowed the French commitment to Pretoria by affirming that France would not sell "long-range or aerial" arms to South Africa although then-existing sales contracts would be honored.[22] Only naval armaments would be sold.[23] Finally, under intense pressure from black African states, which threatened to take economic reprisals against France, President Giscard d'Estaing declared in Mali on February 14, 1977, that every effort had been taken by France "not only to prohibit any new provision of ground or air materiel destined for South Africa but equally to assure that no delivery might take place."[24] Consistent with this declaration, orders for warships (two submarines and two 1200-ton corvette escort and patrol ships) were cancelled.[25]

Table 7-5
French Arms Transfers to Sub-Saharan Africa, 1950–1978

	Tanks	Armored Vehicles and Personal Carriers	Patrol Boats and Ships below 100 tons	Sub-marines	Minor Naval Ships[b]	Supersonic Aircraft	Other Aircraft	Helicopters
South Africa	—	1600[a]	—[c]	3[d]	—[e]	112[f]	13	187[g]
Former French colonies and mandates[h]	10[j]	160[i,j]	30[l]	—	8	5[m]	215[n]	80[o]
Belgian colonies[p]	—	280[q]	—	—	—	17[r]	29[s]	58[t]
Non-Francophone Africa	—	211[u]	—	—	—	24[v]	11[w]	110[x]
Totals	10	2251	30	3	8	158	268	435

Note: The basic sources for this table are the annual yearbooks on armaments of the Stockholm International Peace Research Institute (SIPRI) and the annual review of military inventories of the International Institute for Strategic Studies (IISS). See, for example, SIPRI, *World Armament and Disarmament: SIPRI Yearbook, 1980* (New York: Crane, Russak, 1980), pp. 128–162. For the years 1950–1973, consult SIPRI, *The Arms Trade Registers*, (Cambridge, Mass.: MIT Press, 1975). For the inventory reviews of the IISS, see, for example, *Military Balance 1980–1981* (London, 1980). As the notes indicate, there are considerable discrepancies between these two sources and even within successive publications of the same source. The totals should be used with extreme caution. They are primarily useful, and then only in a restricted sense, to show general patterns, and not totally reliable detailed transfers of weapons from year to year. The higher total, reported by SIPRI or *Military Balance*, is cited where discrepancies appear.

Deliveries of French equipment from third parties are considered retransfers and are not included. For example, South African supply of French helicopters are not cited. See note t.

[a]South Africa was to produce an estimated 800 Panhard AML 60 and 90 armored cars under license in the period 1961–1972. The 1972–1973 *Military Balance* confirms that 800 AML 60/90s were deployed. However, later editions of *Military Balance* report greater quantities of AML 60/90s in service. Three *Military Balances* from 1974 to 1977 report 1000 "AML 245/60, 245/90 Eland" armored cars. Three editions from 1977 to 1981 report 1600 AML although the 1978–1979 issue lists only 1400 60/90s. Aside from the expected 800 to be licensed produced, SIPRI reports only one other delivery of Panhard ACs. See delivery data for 1977.

[b]Includes naval ships which displace more than 100 tons but which are below frigate size, the line between major and minor vessels.

[c]An undisclosed number of French corvettes were ordered by South Africa, but they apparently fell under the embargo imposed by France, following U.N. practice, in 1977. The 1980–81 *Military Balance* lists 12 Israeli Reshef fast attack naval craft have been deployed. These craft are armed with Gabriel II SSMs.

Table 7-5 Continued

d Three Daphne submarines are listed in the 1980–81 *Military Balance*; two others, submarines of the Agosta Class, built by Dubignon of France, are reported as ordered in the 1976–1977 and 1977–1978 editions of *Military Balance*; however later editions do not report delivery and these ships also apparently fell under the French embargo.

e 2 A69 frigates were ordered in the middle 1970s but neither SIPRI nor *Military Balance* indicate delivery. Again these ships fell under embargo.

f The total includes Mirage IIIs and F1s. Figures from Mirage III vary between SIPRI and *Military Balance* and within *Military Balance* from year to year. The highest number reported by SIPRI, namely 72, is cited. (For example, *Military Balance 1975–76* lists 64 Mirage III; *Military Balance 1976–1977*, 57, a lower total possibly due to attrition. The F1s included in the total comprise 16 F1Cs and 32 F1As. Both Mirage IIIs and F1s can be produced in South Africa. The bulk of F1s are apparently indigenously produced under license.

g The 1971–1972 *Military Balance* reports 106 Alouette II/IIIs in service in South Africa. To this date, SIPRI accounted for only 80 Alouette II/IIIs. The 1972–1976 editions report 60 Alouettes. In 1976–1978, 80+ Alouettes are mentioned, while in the 1978–1979 *Military Balance*, 107 Alouette IIIs and 2 Alouette IIs are cited. Finally in 1979–1980 and 1980–81, the *Military Balance* mentions only 67 Alouette IIIs and an unspecified number of Alouette IIs. SIPRI does not account for these variations.

The 1972–1973 *Military Balance* confirms the delivery and deployment of 16 SA–330 Puma helicopters, implying that the other 4 may have been delivered or deployed after July 1972. The 1973–1974 *Military Balance* accounts for all 20 helicopters. Later editions report more Pumas in service. Finally the 1980–81 issue lists 80 SA–330 Pumas. SIPRI cites no further deliveries of Puma helicopters beyond those in 1971.

h Includes Benin (formerly Dahomey), Cameroon, Central African Republic, Chad, Congo (Brazzaville), Gabon, Guinea, Ivory Coast, Madagascar, Mali, Mauritania, Niger, Senegal, Togo, Upper Volta, and Djibouti.

i To Ivory Coast.

j Four additional deliveries listed by SIPRI of an undisclosed number to CAR, Congo, Djibouti and Gabon are not included. *Military Balance 1980–1981* notes 40 AML 60/90, not 30, as SIPRI reports delivered to Senegal; moreover, 12 Panhard M3 are listed for Senegal in the same issue of *Military Balance.*

k Scout cars to Gabon.

l One delivery to Gabon of an undisclosed number, listed by SIPRI, not included.

m Mirage V's to Gabon; 6 Alpha-jets, trainer and light aircraft ground support are reportedly on order, *Military Balance*, 1980–1981.

n Includes 26 aircraft for Chad and 35 aircraft for CAR that were likely used or left by French armed forces since the forces of either state are not capable of operating the level of aircraft supposedly sent to them.

[o] An undisclosed number of helicopters sent to Congo (Brazzaville) and while noted by SIPRI not included.

[p] Includes Zaire, Rwanda, and Burundi. Arms that are listed are for Zaire unless otherwise noted in the notes below.

[q] SIPRI and *Military Balance* differ on totals for Zaire. SIPRI cites 280 AML 60/90s (armored vehicles); *Military Balance* over the 1970s varies between 135 and 166 AML's. The latest *Military Balance 1980–81* lists 135 (95 AML 60's and 45 AML 90s). An undisclosed number of AML 60/90 to Rwanda is not included; *Military Balance 1980–81* lists 12 AML 60/90 inventory, some of which may have been supplied to Belgium.

[r] Mirage Vs; SIPRI lists 12 deliveries; *Military Balance 1980–81* cites 10 in inventory.

[s] These include 20 Reims Cessna's, a small personnel carrier.

[t] Through 1972, SIPRI has noted delivery of 6 Alouette II and 15 Alouette III helicopters. There is considerable fluctuation in *Military Balance* estimates of Zaire's reserve of Alouette helicopters from 5 Alouette II/III in the 1971–1972 edition to 15 Alouette II/III in 1972 to 1973 to 8 Alouette III in 1973–1974 to 20 Alouette II/III in 1974–1975, back to and stable at 15 Alouette II/III from 1975 to 1980. SIPRI does not account for these fluctuations in terms of new deliveries. *Military Balance 1980–1981* lists 5 Alouettes in Burundi air force and 2 Alouettes in Rwanda air force.

[u] Number excludes up to 60 Eland and AML armored vehicles shipped by South Africa to Rhodesia.

[v] 24 Mirage 50s delivered to Sudan in 1978 *and* 1979.

[w] Includes 2 B–26s sent to Biafra and 3 Noratlas to Angola.

[x] Excludes 54 Alouettes supplied to Rhodesia by South Africa; includes 30 Alouettes in Angolan air force, listed in *Military Balance 1980–1981*. 15 deliveries of Pumas to Sudan, listed by SIPRI of which only 12 are confirmed by *Military Balance 1980–1981*, and 8 Alouettes in Zambian air force listed only once in *Military Balance 1976–1977*.

The French embargo, however, did not touch weapons under license agreement with South Africa. These accords permit South Africa to manufacture French Mirage III's and F1's, ground armor and machine guns, and Crotale, SAM, and Magic 550 air-to-air missiles. The Crotale missile (named Cactus in South Africa) was jointly developed by France and South Africa with Pretoria reportedly supplying 85 percent of the costs of development.[26]

The economic significance of French arms exports is sketched in table 7–6. The benefits of arms sales, even to South Africa, were sufficiently attractive to resist the diplomatic pressures of world opinion, expressed in the United Nations, and of black African states. The value of French arms-transfer deliveries mounted from $800 million in 1972 to almost $3 billion in 1977. More than half of these exports were for supersonic jet aircraft and avionics. Except for armored vehicles, South African purchases were largely made for jet fighters and helicopters. These purchases contributed significantly to overall French receipts for arms in the 1970s. Between 1972 and 1977, the ratio of arms receipts over total French exports grew from 3 percent to 4.6 percent. France was able to cover approximately 24 percent of its oil purchases with arms sales during this period, despite a quadrupling of oil prices. Balance-of-payments deficits would also have been increased each year by the size of arms-sales receipts if an active arms-transfer policy had not been pursued. Upwards of 300,000 workers and technicians are employed by the arms industry. The aircraft and electronics industries would be especially hard hit if they were forced to cut back on foreign sales. These economic indicators explain much of the reluctance of successive French administrations to reduce arms sales. The recent election of a Socialist president and a Socialist majority in the National Assembly has not fundamentally changed France's orientation toward arms exports. On September 8, 1981, President Mitterrand essentially affirmed France's previous policy on sales of arms to other countries. He assured recipients that existing contracts would be honored. He also justified French sales as an indispensable means of assuring modern weapons at reasonable cost to France's armed forces, and as providing an alternative supplier for developing states that would otherwise be largely confined to purchases from the superpowers.[27]

In contrast to large sales of advanced arms to South Africa, including extensive licensing agreements to permit indigenous production, French deliveries of arms to the rest of sub-Saharan Africa have been appreciably lower in number and degree of sophistication. As table 7–6, which covers arms transfers from 1950 through 1978, suggests, French transfers have been largely concentrated in support aircraft, armored and ground vehicles, and helicopters. Support aircraft have been composed, in significant part, of obsolete transport airplanes, including American World War II

Table 7-6
Arms Transfers Related to Exports, Oil Imports, and Commercial Balances
(billions of dollars)

	1972	1973	1974	1975	1976	1977
Exports						
Arms deliveries/exports	26.43	36.48	46.16	53.01	57.16	64.97
	3	3.2	3.0	3.7	4.3	4.6
Oil Imports						
Arms deliveries/oil imports	2.7	3.5	9.8	9.7	11.5	11.9
	29.6	33.6	14.1	20	21.2	25.1
Imports	27.0	37.55	52.84	53.94	64.46	70.50
Balance: exports and imports	-.57	-1.07	-6.68	-.93	-7.30	-5.53
Arms sales	.80	1.175	1.386	1.944	2.435	2.992
Deficit without arms sales	-1.87	-2.245	-8.066	-2.874	-9.735	-7.522

Sources: France, Assemblée Nationale, Commission de la Défense Nationale, *Avis sur le projet de loi de finances pour 1978*, No. 3150, *Défense: Dépenses en Capital*, 11 October 1977, pp. 17–24 and France, Assemblée Nationale, Commission des Finances, de l'Economie Générale et du Plan, *Rapport sur le projet de loi de finances pour 1981*, No. 1976, *Défense: Dépenses en Capital*, 9 October 1980, p. 196. Exchange rates for francs based on International Monetary Fund, *International Financial Statistics*, XXII, July 1979, p. 144 and idem, May 1981, pp. 152–154.

equipment transferred from French stocks to local forces. France assigned an appreciable number of Max Holste, Broussard, Noratlas, and American C–47s to each of its former colonies at independence. These were outright grants and should properly be categorized as French military assistance rather than arms sales. Many older Alouette helicopters were also given to local forces during this early period. Only later were the African states, and then only those with adequate resources, expected to purchase their own equipment. As for ground and armored vehicles, South Africa again received more equipment. What is also interesting to note is that the former Belgian colonies, especially Zaire, and non-Francophone African states received more ground equipment than did the Francophone states.

Few supersonic aircraft have been sold to sub-Saharan states other than South Africa. Deliveries have been restricted to small numbers of aircraft to Gabon (five Mirage V),[28] Zaire (seventeen Mirage V),[29] and Sudan (twenty-four Mirage 50s). Even when deliveries, in 1980, of Alpha-Jets to Nigeria (twelve) and Ivory Coast (approximately six)[30] are taken into account, the number sold to sub-Saharan regimes is only slightly more than half the number of 112 Mirage aircraft, including the more advanced F1 over Mirage III and V, delivered or licensed to South Africa.

This pattern of arms transfers makes several implications. First, France has had little economic interest in selling arms to the black African states, since they have had neither the resources nor the technical cadres capable of absorbing large amounts of advanced military equipment. It is no accident that recent transfers of jet aircraft and late-model helicopters to black Africa have been made to countries with resources at their disposal to pay fully or partially for these weapons (Gabon, Ivory Coast, Nigeria.)

Second, what equipment has been transferred has been, in significant part, old or obsolete. The development of efficient and increasingly sophisticated local forces has thus been retarded since training must be largely confined to small and basically simple arms.

The restrictive arms policy pursued by France, whether wittingly or not, has had the effect of enhancing the relative strength of French armed forces stationed on the African continent or included in France's intervention force vis-a-vis local armed forces. France has had little to fear from these forces when it has chosen to intervene. One of the ironic consequences of what might be termed a policy of *chasse gardée* is that French political and military influence has been greatest where it has delivered the fewest number of weapons. In contrast, it has sent the largest percentage of its arms exports to the Middle East where its position remains tenuous and uncertain. This result runs counter to expectations of many arms-transfer proponents who see a link betwen political influence and expanded arms sales. Nor has French influence in Mali, Benin, or Congo been foreclosed despite the reliance of these states on Soviet arms and advisors. They remain members of the franc zone and rely on French economic assistance and trade to develop their economies.

It might also be noted that the most risky interventions that France has mounted—in Zaire, Chad, and Mauritania—have involved the possibility of outside support from the Soviet Union or its surrogates to rebellious or dissident elements opposed to French intrusion. These risks are likely to increase in the future as the Soviet Union and other arms suppliers increase their deliveries to sub-Saharan states. Incentives are also heightened in the Francophone states to diversify their arms supplies, to modernize their forces, and to become less dependent on a single supplier whose monopoly position has slowed their movement toward independence and greater freedom of maneuver. It would appear that France is sensitive to these pressures, since it has substantially increased, as table 7–2 suggests, its military aid in the form of arms and equipment to Francophone states since 1978.

Prospects for France's Security Role in Sub-Saharan Africa

Several key factors will shape the range and significance of the security role that France will be able to play in sub-Saharan Africa. These include the presence of Soviet-bloc military power, the inability and, until recently, indifference of France's allies in the Atlantic Alliance to bolster France's position, the resistance of African leaders to French military intervention, and the demands of black African states for economic development, an end to racial discrimination, and freedom to manage their own affairs. The Socialist government of François Mitterrand is also torn between its own supporters and the security imperatives posed by the possibilities of continued internal upheaval, external aggression, and third-state intervention into the domestic affairs of the states of Francophone Africa. The Socialist Party's platform in the 1981 elections condemned previous military intervention in Africa, singling out French recourse to military force in Gabon, Zaire, the western Sahara, Chad, and Central Africa. The Giscard d'Estaing regime was criticized for playing African gendarme and for supporting only the most corrupt regimes.[31] Jean-Pierre Cot, President Mitterrand's Minister of Cooperation and Development, characterized Socialist policy aims as an effort to decolonize "French relations in Africa after they had been progressively recolonized."[32] Both French Defense Minister Charles Hernu and Foreign Minister Claude Cheysson rejected any return to neocolonialism.[33] President Mitterrand also voiced opposition to an expansion of intervention forces as incompatible with France's objectives in the developing world.[34]

The Socialist government prefers to emphasize the need for a "new internationalism," symbolized by French support for the Cancun Conference in fall, 1981, to spur aid to developing states from the developed world. The Mitterrand government has downplayed security problems in Africa in favor of multilateral efforts to combat hunger, poverty, illiteracy, and slow economic growth that are perceived as the principal determinant of domestic unrest, which provides the conditions for external intervention. Like its Gaullist predecessors, it seeks the dissolution of bloc politics and the gradual emergence of a multipolar system congenial to French national interests. It is also more assertive in its rejection of South African apartheid. In contrast to America's policy, it has recognized the left-leaning South-West African People's Organization (SWAPO) as the legitimate representative of Namibia and has called for independence by 1982.[35]

French reaction to crises in CAR, Cameroon, and Chad suggest, however, that it is by no means ruling out an active role for itself in conflict management. The French gave tacit approval to President Dacko's discreet ouster, although French troops in the CAR could have prevented his departure. French diplomacy forestalled an open clash between Cameroon and Nigeria. In Chad, the Socialist government has cooperated in extending financial and logistics support, along with the United States, to the OAU police force to replace Libyan troops, which have been withdrawn. The Mitterrand government's initial approach to the Chad problem evinces much of the hesitancy and ambiguity characterizing the policy of its predecessor. It views Tripoli as a destabilizing agency in Africa, but it has avoided a direct confrontation with the Kaddafi regime. Previously signed armed contracts are being honored, including the despatch to Libya of naval vessels that had been embargoed by President Giscard d'Estaing. To balance Libyan influence, President Mitterrand also met with Chadian President Goukhouni Oueddei. While refraining from offering military assistance or of committing France to train the Chadian army, he has pledged economic aid and diplomatic support for a unified and independent Chad. However, the capture of N'Djamena by the forces of Hissène Habré weakens French influence over Chadian developments. Meanwhile, new arms contracts with Libya are being ruled out, although this reservation, partly conditioned by American pressures and by the existence of ample arms contracts to be filled elsewhere, may well be relaxed if Libyan oil again becomes desirable, or if its role in black or North African security becomes less threatening.

The Socialist government appears to have particular interest in developing multilateral regional approaches to African security. These have assumed the form either of encouraging the creation of regional forces from states closely associated with France (such as Senegal, Ivory Coast, and Gabon) or of working directly through the OAU or through its OAU clients in Francophone Africa. The Zairian intervention and the Chadian peacekeeping force illustrate, respectively, these multilateral approaches. On the other hand, the Mitterrand government has refrained from implementing the call of the Socialist Party platform to renegotiate France's bilateral security and miliary assistance accords with black African states. While it is keeping its options open, its vacillation is a source of anxiety for its Francophone allies.

French assets and *points d'appui* in Africa are not neglible even though France's relative position to real and potential competitors in the region has declined. The franc zone provides monetary stability and external convertibility; 22,000 French *coopérants* form a network of bonds between the metropole and sub-Saharan clients along which flow critical learning, language, and technical skills; French foreign investment and aid bolster shaky economies and provide employment. France's historic ties and reservoir of good will are still marketable assets. France can hardly be dismissed as an important actor in African affairs,[36] but it needs help to hold on to the positions that it has laboriously developed if the secular decline of its position is to be arrested or reversed. It needs help but the prospects of receiving added financial, military, or diplomatic support from its allies are not bright. Nor, ironically, does it have much incentive to align on an American position, focused narrowly on East-West issues, that is viewed in Paris as misguided and mischievous. Barring help from allies or a major change in the current state of France's economic-resource base, military capabilities, and public support for regional-security roles in Africa, the French position faces continued erosion in Africa in favor of other powers in the region. These include the Soviet bloc, France's western allies, (particularly an active United States ready to replace, but not necessarily to assist, France), and the black African states—or all three.

Notes

1. Charles de Gaulle, *Discours et Messages* (Paris: Plon, 1970), pp. I, 3–4.

2. Raoul Girardet, *L'Idée coloniale en France (1871–1962)* (Paris: Table Ronde, 1972), pp. 195–196.

3. For a discussion of French revolutionary doctrine, see Peter Paret, *French Revolutionary Warfare from Indochina to Algeria: The Analysis of a Political Military Doctrine* (New York: Praeger, 1964), and Girardet, *L'idée colonial.*

4. General Paul Ely, "Notre politique militaire," *Revue de Dé-*

fense Nationale (July 1957), pp. 1035–1050. See also the views of Ingénieur Général Combaux, "Nécessité d'une Eurafrique," ibid. (December 1957), pp. 1814–1826; and Colonel Müller "La Subversion menace-t-elle aussi l'Afrique noire Française?" ibid. (May 1958), pp. 754–770.

5. Michel L. Martin, *Warriors to Managers: The French Military Establishment Since 1945* (Chapel Hill: University of North Carolina Press, 1981), p. 19. See also citations to the French literature of revolutionary warfare in Martin's discussion, n. 20, chapter 1.

6. Quoted in Guy de Carmoy, *The Foreign Policies of France: 1944–1968*. trans. Elaine P. Halperin (Chicago, Ill.: University of Chicago Press, 1970).

7. P.F. Gonidec, *Droit d'outremer* (Paris: Montchrétien, 1959), p. II, 217.

8. For a more extended analysis than can be developed here of deGaulle's critique of the Cold War conflict, see Kolodziej, *French International Policy under De Gaulle and Pompidou: The Politics of Grandeur* (Ithaca, N.Y.: Cornell University Press, 1974).

9. These points are developed in Pierre Dabezies, "La Politique Africaine du Général de Gaulle: 1958–1969," Centre Bordelais d'Etudes Africaines, mimeograph, 18–20 October 1979.

10. The twelve included Central African Republic (CAR), Chad, Congo, Gabon, Senegal, Madagascar, Ivory Coast, Niger, Mauritania, Togo, and Cameroon. Those not signing such agreements were Guinea, Mali, and Upper Volta.

11. These accords are described in detail by Jacques Guillemin in his "Coopération et Intervention, la Politique Militaire de la France en Afrique Noire Francophone et à Madagascar," dissertation (Nice, 1979), pp. 1–32.

12. Ibid., pp. 32–33.

13. For a discussion of these accords, see Jacques Guillemin, *Coopération et Intervention;* Lellouche and Moisi, "French Policy," pp. 111ff, table 7–3, this chapter.

14. See Kolodziej, *French International Policy*, for an elaboration of this argument.

15. Dabezies, "La Politique Africain."

16. Guillemin, *Coopération et Intervention*, p. 63.

17. Antoine Sanguinette, "Les Interventions Militaires Françaises" *Tricontinental*, I (1981); *La France contre l'Afrique*, Numéro special, pp. 94–104; and Thomas Jallaud, "La Coopération Militaire, Outil ou Contrôle," ibid., pp. 105ff.

18. For a more extensive analysis of recent French strategic policy, see Kolodziej, "French Security Policy: Decisions and Dilemmas," *Armed Forces and Society* 8, no. 2 (Winter 1982): 185–221.

19. Quoted in Lellouche and Moisi, "French Policy," p. 118.

20. Quoted by Jean Klein in his "Commerce des Armes et Politique: Le Cas Français." *Politique Etrangère* 41, no. 5 (1976): 578.

21. *Le Monde,* 5 March 1977.

22. Ibid.

23. Klein, "Commerce des Armes," pp. 578–579.

24. *Le Monde,* 5 March 1977.

25. Ibid., 10 November 1977.

26. For an extensive discussion of French arms trade with South Africa, see SIPRI, *Southern Africa: The Escalation of a Conflict* (New York: Praeger, 1976).

27. Foreign Broadcast Information Service, *Western Europe,* September 8, 1981, p. K1.

28. The 1977 SIPRI *Yearbook* indicates five Mirage V interceptor/reconnaissance aircraft were delivered instead of Mirage III as earlier SIPRI data had noted.

29. The number of Mirage aircraft sent to Zaire is not fully certain on the basis of SIPRI and IISS sources as outlined in table 7–5. The 1976 SIPRI *Yearbook* reports seventeen Mirage V delivered from 1975 to 1976. The 1977 SIPRI *Yearbook* reports fourteen Mirage V delivered in that time. The 1977–1978 and 1978–1979 *Military Balances* list seventeen Mirage V's in the force structure. The 1979–1980 and 1980–1981 editions, however, report only thirteen and ten, respectively. Lower numbers are possibly due to attrition since delivery.

30. The 1981 SIPRI *Yearbook* lists four Alpha Jet deliveries in 1980, leaving two to be delivered of the 1977 order of six. The 1980 SIPRI asserts that six Alpha Jets were ordered in 1977 and six again in 1978. The 1980–1981 *Military Balance* only confirms an order of six Alpha Jets. The two preceding editions cite the orders of twelve Alpha Jets.

31. *Projet Socialiste:* Pour la France des Armées 80 (Paris: Club Socialistes du Livre, 1980), pp. 165, 351, 359. See also paper by David Yost," French Policy in Chad and the Libyan Challenge," delivered at Biennial Conference of the Section on Military Studies of the International Studies Association, November 5–7, 1981.

32. *Le Monde,* 19 August 1981, p. 3.

33. *Le Monde,* 11 July 1981, p. 11 and *Le Nouvel Observateur,* 4 July 1981, p. 33.

34. *Le Monde,* 8 October 1981, p. 16.

35. U.S., Foreign Broadcast Information Service, 6 January 1982, p. K.3.

36. This is essentially the conclusion of one recent evaluation by June Kronholz for the *Wall Street Journal,* 22 July 1981. She cites 14,200 French troops and advisors in Africa. See table 7–3 for a different breakdown and lower figures.

8

West German Arms Transfers to Sub-Saharan Africa: Commercialism versus Foreign Policy

Regina Cowen

Against the background of increasing arms transfers to less developed countries in Africa, Latin America, the Middle East, and Asia, the Federal Republic of Germany finds itself engaged in redefining the rules that have thus far governed the arms-export trade. The need for reviewing the principles of arms-export policy arose from the desire of Saudi Arabia to purchase Leopard II tanks and other defense equipment, and the proposed sale of two 209-class submarines to Chile, which met widespread and open concern among German politicians and the German public. In early 1981 an SPD-FDP working group was formed to investigate the continued viability of the cornerstone of West German arms-export policy: that is, not to export weapons of war to areas of tension.

Yet the export of tanks to Saudi Arabia and the sale of submarines to Chile constitute only the tip of the proverbial iceberg. In devising a new arms-export policy, the German government is called upon to find answers to a variety of questions pertaining to political costs and benefits of German arms exports to countries outside the NATO alliance. Furthermore, since the discussion is taking place with open governmental support, the German government, for the first time in ten years is making a genuine attempt at reconciling the existing credibility gap between its declaratory and its action policy.

This chapter investigates the beginnings of German military aid to Third World countries in the early 1960s and the increasing change from military aid to commercial transactions from the end of the 1960s onwards. We shall also take a look at the legal and political framework in which these arms exports have been taking place, and give particular attention to the role played by the government not only in controlling the export of arms, but also in managing the procurement process for the armed forces and in actively influencing the structure of the West German defense industry.

Military Aid

Most West German arms exports during the 1960s took place within a program of military aid and most of that aid went to African states. India,

Iran, Israel, and Jordan were the only countries outside of Africa to receive military aid during that period.[1] As reasons and objectives for giving military aid changed in the course of events, so did the kind and extent of military aid. It may therefore be useful to try and categorize the different kinds of military aid given by Germany, and the objectives aimed at by the German government.

It is not quite clear how the idea of giving military aid to developing and usually newly independent African countries was perceived by the German government. It seems certain, however, that alliance politics played a major part.[2] Military aid must also be seen as part of the German effort to take on the responsibility of financing NATO defense aid to Greece and Turkey at around the same time, and should therefore be regarded as the German contribution to alliance burden sharing. Even if Germany had not begun to use military aid for her own interests, this German effort at taking some responsibility from the United States would have helped greatly in consolidating Germany's position among her Western allies. The fact that Washington had been informed of West German military-aid projects in Africa and had openly consented to such undertakings, was first reported in 1963 in connection with German engagement in Nigeria. The U.S. Embassy in Bonn confirmed rumors of Bundeswehr officers stationed in Nigeria setting up and training a new Nigerian air force. Furthermore, the Embassy also disclosed the existence of other military-aid agreements between Germany and African states, namely the Sudan, Somalia, Madagascar, and Guinea. As for the reason behind German aid, the U.S. embassy officials remarked on German assistance in warding off Soviet influence in Africa.[3]

The first African country to receive German defense equipment and training was the Sudan; an agreement to that effect was concluded between the two countries at the end of 1961.[4] The Sudan, Nigeria, and Tanzania received the largest shares of German military aid, for which between 1962 and 1970 some DM 400 million were made available.[5] These countries also received patrol and coast-guard boats, some small trainer aircraft, rifles, and ammunition.[6] Apart from that, the German armed forces provided facilities at home and in the respective countries for military training and the organization of air-force personnel and coast guards.[7] Although it was important for West Germany at the time to support United States-Third World military-aid programs, there were interests close to home that persuaded Germany to use military aid as an instrument of foreign policy. In the first instance, the on-going Cold War between East and West highlighted the political and psychological uncertainties pertaining to the "German Question". Both Germanys were faced with the problem of legitimate coexistence and each laid claim to being the sole representative of a legitimate German state. Thus military aid to newly independent African states appeared to be a useful instrument in pursuing three interrelated objectives. First, it was reported in 1966 that all military-aid agreements contained a clause with respect to the maintenance of friendly relations between donor and recipient.[8] For the countries receiving West German aid this meant not to recognize the German Democratic Republic (GDR). Second, since the armed forces of African states appeared to be a most significant factor in shaping the future of their countries, good relations with those armies via military aid could result in valuable support for West Germany.[9] Third, the competition between the two Germanies provided an incentive for West Germany to consolidate her claims and, with the first-generation surplus weapons, almost all of American origin, at hand, opportunities and capabilities coincided.

During this first period of military aid to Africa, events outside and inside Germany led to a first review of policy. In March 1960, the Federal Republic and the state of Israel had concluded a secret military-aid agreement and between 1962 and 1965 Germany supplied weapons valued at DM 149 million.[10] The agreement became public knowledge in 1965 and soured relations with Arab states considerably. Parallel to disclosures of secret arms supplies to Israel, German-Arab relations became strained further through the announcement of the GDR's State Council Chairman Walter Ulbricht's visit to Cairo. As a direct consequence of these events, the Sudan broke off diplomatic relations with Bonn. When Tanzania permitted the GDR to open a consulate, German military aid was cancelled. Thus, within a relatively short time, two of Germany's most valued military-aid projects had proved ineffective in persuading the recipient country of German desires, and certainly showed the ineffectiveness of linking foreign-policy objectives with the supply of military aid. Germany's still modest military-aid record may have been at least in part responsible for that failure. But there is no evidence that Germany, during this first phase of military aid, ever wanted to contribute more than she actually did. Furthermore, it is doubtful, given the substantial commitment to Greece and Turkey, and, given that during the early 1960s most West German defense equipment still had to be imported, whether more military aid to Africa could have been made available. In fact the ensuing domestic debate of the deal with Israel, which also involved discussion of military aid to Africa showed just how uneasy German politicians and the German public felt about the German involvement. In February 1965, the cabinet of Chancellor Erhard made a decision that may, retrospectively, be called a fateful one, not to deliver arms into areas of tension. The formulation of such a vague principle that was to guide future arms exports was convenient at the time since it allowed Germany to extricate herself from military aid to Israel without undue discrimination of that state.[11]

After these first unpleasant experiences with military aid at home and abroad, the German government continued its efforts in Africa, but the policy objectives, and thus the kind of material supplied, changed. While during the first phase, emphasis had been placed on external security, the government now turned its attention to aiding the formation and supplying the equipment of African police forces. Under this program no weapons or ammunition were supplied. Somalia, Ethiopia, and Niger were the major recipients. But this second phase was short-lived particularly after it became known that the German-equipped and-trained Ethiopian police were used to crush student demonstrations. In addition, Ethiopia and Somalia were frequently engaged in border conflicts and it was believed that both sides also used their police forces.[12]

The last attempt of the German government at providing at least quasi-military assistance began in 1968 and, for a time, Guinea received most of the aid under that program. Germany supplied transport vehicles, liaison aircraft, and road-building and pioneering equipment. On the basis of recommendations by the Foreign Affairs Committee, more emphasis was placed on improving infrastructure and meeting civilian needs.[13] Yet this program too collapsed in 1970 when German experts were expelled from Guinea, allegedly for supporting an invasion attempt staged from Portuguese Guinea.

By the end of the 1960s all major West German military and quasi-military-aid program had been abandoned. Besides the decision not to supply weapons into areas of tension in 1965, other domestic political measures contributed to a tighter political control over military aid. With the beginning of the second phase of the military-aid program no arms were delivered to African states under that program. An opposition SPD party initiative in 1966, which suggested that permission for export of equipment and training of forces personnel under the military-aid program be obtained from the Foreign Affairs and the Budget Committees, was incorporated into the federal budgetary laws. As a result of these improved controls and because of the disappointment with previous major program, the German military-aid program began to drop sharply after 1965.

While in 1965 military aid totalled DM 305 million, in 1966 it came to only DM 108 million,[14] and dropped even further in subsequent years. Altogether, West Germany spent around 1,000 million DM on military aid over the 1960s, but spent some 14,000 million DM on development aid.[15] Indeed, the ratio between military and civilian aid program shows the remarkable figure of 1:13.8 in favor of development aid. This high proportion of development aid is reflected throughout Africa and there was, during that period, no African country receiving military aid that did not obtain substantial amounts of development aid at the same time. One could even suggest that it should have been civilian aid that should

Table 8–1
Total West German Military Aid
(million DM)

Recipient	Years	Military Aid	Totals
NATO-Defense Aid			
Greece	1964–1968	101.0	
Turkey	1964–1970	300.0	
			401.0
Equipment and Training Aid			
Ethiopia	1965–1971	46.0	
Ghana	1969–1971	6.0	
Guinea	1962–1971	47.0	
India	1962	3.5	
Iran	1966–1972	40.0	
Jordan	1964–1965	1.7	
Kenya	1966–1970	16.0	
Madagascar	1962–1964	6.0	
Mali	1969–1970	2.0	
Morocco	1968–1972	16.0	
Niger	1966–1971	8.0	
Nigeria	1963–1967	15.0	
Somalia	1962–1971	18.0	
Sudan	1961–1965	100.0	
Tanzania	1963–1965	6.2	
Togo	1969–1971	4.0	
Chad	1969–1971	6.0	
Tunisia	1968–1972	8.0	
			345.4
Special Program Israel			
Equipment Aid	1962–1965	149.0	
Offset Payment	1965	140.0	
			289.0
Military Training Aid			
Thirty-one Countries		18.772	
			18.772
Total			1054.172

Source: Helga Haftendorn, *Militärhilfe und Rüstungsexporte der* BRD (Düsseldorf: Ber-telsmann Universitatsverlag, 1971), p. 130. Reprinted with permission.

have persuaded some of the African states with whom Germany had established aid programs that were subsequently cancelled, to maintain friendly relations with the Federal Republic. The evidence above, how-ever shows that this did not happen.

With the Cold War abating toward the end of the 1960s the Federal Republic also found herself in a changed international and domestic en-vironment. Within Germany, the Social Democrats, a party known for its outspoken resentment of arms exports had assumed office for the first time. This was reflected in the 1970 white paper on defense,[16] which

Table 8–2
Military Training Assistance

Algeria:	1967–1968	4 Officers
	1969–1970	5 NCOs
Ethiopia:	1965–1969	5 Officers
	1965–1974	9 Cadets
	1966–1972	16 NCOs
Libya:	1965–1968	1 Cadet
	1970–1971	3 Cadets
Morocco:	1966–1972	21 Officers
Sudan:	1964–1967	15 Officers
Togo:	1965–1967	1 Officer

Source: *Die Welt* 10 September 1970.

Table 8–3
Training Assistance—Equipment Aid

Country	Years	Training Received
Ethiopia	1966–1972	9 Police Detectives
		3 Mechanics
Guinea	1962–1971	130 Skilled Workers for Army Factories
		179 Engineers
		90 Mechanics
		23 Radio Operators
Madagascar	1963–1964	55 Coastguardsmen
Morocco	1969	3 Mechanics
Niger	1969–1970	12 Pilots
		10 Engineers
Nigeria	1963–1967	550 Air Force Technicians and Pilots
Somalia	1965–1972	2 Police Officers
		4 Logistics Personnel
		40 Mechanics
Sudan	1962–1965	150 Soldiers
		50 Technicians
		13 Pilots
Tanzania	1963–1965	36 Naval Police
		15 Pilots

Source: Haftendorn *Militärhilfe* p. 117.

again mentions the principle of not delivering arms in areas of tension; further evidence was the small budget of equipment aid to thirteen states (twelve in Africa) that amounted to 74 million DM over "the next few years" and the promise not to supply arms under that program. Outside Germany, the tentative beginnings of détente in Europe and between the two superpowers, the realization that recognition of GDR as an independent sovereign state could not be prevented, and the increasing burden of providing defense aid to Greece and Turkey first, and then to Portugal, brought German interests closer to home. None of the major military-aid program of the 1960s was ever revived. In this context, one should not underestimate the German contribution to the defense of NATO's flanks.

Table 8–4
West German Military and Development Aid: Comparison,
1960–1968
(DM million)

Recipient	Military Aid	Development Aid	Ratio
Ethiopia	46.0	65.4	1:1.4
Ghana	6.0	200.1	1:33
Greece	101.0	357.7	1:3.5
Guinea	47.0	83.2	1:1.8
India	3.5	2,457.7	1:702
Iran	40.0	239.3	1:6
Israel	289.0	2,108.8	1:7.3
Jordan	1.7	75.6	1:44.5
Kenya	16.0	76.9	1:4.8
Madagascar	6.0	58.4	1:9.7
Mali	2.0	17.2	1:8.6
Morocco	16.0	240.1	1:15
Niger	8.0	17.9	1:2.2
Nigeria	15.0	148.2	1:9.8
Somalia	18.0	70.9	1:3.9
Sudan	106.0	97.4	1:0.9
Tanzania	6.2	117.5	1:18.0
Togo	4.0	100.9	1:25.2
Chad	6.0	15.2	1:2.5
Turkey	300.0	843.6	1:2.8
Tunisia	8.0	119.2	1:14.9
Total	1035.399	14,351.2	1:13.8

Source: Haftendorn, *Militärhilfe*, p. 137, and adjustments by author.

While, in the mid-1960s German NATO aid totalled one third of all German military and equipment aid, by 1970 two thirds went to NATO.

The Commercial Take-Over versus Legal and Political Guidelines

During the military/equipment-aid period, the government of the Federal Republic did conclude agreements for arms supply. Political control over arms and equipment exports had been established through parliamentary committees and the main political guideline was not to deliver arms into areas of tension. Thus for all its purposes, the flow of military aid to African countries as part of German foreign policy was tightly controlled. What happened over the next decade, and continued happening, is a direct result of government first failing to enforce arms-export principles as developed in the 1960s vis-a-vis commercial-arms exports; second, adapting its internal decision-making structure to maintain political control over quantity and quality of arms exports, and, third, tolerating the vast increases in arms exports to the Third World, and, through coproduction agreements with other Western European nations, even encouraging the arms flow. In 1982 Germany ranked fifth on the list of major arms suppliers to the Third World,[17] behind the United States, the Soviet Union, France, and Britain; export figures have reached an all-time high of $875 million, two-thirds of which account for deliveries to the Third World.[18] An investigation of the regional distribution of West German arms exports to the Third World[19] shows Africa in third place behind the Near East and Latin America for the period 1965–1974, and for both the 1973–1977 period and 1974–1978 period. (See table 8–5.) During the same periods, the monetary value of arms delivered to Africa jumped from $73 million to $575 million. The largest increase is recorded for the years within the second period (from $75 million to $425 million), an observation also reflected in the annual total figures of German arms exports; where a distinct take-off point can be identified in 1975. This record becomes even more impressive if one considers the

Table 8–5
Regional Distribution of West German Arms Transfers, 1965–1978
(U.S. million current)

Recipient	1965–1974	1973–1977	1974–1978
NATO Europe	628	510	675
Other European	47	80	90
East Asia	23	80	100
Near Asia	181	—	950
South Asia	36	20	20
Middle East	—	715	—
Africa	73	425	575
North America	96	30	120
Latin America	137	325	360
Oceania	—	40	130
Total	1,221	2,225	3,020
NATO Europe	628	510	675
Other European	47	80	90
North America	96	30	120
Oceania	—	40	130
Developed Total	771	660	1,015
East Asia	23	80	100
Near Asia	181	—	950
South Asia	36	20	20
Middle East	—	715	—
Africa	73	425	575
Latin America	137	325	360
Developing Total	450	1,565	2,005

Source: US Arms Control and Disarmament Agency, *World Military Expenditures and Arms Transfers 1965–1974, 1968–1977, 1969–1978.*

time-span 1975–1978 during which a doubling of arms exports took place.[20]See tables 8–6, and 8–7.

In the search for an explanation for these extraordinary developments it is proposed to investigate three factors that together have made Germany become one of the foremost European arms exporters.

Table 8–6
West German Arms Transfers to Africa, 1965–1978
(current U.S. $)

Recipient	1965–1974	1973–1977	1974–1978
Algeria	—	210	280
Angola	—	10	10
Burundi	—	5	5
Chad	1	—	—
Ethiopia	10	5	5
Ghana	4	10	10
Kenya	—	5	5
Libya	7	80	140
Morocco	6	40	50
Niger	1	5	—
Nigeria	18	10	10
Somalia	3	10	10
South Africa	1	—	—
Sudan	3	—	30
Togo	2	—	5
Tunisia	2	10	10
Zaire	13	20	10
Zambia	2	5	5

Source: *World Military Expenditures and Arms Transfers* U.S. Arms Control and Disarmament Agency, 1965–1974; 1968–1977; 1969–1978.

Table 8–7
West German Arms Exports, 1965–1978

Year	Current U.S. $	Constant U.S. $
1965	102	142
1966	689	92
1967	58	76
1968	98	124
1969	101	122
1970	189	216
1971	130	142
1972	226	239
1973	140	177
1974	223	202
1975	420	442
1976	650	650
1977	800	758
1978	875	814

Source: *World Military Expenditures and Arms Transfers* US Arms Control and Disarmament Agency, 1965–1974; 1968–1977; 1969–1978.

The first factor we shall call the legal and political provisions governing the commercial production and sale of armaments (weapons and weapon systems) and defense-related material (nonlethal, such as trucks and trainer aircraft, but also such items as blueprints for the initiation of military production outside Germany and dual-purpose equipment such as observation equipment to determine harvest time or to spy across borders).

The first reference to the production of armaments by the Federal Republic is found in article 26, paragraphs I and II of the German Constitution. Paragraph I states that actions suitable for and intended to disrupt peaceful international conduct, particularly actions for the purpose of aggressive warfare, are contradictory to the Constitution. Paragraph II states that weapons of war may only be produced, transported, and marketed by permission of the Federal Government,[21] It was not until April 1961 that the law regarding the practical meaning of Article 26 was introduced. The Law on the Control of Weapons of War (KWKG) spells out in detail what "weapons of war" are, and a list of such weapons is attached to that law.[22] It states further that when licenses for export are required (Articles 2, 3, 4, 4a), and gives reasons for denial of license. Licenses are not granted if there is reason to believe that weapons exported from Germany will "disturb friendly relations with other states," or if there is a danger that such weapons would be "used to fight a war of aggression." On April 28 of the same year, the Foreign Trade Act (AWG) was passed through Parliament and it is meant to complement the KWKG. It covers industrial products that have a militarily useful potential. The Export List contains all goods, including those on the Weapons of War List (since for those both a production and an export license has to be obtained), that cannot be exported freely, and they accordingly range from bombs to particular electrical circuits. For all weapons and materials defined by the KWKG and the AWG, the applicant for producing or exporting licenses has no right of enforcement. Such decision-making authority lies with the government—for weapons, according to the KWKG and for material, with a federal agency of the Ministry of Economics. The export decision on commercially exported weapons is taken by the Minister of Economic Affairs in consultation with the Foreign Office and the Ministry of Defence. Transactions that are believed to be of political significance may be referred to the Federal Security Council (cabinet committee consisting of the Chancellor, Ministers of Defense, Foreign Affairs, Economics, Finance and Domestic Affairs).

There are also certain Western European Union (WEU) restrictions dating back to 1954 still in operation, although over the years these restrictions have been widely relaxed for the production of conventional weapons.

Yet the most widely used, abused, and neglected (according to convenience) provisions that express most firmly the German government's approach to the transfer of armaments are the political principles of June 1971. These principles permitted unrestricted export of weapons of war and defense material to NATO member states. Communist countries were to receive weapons of war and defense material only by agreement of all COCOM (Coordinating Committee) members. Countries in areas of tension (to be decided on by the Foreign Office), would receive no weapons of war either; the supply of defense material should also be refused if a disruption of peaceful international relations or damage to the Federal Republic's foreign relations is to be expected. All other countries should not receive any weapons of war except where political considerations permit the rule of exception. Permission to export defense material should only be granted if other legal provisions are not infringed.[23] In 1978, Article 4a was made part of the Weapons of War Control Act and requires all citizens of the Federal Republic who intend to conclude contracts for the sale of weapons or provide facilities for the conclusion of such contracts, to obtain permission of those weapons are outside the Federal Republic. This particular provision seems to have been introduced only to increase the ability of the federal government to keep a record of what is sold and to whom through industrial branches of German-based companies abroad. It certainly has not helped to lower German arms-export figures and has done nothing to prevent the use of foreigners as salesmen or the transfer of the German-French-produced HOT, Milan and Alpha-Jet trainers of which more will be said below.

This most impressive list of self-imposed restrictions on the transfer of weapons and defense material gives us reason to believe that the Federal Republic should have been well-equipped to cope satisfactorily with almost every request for the exportation of armaments. Before analyzing in more detail how these restrictions have been circumvented, ignored, or have encouraged the search for loopholes, it is useful to look at just when and why some of these restrictions were introduced.

The Weapons of War Control Act (KWKG) was finally passed as a consequence of an incident involving a German freighter transporting weapons for the Algerian resistance movement in 1960.[24] Chancellor Erhard's cabinet conceived the phrase "areas of tension" in order for Germany to withdrawn from the secret arms deal with Israel. The aforementioned military- and equipment-aid programs had almost all collapsed before a significant change of policy in the light of newly available guidelines could have made a significant contribution to the states supplied. That number of countries dropped because of unrealistic policy objectives, not because such countries were designated "areas of tension". The notable exception, of course, was Nigeria where the aid program was suspended just before the outbreak of the Biafran War, and two transport planes were repurchased.[25] Thus two most important provisions regulating the export of armaments were introduced as a necessity rather than as a precaution. This obvious lack of foresight on the part of the German government helps to explain the ensuing conflicts of priorities that eventually resulted in a credibility gap between declaratory and action policy.

It has been shown above that until the late 1960s, arms exports were dealt with on a government-to-government basis. The number of weapons and related material was still small and West Germany was importing more than one-third of Bundeswehr equipment. Most of the military production that did take place in Germany was done under license and financial offset agreements with the United States. This gave the German defense industry the opportunity to gather expertise and experience in areas of high technology. Production was geared toward the needs of the Federal armed forces in order to fulfill Germany's military role in NATO. As those needs increased, the defense industry became more and more able to satisfy them. West Germany now imports only one-fifth of its defense equipment,[26] and the defense industry provides work for some 200,000 people.[27] As an example of the fast growth of the defense industry one can cite the aerospace industry. In 1960 it employed 20,000 people, achieving a turnover of DM 384.6 million; and in 1965 it employed 41,000 people and increased its turnover to DM 1,053 million. In 1970 it employed 57,253 people and the turnover came to DM 2,882 million.[28] In 1979, 65,853 people were employed and the turnover had more than doubled to reach DM 7,235 million.[29]

Currently Germany is producing most weapons and materials in service with the Bundeswehr either on its own or in cooperation with European NATO partners. Particularly in the fields of tanks, antitank weapons, helicopters, submarines, and most recently, high-technology aircraft such as the Alpha Jet and Tornado, the production of such equipment shows that the Federal Republic has closed the technology gap that had existed between Germany and other European NATO members throughout the 1960s.

With the West German defense industry becoming internationally competitive, the federal government has begun to relax the strict interpretation of what constitutes an "area of tension." Judging by the continuously increasing value of German arms exports, some would argue that the area-of-tension rule was never applied strictly. This is not the case. A strict interpretation of the rule would have meant a literal disengagement from the international arms market, since tensions between two or more countries may be found in abundance at any time period one wishes to consider. Second, some significant requests for arms were refused by invoking the nondelivery-into-areas-of-tension rule. In 1969, Iran wanted to negotiate the purchase of 1,000 Leopard I tanks and in 1977 Saudi Arabia also inquired about the same tanks. Both requests were turned down. What is more important, in this context, is to point out the inconsistency of interpretation criteria used by the foreign office to determine what an area of tension is or what factors have to be present to put a country into that category. How international situations are assessed in the light of arms transfers is not known, and the number of countries to which delivery of weapons was granted makes a mockery of Chancellor Schmidt's speech before the U.N. disarmament session in May 1978: "Only in altogether minor exceptional cases do we permit the delivery of weapons to states outside our own alliance . . . As a principle, delivery of weapons into areas of international tension is not permitted."[30]

Such statements make it difficult to understand how German weapons, parts of weapons, blueprints, helicopters most adaptable for counterinsurgency missions, and vast numbers of G–3 rifles could have been exported to Third World countries (see table 8–8). In this way, Iran, after the oil embargo in 1974, received equipment for tank maintenance, ammunition plants, tank engines, tracks and guns, supplied by the same company that supplies the Bundeswehr with Leopard II parts.[31] By spring 1979, Kenya and Brunei had both received weapons and parts of weapons. Ethiopia and Niger were supplied with equipment to produce weapons, Nigeria and the Sudan had obtained weapons, parts and equipment to produce weapons.[32] Ammunition was sold to Tanzania, a frigate costing DM 314 million to Nigeria, 5,000 chassis for trucks to South Africa,[33] for civil use only—yet the same trucks are used within NATO for military purposes and the Export List states specifically that vehicles of "military construction" need an export license.[34] While the Federal Republic was granting licenses to export weapons and defense material, Africa, and in particular the sub-Saharan states, constituted an area of tension in almost anybody's vocabulary. Apart from the border conflicts between Ethiopia, Somalia and Kenya, the uncertainties about the future of Zimbabwe, the conflicts concentrated in the Horn of Africa, and the ever-increasing hostilities between the Republic of South Africa, and black African states to the North, the major threat to peace on the African continent in the view of the West stems from Soviet, Cuban, and East German involvement. Mozambique, Angola, Benin, Congo, and Ethiopia now conform

Table 8-8
West German Arms Sales and Military Aid to African Countries, 1958–1979

Year	Recipient	Item	Commercial Sales/Military Aid	Details
1958	South Africa	2 Dornier DO–27B	Commercial Sale	
1961	Katanga	5 Dornier DO–28	?	
1961	Tunisia	1 Patrol Boat	Commercial Sale	75 Tons
1962	Zaire	1 Dornier DO–27	Military Aid	
1962–1965	Sudan	97 Saladin	Military Aid	
1963	Tunisia	1 Patrol Boat	Commercial Sale	75 Tons
1963	Malagasy	3 Patrol Boats	Military Aid	
1963	Nigeria	2 Noratlas	Military Aid	
1963	Nigeria	14 Piaggio P.149D	Military Aid	
1963	Zaire	2 Dornier DO–27	Military Aid	
1964	Nigeria	20 Dornier DO–27	Military Aid (15)	Commercial Sale (5)
1964	Rwanda	1 Dornier DO–27	?	
1964	Sudan	3 Dornier DO–27	Military Aid	50 Tons
1964	Tanzania	2 Coastguard Boats	Military Aid	112 Tons
1964	Tanzania	4 Patrol Boats	Military Aid	later transferred to Kenya
1964	Togo	10 Piaggio P.149D	?	
1965	Ghana	1 Fast Patrol Boat	Commercial Sale	
1965	Nigeria	5 Fouga Magister	Military Aid	delivery uncertain
1965	Tanzania	8 Piaggio P.149D	Military Aid	
1965	Tanzania	2 Dornier DO–28	Military Aid	
1966	Niger	2 River Gunboats	Military Aid	
1967	Tunisia	1 Patrol Boat	Commercial Sale	75 Tons
1968	Morocco	24 Fouga Magister	?	
1968	Morocco	2 Patrol Boats	?	
1968	Cameroon	1 Dornier DO–28	Commercial Sale	
1968	Ghana	5 Fast Patrol Boats	Commercial Sale	
1969–1970	Tunisia	1 Patrol Boat	Commercial Sale	325 Tons Ex-French
1970–1971	Niger	4 Noratlas	Military Aid	Ex-Luftwaffe
1971	Ethiopia	1 Reims-Cessna	Military Aid	
1971	Niger	1 Aero Commander 500	Commercial Sale	
1971	Niger	2 Douglas DC–6B	Commercial Sale	Ex-Luftwaffe
1974	Ethiopia	2 Dornier DO–28	Military Aid	

Year	Country	Quantity / Type	Transfer	Notes
1974	Ghana	1 or 2 Patrol Boat(s)	Commercial Sale	160 Tons
1974	Nigeria	8 Dornier DO–28	Commercial Sale	
1974	Nigeria	4 MBB BO–105	Commercial Sale	
1974	Zambia	10 Dornier DO–28	Commercial Sale	
1976	Gabon	(2 Fast Patrol Boats	Commercial Sale	Jaguar Class–2
		(2 Fast Patrol Boats	Commercial Sale	Jaguar Class–3
1976	Tanzania	1 Survey Ship	Commercial Sale	Delivered 1979
1976	Nigeria	2 Tank Landing Ships	Commercial Sale	Delivered 1979
1977	Ghana	(2 Patrol Boats	Commercial Sale	Delivered 1979
		(2 Patrol Boats	Commercial Sale	
1977	Kenya	6 DO–28D–2	Commercial Sale	Delivered 1978
1977	Nigeria	(1 Frigate	Commercial Sale	
		(1 Tank Landing Ship	Commercial Sale	Delivered 1980
		(3 Fast Patrol Boats	Commercial Sale	
1977	Sudan	20 MBB BO–105C	Commercial Sale	Delivered 1977 (10)
1977	Togo	5 Panavia Tornado (Fighter)	Commercial Sale	Delivered 1979
1977	Togo	5 Alpha Jet Trainers	Commercial Sale	Delivered 1980
1977	Nigeria	1 Frigate	Commercial Sale	
1977	Nigeria	3 Fast Patrol Boats	Commercial Sale	
1978	Malawi	4 Dornier DO–28D–2	Commercial Sale	Delivered 1980
1978	Sierra Leone	1 BO–105CB	Commercial Sale	Delivered 1978
1978	Ethiopia	2 Dornier DO–28D–Z	Commercial Sale	Delivered 1978
1978	Malawi	6 Dornier DO–27	Commercial Sale	Delivered 1979
1979	Brunei	6 BO–105C	Commercial Sale	
1979	Cameroon	2 Dornier DO–28D–1	Commercial Sale	
1979	Malawi	6 Dornier DO–28–2	Commercial Sale	
1979	Morocco	Dornier DO–28D–2	Commercial Sale	
1979	Nigeria	12 Alpha Jet Trainers	Commercial Sale	

Source: *SIPRI Yearbook 1968–1969, 1974, 1979, 1980. SIPRI Arms Trade Register 1975.* H. Rattinger "West Germany's Arms Transfers to the Non-Industrial World" in U. Ra'anan et al., eds. *Arms Transfers to the Third World: The Military Build-up in Less Industrial Countries* (Boulder, Colo., Westview Press, 1978).

to Marxist-Leninist rule. In 1978, U.S. government estimates numbered 41,000 communist military personnel in sub-Saharan Africa; 3,800 of these were believed to come from Eastern Europe. The largest force concentrations were found in Angola and Ethiopia, mostly Cubans numbering approximately 37,000: 19,000 in Angola and 16,500 in Ethiopia. Next in line was Mozambique where 1,130 communist personnel were found to be present. More Communist forces were stationed in Equatorial Guinea, Guinea, Guinea-Bissau, Mali, and Zambia. The number of Communist technical experts came to 37,000 (11,000 Chinese) and their presence was recorded in twenty-three countries, with the largest concentration in Angola (some 10,000, mostly Cubans), followed by Nigeria with Soviet personnel numbering 1,600.[35] The Soviet Union provides most of the military hardware and the Cubans concentrate on providing the manpower.

Thus far Communist weapons and forces have been used to bring about the settlement of indigenous African disputes. The danger that lies in any kind of foreign involvement, however, is the export of conflicts and conflict behavior, which are not dependent on geography. The prime example of such conflict is the East-West conflict, which is not tied to geography but can make its presence felt anywhere on the globe. Thus the settlement of conflicts in Africa is potentially less important than the establishment of the winning party. If this becomes the general approach to conflict resolution in Africa, and many would argue that this is already the case, regional and continental stability will rest on weak pillars.

Nigeria provides an excellent example for the increasing import of foreign-designed weapons into Africa. Starting a major modernization program for its armed forces, Nigeria began a series of large-scale purchases. In February 1979, twelve Dornier Dassault-Breguet Alpha Jet-trainer light-ground-attack aircraft were ordered to be delivered in 1981 and 1982.[36] The Nigerians further ordered sixteen Franco-German Roland ground-to-air-missile units.[37] Both contracts were won by the Germany industry against fierce international competition.

It is, of course, difficult to ascertain whether, in the instances thus far cited, the federal government used or abused the principle of non-delivery of weapons into areas of tension, whether export licenses were granted because decision makers were not aware of political repercussions (which would point to a weakness of executive organizaton), whether weapons components were exported to NATO countries and then reassembled for export to Third World countries (which would indicate a weakness of the existing legal framework), or whether deals were concluded by transfer of production licenses for which no permission has to be obtained by industry.

The delivery of weapons into areas of tension can also have a stabilizing effect in that it might dissuade an enemy from escalating a conflict. Weapons, therefore, can play a deterrent role or even diffuse existing conflicts. At the same time expensive arms imports tie up scarce financial resources that could be spent on civilian-development projects, and they have led to a growing militarization of less-developed countries and of their relations with one another.

The most surprising fact in the Federal Republic's handling of arms exports is an overall lack of policy design. As has been amply shown above, if government officials had acted strictly within the legal framework, German arms exports to the developing world could not have reached a value of $2,000 million. But even competent bureaucrats must find it difficult to act if they are not advised on parameters within which to make a decision. The classification of a region as an ''area of tension'' is a political judgment and has to be oriented on the exporting state's foreign policy. Without this conceptual link between arms exports and foreign policy, there can be no coherent and consistent arms-export policy. As has been discussed previously, during the military- and equipment-aid phase of the 1960s, German foreign-policy interests were reflected in its approach to providing military aid and in conducting the projects military aid was used for. With the ending of these programs, government policial involvement ceased and the vital foreign-policy link was lost. Not only have German arms exports become commercialized but this commercialization has in turn shaped the conceptual approach to arms transfer. The organizational decision-making structure exemplifies this. In the Ministry of Economics, only one civil servant and his assistant deal with all commercial arms export applications that fall under the Weapons of War Control Act. Only if these two officials have doubts about a request do they refer to the Minister himself, who might then refer to the Federal Security Council[38]—a procedure one would not have epxected in the light of the magnitude of German arms exports. Thus the Federal Government has failed to actively guide arms exports in the context of foreign policy and failed to adapt the decision-making structure to the amount and variety of arms exports taking place.

Far from resisting the trend toward commercialization of arms exports, the federal government is indirectly responsible for creating increased export opportunities for the German defense industry. There are rumors of federal cabinet decisions in 1972 and 1977[39] relating to the German position vis-à-vis exportation of German-French weapons by France. The possibility that such decisions were taken is strongly supported by German acquiescence to exports of jointly produced weapons and, most recently, by Chancellor Schmidt's address to the Bundestag.[40] He said it would be very difficult to prescribe Germany's export principles to other partners in a cooperative project.

Joint defense production is undertaken for reasons of standardization of equipment within the alliance and cost-effectiveness. In the case of Germany, defense cooperation has served the additional purpose of acquiring a competitive defense-industrial base and, after this objective had been achieved, cooperation (this time primarily for reasons of cost) had to be continued. Suspension of cooperative projects would have meant the loss of ability to cooperate within a very short time and the even more immediate result of overcapacity in defense-related industries and the loss of jobs. Against this background it is unlikely that the on-going discussion on new arms-export guidelines will change the currently practised exporting of jointly produced equipment.

In the past this practise has resulted in Franco-German weapons such as the antitank-guided weapons HOT and MILAN being exported to Lebanon, People's Republic of China, Syria, Egypt, Iraq, South Africa, (MILAN), and Egypt, Kuwait, Syria, Iraq and People's Republic of China (HOT). The antiaircraft system ROLAND has been sold to Brazil and Nigeria. Alpha Jet trainer-light-ground-attack aircraft have been sold to Egypt (two hundred), Togo (five), Ivory Coast (six), Morocco (twenty-four).[41] Since France handles all export business outside NATO, there is no reason to assume that the export of jointly produced weapons should not continue.

Thus far the West German defense industry has only produced weapons and equipment for the federal armed forces; the potential export possibilities have not been the initiating factor for production. Whether this remains the case is open to question. There will undoubtedly be pressure on the German government that it will find difficult to resist. Existing capacities for defense production will cause problems in the late 1980s. The rising cost of defense equipment, particularly the expenditures on research and development will make even the European defense-equipment market appear too limited. The cost explosion experienced with the multi-role-combat-aircraft TORNADO only proved a disincentive to similar collaborative projects. The production of another two 122-class frigates was postponed, as was the development of a new tactical fighter, and talks with France on the Main Battle Tank 3. Another problem is posed by the large amount of surplus equipment that is now becoming available. All surplus Bundeswehr equipment is dealt with by VEBEG, the state owned surplus weapon disposal company. What is not scrapped is usually available for sale. With the phasing in of new systems into the Bundeswehr, hundreds of F–140 starfighters and G–91s, thousands of Leopard I's and armored personnel carriers and ten destroyers and frigates will somehow have to be disposed of.[42] Part of the surplus equipment will be delivered to Turkey, Greece, and Portugal within Germany's NATO defense-aid program. Since 20 percent of the aid volume is usually set aside to be taken up by the delivery of surplus material, 80 percent is new equipment. In 1981 agreements on new installments were signed with all three countries: Turkey will receive DM 130 million, Greece DM 70 million, Portugal DM 5 million. Thus for DM 30 million, Turkey will receive mainly F–104 fighters and other surplus material, Greece a destroyer and also F–104 Gs for its 14 million. The nature of material to Portugal has as yet not been decided. The industrial agreements cover an eighteen-month period and will be renewed in due course.[43] Under an additional aid program, the Special Defense Aid, Turkey was also to receive seventy-seven Leopard I and 249 MILAN antitank systems with 5,000 missiles between 1980–1983.[44] The supply of surplus and new equipment (20 percent surplus and 80 percent new) to NATO's militarily less-developed members will reduce the amount of surplus material available for export outside NATO and new equipment will be offered, at least at first, to NATO partners. Yet the monetary value of NATO defense aid is not likely to be a satisfactory outlet for German surplus weapons in the short, or even medium, term and given France's pronounced export interests, joint developments have, to date, found their most lucrative markets in the Third World.

The Economic and Political Importance of the German Defense Industry

In the previous sections of this chapter we analyzed the development of German arms exports and military aid, their legal and political restrictions and guidelines. It was found that the political guidelines were especially ill-defined and that the organization of the decision-making structure could be substantially improved. In addition it was found that governmental disengagement and the consequent divorce of arms-export practices from foreign policy greatly encouraged the commercialization of arms transfer.

The 1979 white paper on defense mentions peace as "the governing condition fundamental to our life".[45] And indeed, for the past decade, the Social-Democrat/Free-Democrat government has prided itself on its "peace policy" (Friedenspolitik), and has pursued a policy of detente with the East. At present the federal government is trying hard to save the fruits of detente in the light of Soviet military build-ups and domestic opposition to the stationing of American cruise missiles and Pershing-IIs on German soil. The Government's peace policy is questioned by those who see peace threatened through the proposed missile deployment and by those who see West German arms exports as a contradiction of the government's claim to pursue a policy of worldwide detente. With respect

to arms transfer we have seen how the existing credibility gap has occurred; we shall now turn to investigate why the German government has
failed to close this gap.

There is no doubt that the share of arms exports in total manufacturing
is small; at present the figure is 2.03 percent. Some 200,000 people are
employed in the defense industry or 2 percent of the total work force in
manufacturing. The overall contribution of arms exports to total exports
is 0.7 percent.[46] While the German economy as a whole does not depend
on the successful sale of weapons, there are structural industrial problems
that cannot be ignored.

The Federal Republic of Germany does not own any part of the
defense industry. Ever since defense production was undertaken in postwar Germany, it has been the policy of successive governments to leave
defense production to private enterprise. The experience of World War
II, where vast numbers of people were employed in the war effort (by
1945, employment in the aircraft industry alone had reached one million)
did not permit new democratic German governments to be seen to be
directly involved in the production of military hardware. This circumstance also accounts for commercial interests increasingly dominating
German defense production. In the main, government is in a position that
permits only partial control via the procurement process and funding of
research and development.

The biggest problem facing any defense industry, public or private,
is that of coping with an erratic government-procurement cycle. Most
modern weapon systems take a decade or more from concept to production
phase, and two decades or more will pass before similar projects are
undertaken. Germany's role in NATO determines the kinds of weapons
procured, and it is this factor that has led to severe problems for the
German shipbuilding industry where the last submarines for the Navy
were procured in the 1960s and further demand is not to be expected
before were into the 1960s. The German navy has ordered six frigates,
which are being built in five shipyards; the spread of orders is to reduce
excess capacities. Civilian outlets for shipyards have been steadily de-
creasing over the past decade and the German government found itself
in the position of either accepting unemployment (60,000 people are
employed at shipyards) in regions that do not support alternative industries, or relaxing its restrictive military-export policy. Shipyard order
books show that the latter was opted for. At the beginning of 1981, eleven
frigates, four corvettes, six submarines and thirty-nine fast patrol boats
were on order from mainly Third World countries.[47] If the federal government during a later review of arms-export policy should decide on
curtailing the export of submarines and surface ships, some shipyards
might be forced to shut down.

The prospects for Maschinen GmbH Kiel (MAK) and Krauss-Maffei are positive. Production of the Leopard II tank is shared between the two—another sign of governmental management of the industrial structure. MAK, which has a 30 percent military-production share in its turnover, would have incurred great financial losses if Krauss-Maffei alone had been awarded the contract.[48]

The aircraft/aerospace industry, cited before as an example of the rapid growth of defense industry, faces structural problems similar to those of the shipbuilding industry. Again we find a concentration of aerospace companies, only this time in the south of Germany. Messerschmitt-Bölkow-Blohm (MBB) is the product of a merger of a dozen smaller companies that has been achieved over the last twenty years. MBB's largest project is the MRCA Tornado. Its only domestic competitor is Dornier, a family enterprise currently producing the Alpha Jet. The Maschinen-Turbinen-Union (MTU) and Klöckner-Humboldt-Deutz (KHD) are the only aircraft-engine producers of note. Some 60 percent of MBB's production is in defense; Dornier shows the same dependence on military orders. If the Federal Armed Forces had been able to order required equipment, this dependence would not automaticlly cause problems for the industry. However, the cost explosion in defense material has hit the aerospace industry the hardest. In December 1974, the federal government created the position of Aerospace Coordinator, subsequently taken by State Secretary Grüner, based in the Ministry of Economics, whose task it was to assess the needs of the industry, to coordinate civil and military programs and advise government of all decisions that might have an impact on the industrial structure. In practice, he acts as the government spokesman on aerospace matters. Under his auspices, two reports were compiled, one in 1975 and the next in 1977.[49] Both reports show an acute awareness, but it is clear that some difficult choices will have to be made soon. How can economies be achieved if production series are not increased at the same time? An increase in production series would invariably lead to a growth in capacity. How can growth of capacity be avoided particularly in the light of irregular procurement by the Federal Armed Forces?

Germany does not want to become self-sufficient in the procurement of defense equipment.[50] What may be added, however, is that the federal government might not have enough room in which to maneuver. The choice might not be between capacities and series production, but between being able to supply the armed forces in the years to come with German-produced (or at least German-coproduced) equipment or of returning to licensed production of foreign-designed equipment. The realization that defense cooperation will force itself on the European defense industries eventually has inspired German efforts toward collaborative projects. The experience with joint projects is mixed; the learning process is often slow and, therefore, the payoffs cannot yet be seen in monetary terms.

Using the procurement process, the federal government has been trying to control capacities and increase economies. In 1979, the Federal Procurement Agency awarded 87 percent of the contracts without tender, a total of DM 7,200.[51] Continuous encouragement of industry by the government to engage in collaborative projects has also helped to reorient defense production: in 1979, 50 percent of the expenditure on procurement and 60 percent of the expenditure on research and development were taken up by equipment produced on a joint basis.[52]

This review of the German defense industry, although brief, nevertheless shows where the problem areas are and how difficult it will be for the German government to make the right choice. Increased cooperative projects may be a temporary solution to the problem of achieving economies; such projects will increase series production and might not lead to successive expansion of capacity. In the long run, however, not even joint ventures may prove cost effective and the indirectly resulting arms exports do not make good foreign policy, not even in the short run.

In Search of a New Policy

No political party and no one in the German government wants to abandon the traditionally restrictive approach to arms sales. Opinions are, in the main, split over what role arms sales should play in the context of foreign policy, and, second, to what extent they should be allowed to play a role. The obvious need for government to incorporate arms transfers into a policy framework has been stated before. What has prolonged the search for new guidelines for so long are the doubts that seem to exist with respect to an active foreign policy, regardless of arms transfers.

For the past decade and beyond the Federal Republic has realized her foreign-policy interest and her security interests through the North Atlantic Alliance and the European Community. For Germany, the need to define extra-European interests did not arise and friendly relations with other states was the most clearly defined foreign-policy objective. But in recent years Germany has had to realize the existence of interests outside Europe, interests that are vital to Germany as an independent sovereign state and as a member of the Western alliance.

In the first instance, Germany imports almost one third of her oil requirements from Saudi Arabia, which is also Germany's biggest trading partner in that region. There is no doubt that friendly relations with Saudi Arabia will have to be maintained—but at what price? Does the maintenance of friendly relations include the supply of Leopard tanks? Thus far, Germany has refrained from exporting tanks to countries outside the alliance and would a departure from this practice not set a significant precedence? What would be the military and political effects on the Gulf region? Yet is it not a more preferable option for Germany to send weapons to the Gulf instead of Bundeswehr soldiers?

These are just some of the questions out of the multitude of questions raised within Germany as the 1980s began. In December 1980, the SPD working group concluded its proposals for new guidelines on arms exports. These proposals accepted by the cabinet, the licences for the export of weapons to countries outside NATO will be granted if vital foreign policy and security interests demand it.[53] Furthermore, the report also suggests consultation with the Federal Parliament before a license for arms export is given, a condition that would undoubtedly curtail the maneuverability of the executive.

It is not entirely certain at present, how much government involvement in the transfer of arms proposed under these new guidelines can be expected. Yet judging by the open interest and concern government has shown in arranging an official forum for discussion of policy, it seems likely that existing legal and future political guidelines will be adhered to—as far as this is possible. We have seen above, that the survival of the shipyards will depend on the export of submarines, frigates, and patrol boats, that the procurement process has restructured defense industry toward European-defense cooperation, resulting in more exports. The new arms-export guidelines, whatever their final form, can do nothing to alleviate these problems.

Equally important in the present context is, however, the reestablishment of the link between arms-export practice and foreign policy. Given domestic economic pressures, it will be a hard task for the federal government to synchronize economic realities and foreign-policy objectives.

Notes

1. Helga Haftendorn, "Militärhilfe als Problem deutscher Aussenpolitik," *Aus Politik und Zeitgeschichte,* 28, no. 71 (10 July 1971): 41.

2. Helga Haftendorn. "Militärhilfe im aussenpolitischen Instrumentarium der BRD und der USA," *Politische Vierteljahresschrift,* 13, no. 3 (November 1972): 384–385.

3. Hinrich Grote, "Die Bundeswehr ist in Afrika gefragt," *Die Welt,* 10 September 1970.

4. Haftendorn, *Aus Politik und Zeitgeschichte,* p. 39.

5. Ibid., p. 39.

6. Ibid., p. 39.

7. Ibid., p. 39.

8. Wolfgang Wagner, "Deutsche Ausrüstungshilfe in Afrika," *Europa Archiv*, 6 (1966): 228.

9. M.J.V. Bell, "Army and Nation in Sub-Saharan Africa," *Adelphi Paper*, 21 (August 1965): 2–4.

10. See table 8–1. It was not felt necessary to convert Deutsche marks into U.S. dollars. Where Deutsche marks are used, it is for the purpose of indicating a trend only.

11. Wagner, "Deutsche Ausrüstangshilfe," p. 229.

12. Haftendorn, *Aus Politik und Zeitgeschichte*, p. 40.

13. Ibid., p. 40.

14. Helga Haftendorn, *Militärhilfe und Rüstungsexporte der BRD* (Düsseldorf: Bertelsmann Universitatsverlag, 1971), p. 129.

15. See tables 8–1—8–4.

16. Federal Ministry of Defense, *White Paper on the Security of the Federal Republic of Germany and on the State of the German Federal Armed Forces* (Bonn: 1970), p. 157.

17. Joachim Krause, Arbeitspapier 2286: *Die Rüstungsexportpolitik der Bundesrepublik Deutschland* (Ebenhausen: Stiftung Wissenschaft und Politik, 1981), p. 32.

18. See table 8–5.

19. See table 8–5.

20. See table 8–7.

21. *Grundgesetz für Bundesrepublik Deutschland*, 47th revised edition (Munich: C. H. Beck Verlagsbuchhandlung, 1981), p. 30.

22. *Gesetz über die Kontrolle von Kriegswaffen*, 4th edition (Munich: C. H. Beck Verlagsbuchhandlung, 1981), pp. 235–266.

23. *Militärpolitik Dokumentation*, 4, no. 18, 1980. "Rechtliche Grenzen von Rüstungsproduktion und Rüstungshandel," p. 33. An overview is also provided by Ch. Loeck, "Die Politik des Transfers Konventioneller Rüstung," in H. Haftendorn et al., *Verwaltete Aussenpolitik* (Cologne: Verlag Wissenschaft und Politik, 1978), pp. 209–210.

24. John Stanley and Maurice Pearton, *The International Trade in Arms* (London: Chatto & Windus, 1971), pp. 25–27.

25. Haftendorn, *Aus Politik und Zeitgeschichte*, p. 40.

26. Siegfried Sadtler, "Fragen der Verteidigungswirtschaft im Rahmen der Volkswirtschaft," *Bundeswehrverwaltung*, 7 (July 1976): 146.

27. Sadtler, "fragen der Verteidigungswirtschaft," p. 148.

28. Estimated figures given to the author on request by the Federal Association of Aerospace Industries, December 1981.

29. Federal Association of Aerospace Industries, *Statistical Archives*.

30. White Paper 1979, p. 38.

31. *Der Spiegel,* 7 (1974): 22.

32. *Der Spiegel,* 14 (1979): 67.

33. *Der Spiegel,* 14 (1979): 67–69. *Der Spiegel,* 42 (1981): 60–61.

34. *Der Spiegel,* 42 (1981): 62.

35. David D. Newsom, ''Report by the U.S. Under Secretary of State for Political Affairs to the African Affairs Sub-Committee of the House Committee on Foreign Affairs,'' *Internatinal Communication Agency,* 19 October 1979.

36. ''Nigerian Air Force Orders 12 Alpha Jets,'' *Aviation Week and Space Technology,* 5 February 1979, p. 18.

37. ''Armed Forces a Cash Priority,'' *Financial Times,* 2 November 1981, p. 2.

38. Information given to author by the Federal Ministry of Economics, October 1981.

39. The 1972 decision was reported in ''Reichlich Kriegsgut für die Dritte Welt,'' *Süddeutsche Zeitung,* 3 May 1978.

The author was informed of the 1977 decision during a visit to the Federal Ministry of Economics in October 1981. It is not clear whether the federal government has tried to keep these decisions secret or whether the lack of information on them indicates German research gaps.

40. *Deutscher Bundestag, Plenary Protocol 9/19,* 9. Wahlperiode, 19. (Sitzung, Bonn: 30 January 1981), p. 821 (C).

41. There are conflicting reports on the number of Alpha Jets sold to these countries. For figures used in the text: Michael Brzoska und Herbert Wulf, ''Offensive im Rüstungsexport,'' in Studiengruppe Militärpolitik, *Aufrüsten um Abzurüsten?* (Hamburg: Rowohlt Verlag, 1980), p. 266. From a different source, Togo has bought five Alpha Jets, Ivory Coast twelve, Morocco twenty-four, and Egypt has signed a memorandum of understanding for producing 160 Alpha Jets under license: *Aviation Week and Space Techniology,* 5 February 1979, p. 18.

42. Hans Rattinger, ''West Germany's Arms Tramsfers to the Non-industrial World,'' in *Arms Transfers to the Third World,* Uri Ra'anan, R.L. Pfaltzgraff, Jr., and G. Kemp, eds., (Boulder, Colo.: Westview Press, 1978), p. 246.

43. Information given to author on request by Federal Ministry of Defense, October 1981.

44. Ministry of Defense information, October 1981.

45. White Paper 1979, p. 3.

46. Sadtler, ''fragen der Verteidigungswirtschaft,'' p. 148.

47. Volker Wörl, ''Deutschlands Rüstungsindustrie—weder Koloss noch Zwerg,'' *Süddeutsche Zeitung,* 4/5 July 1981, p. 36.

48. Ibid., p. 36.

49. Ministry of Economics, *Bericht des Koordinators für die deutsche Luft- und Raumfahrt 1975* (Bonn, December 1975) and Ministry of Economics, *Bericht des Koordinators für die deutsche Luft- und Raumfahrt 1977* (Bonn, March 1977).

50. White Paper 1979, p. 35.

51. Information given to the author on request by the Federal Ministry of Defense, Procurement Section, October 1981.

52. White Paper 1979, p. 35.

53. *Der Spiegel*, 49 (December 1981): 27. *Die Zeit*, 50 (4 December 1981): 5.

U.S. Arms Transfers and Security-Assistance Programs in Africa: A Review and Policy Perspective

Joseph P. Smaldone

Although the United States was the leading arms supplier to the Third World until its dominant position was closely contested, if not eclipsed, by the Soviet Union in the late 1970s, Africa is the only region where U.S. arms transfers have never reached notable proportions. The American share of the African arms market does not even begin to compare with that captured by the Soviet Union. In fact, Moscow's preponderance is so overwhelming that it enjoys the singular distinction of being in a class by itself, far ahead of the United States and several European suppliers, which form a minor category of their own. The strands of the African-American military connection have been few and tenuous indeed. Since the 1960s, Africa has acquired only about 5 percent of its imported arms from the United States, and conversely, Africa has accounted for only 1.5 percent of worldwide U.S. military transfers. Even during the late seventies, when U.S. arms exports to the region accelerated rapidly, Africa received only 3 percent of America's foreign military transfers.

Nevertheless, U.S. arms transfers to Africa deserve study on the grounds of intrinsic interest, timeliness, and relevance. As we shall see, relatively little has been published on the subject, and previous works have not provided a thorough exposition and synthesis of the data and literature from both an American and African perspectives. Moreover, considering the intense interest in the international arms trade in both the official and academic communities, this chapter offers a timely and modest contribution to the continuing public debate.

This chapter is organized into five parts. The first section presents a brief description and summary of current U.S. arms-transfer and security-assistance programs. Part two examines in detail the changing

This is a revised version of a paper originally presented at the Twenty-fourth Annual Meeting of the African Studies Association, Indiana University, Bloomington, Indiana, 21–24 October 1981. Views and conclusions are those of the author, and do not necessarily represent those of the Department of State or the U.S. government. Special thanks are due to Bonnie L. Moss for her expert typing of the manuscript. Without her prompt and efficient service, this chapter would never have seen the light of day.

patterns of U.S. military transfers to Africa during the last three decades, using a series of statistical tables and figures. In the third and fourth sections we review the literature on arms transfers to the Third World, especially cross-national and empirical studies, in an attempt to explain international arms flows to Africa in general and U.S. military transfers to the region in particular. The examination concludes with some observations and conjectures on the prospects for the African-American military connection during the early 1980s.

U.S. Arms-Transfer and Security-Assistance Programs

U.S. military transfers to foreign countries and international organizations are effected through two distinct channels: direct commercial sales by U.S. manufacturers and exporters, and government-to-government security-assistance programs.[1] Commercial arms exports are regulated by a licensing process administered by the State Department's Office of Munitions Control under the statutory authority of the Arms Export Control Act (AECA), section 38, "in furtherance of world peace and the security and foreign policy of the United States." This office prescribes and administers the U.S. Munitions List and the International Traffic in Arms Regulations (Title 22, Code of Federal Regulations, parts 121–130), under which commercial arms exports are licensed. Prior to December 1981 there was a statutory ceiling of $100 million on commercial sales of major defense equipment to other than allies (NATO, Australia, New Zealand, and Japan).[2] The practical effect of this limitation, now repealed, was to place sales of major defense equipment valued at $100 million or more to nonallied countries on a government-to-government basis under the Foreign Military Sales (FMS) program. During fiscal year 1971–1980 the total value of U.S. commercial arms exports was $10.2 billion. However, it is important to note the rather abrupt increase in the average annual value of commercial exports from $464 million during 1971–1975 to $1.6 billion during 1976–1980.

The U.S. security-assistance programs, on the other hand, include grants, loans, and cash sales, and are subject to annual congressional authorization and appropriations. They are carried out under provisions of the AECA and the Foreign Assistance Act (FAA) of 1961, as amended, under the policy and program direction of the State Department's Office of Security Assistance and Sales. In fact, security assistance consists of five separate programs, four military—the Military Assistance Program, the International Military Education and Training Program, and the Foreign Military Sales (both Financing and Cash) Programs; and one economic—the Economic Support Fund.

The Military Assistance Program (MAP) provides military aid in the form of loans or grants of defense articles and services (except training) to eligible countries under the authority of part II, chapter 2, of the FAA. The MAP was the principal arms-transfer program in the 1950s and 1960s, but was phased out during 1978–1981 except as specifically requested by the President and authorized by Congress. It is now used largely in connection with U.S. base-rights agreements; hence more than one-half of the FY 1980 authorization of $110.2 million, and three-fourths of the Fiscal Year 1981 authorization of $106.1 million, were earmarked for Portugal, Spain, and the Philippines. The 1982 MAP proposal had no country programs, but requested the establishment of a $100 million MAP Special Requirements Fund to enable the United States to respond to unforeseen contingencies where U.S. national-security interests or the recipient's economic condition require grant aid. However, Congress authorized only $25 million for this purpose and did not appropriate any funds for it. From 1950 to 1980, $59.8 billion was delivered or expended worldwide under MAP, including MAP Excess Defense Articles and Military Assistance Service Funded programs. The abrupt phase-out of MAP is reflected in the precipitous decline in average annual deliveries/ expenditures from $3.2 billion during 1971–1975 to $267 million during 1976–1980.

The International Military Education and Training (IMET) program, which was carried out as part of MAP until 1976, provides grant education and training authorized under part II, chapter 5, of the FAA. During 1950–1980 IMET expenditures totaled $1.97 billion and more than half a million foreign students were trained. Although program expenditures have declined sharply in recent years, from an average annual value of $58 million during 1971–1975 to $27 million during 1976–1980, the number of countries involved has increased: thirty-eight nations in 1979, fifty-two in 1980, sixty-three in 1981, and seventy-two proposed for 1982. During 1976–1980 an average of 5,450 foreign students were trained each year under the IMET program. Because of this direct personal contact and impact on foreign military establishments, IMET is widely regarded as the most cost effective of the security-assistance programs.

Foreign Military Sales (FMS)—Financing and Cash—the two remaining U.S. military transfer programs, are authorized and carried out under the AECA. The former provides appropriated funds for direct credits and loan-repayment guarantees to enable those countries determined eligible by the president, to purchase defense articles and services, including training. This FMS-Financing program averaged $2.9 billion worldwide during 1976–1980; $3.05 billion was programmed in Fiscal Year 1981, and $3.83 billion has been appropriated for Fiscal Year 1982. The FMS-Cash program permits direct purchases of U.S. defense articles and services by eligible foreign governments. These direct sales have become the largest single arms-transfer program in recent years, averaging $9.5 billion in sales agreements annually during 1976–1980.

In addition to these military programs, the U.S. security-assistance program includes the Economic Support Fund (ESF).[3] The ESF provides economic assistance (loans and grants) in the form of budgetary and resource support to selected countries of special political and security interest to the United States where economic and political stability is threatened, particularly by unusually heavy security and defense burdens. In concept this program dates back to the Marshall Plan, and has borne various names: defense support (1951–1960), supporting assistance (1961–1970), security-supporting assistance (1971–1978), and now economic-support fund. ESF is authorized and carried out under part II, chapter 4, of the FAA, under policy and program direction of the State Department, but is administered by the International Development Co-operation Agency. About $8.6 billion in ESF-type aid was provided in the Mutual Security Act period (1953–1961), and about $19 billion was programmed under the FAA during 1962–1980. The ESF program has increased markedly from about one-half billion dollars annually during the late sixties and early seventies to about $2 billion per year since 1976, the bulk which has been allocated to the Middle East, especially to Israel and Egypt.

To complete the picture, mention should be made of three specialized programs. First, chapter 633 of Public Law 84–1028 authorizes the grant, sale, lease, loan, barter, or disposition otherwise of U.S. naval ships to foreign governments. Since World War II about 4,000 vessels of various types have been transferred to about sixty countries, including one small vessel each to Tunisia and Ethiopia. Second, Peacekeeping Operations provides grant assistance under part II, chapter 6, of the FAA. This provision was added in 1978 for such programs as the Sinai Field Support Mission and the United States contribution to the U.N. force in Cyprus; however, in Fiscal Year 1979–1980 it was included with ESF as a combined Security Supporting Assistance account. Some $22–27 million was appropriated annually from 1979 through 1981 for this program. Finally, in 1979, part II, chapter 7, of the FAA authorized an $800-million grant to Israel for airbase construction to replace the evacuated Sinai airbases at Etzion and Etam.

Table 9–1 provides a statistical summary of U.S. military- and security-assistance transfers worldwide during the period 1950–1980. FMS more than doubled every five years between the 1950s and mid-1970s, and more than trebled during 1976–1980. By the late 1960s, FMS had supplanted MAP as the dominant security-assistance program; the latter was being phased out. The Military Assistance Service Fund (MASF)

Table 9–1
U.S. Military- and Security-Assistance Transfers, Worldwide, FY 1950–1980
(million current dollars)

	1950–1955	1956–1960	1961–1965	1966–1970	1971–1975	1976–1980	Totals 1950–1980
Military							
FMS	389.1	1,075.4	2,587.2	5,114.4	10,967.1	35,433.2	55,566.3
MAP	11,148.6	11,510.9	6,392.9	3,775.2	2,924.9	1,178.1	36,930.6
MAP Excess	794.3	764.0	994.8	1,302.0	1,342.7	136.6	5,334.4
MASF	—	—	—	5,099.5	11,349.3	20.4	16,469.2
MASF Excess	—	—	—	751.7	278.6	—	1,030.3
MASF Training	—	—	—	97.1	149.8	—	246.9
IMET	291.2	298.5	591.8	267.9	141.1	132.8	1,723.2
Commercial	NA	NA	NA	NA	2,319.0	7,898.2	10,217.2
Total Military	12,623.2	13,648.8	10,556.7	16,407.8	29,472.5	44,799.3	127,518.3
ESF	348.0	8,853.0	2,370.0	3,226.0	3,686.0	10,140	28,623
Grand Totals	12,971.2	22,501.8	12,935.7	19,633.8	33,158.5	54,939.3	156,141.3

Source: U.S. Defense Security Assistance Agency, *Fiscal Year Series, 1982*; for ESF, U.S. Agency for International Development, *U.S. Overseas Loans and Grants*, annual, various issues; FY 1980 data from *Congressional Presentation: Security Assistance Programs, FY 1982*, p. 3.

Notes: Figures represent actual value of deliveries/expenditures, not programmed or pipeline costs; ESF figures are commitments. The ESF data shown in the first three columns are actually for the periods FY 1949–52, FY 1953–61, and FY 1962–65, and could not be aggregated by five-year intervals because of the statistical-reporting format used in the source. MAP Excess refers to grants of excess defense articles rather than new procurements. MASF—Military Assistance Service Funded programs (FY 1966–75)—consisted of grant aid of military equipment and related services and training to countries allied with the United States in the southeast-Asian conflict, that is, Korea, Laos, Philippines, Thailand, and South Vietnam.

NA = not available.

programs, despite their bulk during 1966–1975, were directed exclusively to the Vietnam war effort and have been defunct since 1975. On the other hand, IMET has consistently been the smallest program; it peaked during the early 1960s, then declined abruptly, and has totaled only $1.7 billion since 1950. Notable also has been the rapid growth of commercial sales in the late 1970s, paralleling the threefold FMS expansion during 1976–1980. The overall picture shows that total military transfers rose sharply after the mid-1960s; in fact, 35 percent of all transfers during the last three decades were made during 1976–1980. The ESF program has also assumed a new and enlarged role in recent years, accounting for almost one-fourth of total security assistance during 1976–1980. Again, the cumulative figures show that 35 percent of total U.S. security assistance since 1950 was delivered during 1976–1980.

It is also interesting to examine the types of defense articles and services provided under these various programs. Table 9–2 shows worldwide FMS and MAP orders and deliveries by category during fiscal years 1950–1980. The data indicate that 57 percent of FMS orders (64 percent of deliveries) and 61 percent of programmed MAP are weapons-related, that is, the first five categories. Army FMS orders are the largest (43 percent), followed by Air Force (35 percent) and Navy (21 percent). Most striking is the huge FMS pipeline of undelivered material, the value of which equals total deliveries during the last thirty years. On the other hand, the military-assistance programs, of which MAP was the largest, have been nearly exhausted.

The African Connection: Historical and Statistical Summary

Against this general background and global pattern, we can now consider U.S. arms-transfer and security-assistance programs in Africa. It is worth noting at the outset that military tranfers to sub-Saharan Africa have been subject to specific statutory restrictions since the 1960s. Section 508 of the FAA (originally section 512) imposed a $25 million annual ceiling on military assistance and sales for sub-Saharan Africa. This limitation was raised to $40 million in 1967. A year later sales were exempted from the ceiling, but aid was limited to $25 million. Although section 508 was repealed in 1973, section 33 of the Foreign Military Sales Act of 1968 (predecessor of the AECA) restricted the aggregate of military grants, credits, loan guarantees, and cash sales (excluding training) to $40 million annually. Cash sales were exempted from this ceiling in 1973, and in 1974 the president was authorized to waive the ceiling whenever it was determined ''important to the security of the United States'' and promptly

Table 9–2
Foreign Military-Sales and Military-Assistance Programs, by Category—FY 1950–FY 1980

Categories / Implementing Agencies	Foreign Military Sales			Military Assistance—Grant Aid[a]		
	Ordered	Delivered	Undelivered	Programmed	Delivered	Undelivered
Total	110,524,421	55,566,305	54,958,116	55,979,062	55,369,943	609,119
Aircraft (including spares)	32,003,394	19,169,776	12,833,618	9,579,219	9,430,415	148,804
Ships (including spares)	3,903,821	1,086,719	2,817,101	2,301,304	2,285,645	15,659
Vehicles and Weapons (including spares)	9,672,255	6,010,002	3,662,253	9,847,901	9,756,778	91,124
Ammunition	4,573,697	3,242,911	1,330,786	11,241,060	11,212,410	28,650
Missiles (including spares)	12,334,685	5,891,493	3,921,192	1,541,189	1,394,091	147,098
Communication Equipment (including spares)	2,589,250	1,482,495	1,106,755	2,813,263	2,737,803	75,459
Other Equipment and Supplies	2,983,206	2,187,973	795,233	5,280,649	5,233,850	46,799
Construction	18,605,345	5,842,843	2,762,502	1,027,289	1,027,289	—
Repair and Rehabilitation of Equipment	1,187,571	705,890	481,681	1,014,859	980,967	33,893
Supply Operations	3,712,822	1,854,650	1,858,172	4,827,112	4,817,206	9,906
Training	3,195,955	1,956,242	1,239,713	1,972,681	1,970,128	2,552
Technical Assistance and Special Services	12,742,526	6,019,406	6,723,120	4,532,155	4,523,097	9,058
Books, Maps, and Publications	150,780	71,903	78,877	382	264	118
Undefinitized and Adjustments	2,869,115	44,002	5,347,113	—	—	—
Army	47,626,965	24,043,244	23,583,721	31,639,245	31,274,950	364,295
Navy	23,656,029	10,383,612	13,272,417	5,678,693	5,575,618	103,076
Air Force	38,677,361	20,739,377	17,937,984	16,823,053	16,682,304	140,749
Other Agencies	564,065	400,072	163,994	1,838,071	1,837,071	1,000

Source: U.S. Defense Security Assistance Agency, *Foreign Military Sales and Military Assistance Facts*, December 1980, p. 69.
[a]Includes MAP, MASF and IMET.

so reported to the Congress. The president exercised this waiver authority
every year until 1979, when the ceiling was repealed and replaced by the
mild "sense of the Congress" injunction now in effect: "It is the sense
of the Congress that the problems of sub-Saharan Africa are primarily
those of economic development and that United States policy should assist
in limiting the development of costly military conflict in the region.
Therefore, the President shall exercise restraint in selling defense articles
and defense services, and in providing financing for sales of defense
articles and defense services, to countries in sub-Saharan Africa."

The next series of tables and figures summarizes the salient trends
in the African-American military connection in progressively finer detail.
Table 9–3 shows that the total value of U.S. military transfers to Africa
during the last three decades is about $1.9 billion, or only 1.5 percent
of the worldwide total. However, it is important to note the recently
increasing absolute and relative value of military transfers to Africa,
which totaled more than $1.3 billion during 1976–1980. Although the
latter figure represents only 3 percent of U.S. military transfers during
this five-year period, it amounts to almost a threefold increase over the
historical figure of about 1 percent. Overall, the five North African states
have obtained more than three-fifths of all U.S. military transfers to the
continent. This dominance by North Africa, however, was achieved only
during 1976–1980, when this region not only surpassed sub-Saharan
Africa for the first time, but also received nearly three times more in
military material and services.

When U.S. military transfers to Africa are examined by program, as
indicated in table 9–4, the aggregate growth pattern subsumes a number
of erratic program histories. FMS in particular surged sharply since the
late 1960s, to $1.1 billion during FY 1976–1980, comprising 84% of
U.S. military transfers during this period. MAP, in contrast to the worldwide trend of secular decline, shows rapid growth through the late sixties,
followed by decline thereafter. The African IMET program increased
sharply through the sixties, then dropped by one-half during the early
seventies, before rising during 1976–1980 to the nominal peak of the
1966–1970 period. Perhaps most noteworthy about IMET is that Africa's
$23.4 million during the late seventies represents the highest proportion
of all program categories—17 percent of the worldwide total. Lastly,
commercial sales, following the global pattern, also increased more than
threefold during 1976–1980 over the preceding five-year period.

The regional distribution of U.S. military transfers to Africa is also
of interest. As table 9–5 shows, FMS accounted for most of the increase
in the late 1970s, but the sevenfold increase in FMS to sub-Saharan states
was overshadowed by a thirty-five–fold expansion in North Africa.
Overall, FMS comprised 85 percent of North African deliveries, but only

Table 9–3
U.S. Military Transfers to Africa, FY 1950–1980
(million current dollars)

	1950–1955	1956–1960	1961–1965	1966–1970	1971–1975	1976–1980	Total 1950–1980
Worldwide	12,623.2	13,648.8	10,566.7	16,407.8	29,472.5	44,799.3	127,518.3
Africa	5.72	39.7	120.6	192.9	191.5	1,329.7	1,880.1
Worldwide (percentage)	a	a	.1	1.2	a	3	1.5
North Africa	.12	5.75	47.4	93.8	77.4	952.2	1,172.7
Africa (percentage)	2	14	38	49	40	72	62
Sub-Sahara	5.6	33.9	73.2	99.1	114.1	377.5	707.4
Africa (percentage)	98	86	62	51	60	28	38

Source: U.S. Defense Security Assistance Agency, *Fiscal Year Series, 1980.*

Note: Figures represent actual value of deliveries/expenditures, not programmed or pipeline costs.
[a] = less than 1%.

Table 9-4
U.S. Military Transfers to Africa, by Program, FY 1950-1980
(million current dollars)

	1950–1955	1956–1960	1961–1965	1966–1970	1971–1975	1976–1980	Total 1950–1980
FMS	.71	4.0	1.33	48.5	60.5	1,118.2	1,233.2
MAP	4.7	29.7	89.6	99.1	56.4	20.2	299.7
MAP Excess	.086	3.2	18.6	22.9	12.0	.6	57.4
IMET	.2	2.82	11.0	22.4	12.7	23.4	72.5
Commercial	NA	NA	NA	NA	50.0	167.3	217.3
Totals	5.72	39.7	120.6	192.9	191.5	1,329.7	1,880.1

Source: U.S. Defense Security Assistance Agency, *Fiscal Year Series, 1980.*

Notes: Figures represent actual value of deliveries/expenditures, not programmed or pipeline costs.

NA = not available.

Table 9–5
U.S. Military Transfers to North and Sub-Saharan Africa, by Program, FY 1950–1980
(million current dollars)

	1950–1955	1956–1960	1961–1965	1966–1970	1971–1975	1976–1980	Total 1950–1980
Africa	5.72	39.7	120.6	192.9	191.5	1,329.7	1,880.1
Worldwide (percentage)	a	a	1.1	1.2	a	3	1.5
North Africa	.12	5.75	43.4	93.8	77.4	952.2	1,172.7
Africa (percentage)	2	14	36	49	40	72	62
FMS	.12	2.8	.57	44.3	24.1	850.9	992.8
MAP	—	2.5	36.3	28.2	12.5	2.9	82.4
MAP Excess	—	.37	3.3	12.7	4.3	.02	21.2
IMET	—	.12	2.7	8.6	4.8	9.6	25.8
Commercial	NA	NA	NA	NA	31.8	88.8	120.6
Sub-Sahara	5.6	33.9	77.2	99.1	114.1	377.5	707.4
Africa (percentage)	98	86	64	51	60	28	38
FMS	.59	1.2	.76	4.2	36.4	267.3	310.5
MAP	4.7	27.2	53.5	70.9	43.9	17.3	217.3
MAP Excess	.086	2.8	14.8	10.2	7.7	.58	36.1
IMET	.2	2.7	8.5	13.8	7.9	13.8	46.6
Commercial	NA	NA	NA	NA	18.2	78.5	96.7

Source: U.S. Defense Security Assistance Agency. *Fiscal Year Series, 1980.*

Notes: Figures represent actual value of deliveries/expenditures, not programmed or pipeline costs.

NA = not available.

a = less than 1%.

44 percent of transfers to the sub-Saharan region. On the other hand, MAP (including MAP Excess) in sub-Saharan Africa antedates and has consistently exceeded that in North Africa. Over the entire period, sub-Saharan states obtained $253 million in MAP/MAP Excess, whereas North Africa acquired about $104 million. The relative importance of MAP/MAP Excess in sub-Saharan Africa is indicated by the fact that it constituted 36 percent of total U.S. military transfers to this region; the comparable North African figure is only 9 percent. IMET for sub-Saharan Africa has also consistently exceeded the North African share, $46.6 million to $25.8 million overall. Commercial sales, interestingly, expanded more in the sub-Saharan region than the North. Although commercial arms exports to North Africa were 25 percent higher than sub-Saharan sales, and nearly trebled during 1976–1980 over the preceding five-year period, sub-Saharan commercial exports more than quadrupled during the same period.

This general description of aggregate, regional, and program developments needs to be amplified in order to highlight the actual distribution of U.S. military transfers among African states and the key factors that explain these patterns and trends. Accordingly, table 9–6 shows the principal African recipients of U.S. military transfers during 1950–1980. This list reveals quite clearly the importance attached by the United States to maintaining substantial military relations with the strategic North African-Mediterranean littoral states, particularly where the United States has had military access/transit privileges or agreements. Thus Morocco and Tunisia, moderate Arab states that have cooperated with the United States to achieve mutual security objectives in the Middle East and Mediterranean area, formerly hosted American military bases and currently permit port calls by the U.S. Sixth Fleet, including nuclear warships. In Libya, the United States maintained Wheelus Air Force Base until American use of the facility was terminated after the 1969 coup. Likewise, the more recent United States-Egyptian security relationship includes access to port and military facilities for both Mediterranean-based naval vessels and Rapid Deployment Force units responding to regional-crisis contingencies.

The predominance of Ethiopia is to be seen in the same strategic context. Although terminated after Fiscal Year 1977, the Ehtiopian military-assistance program amounted to nearly one-half the sub-Saharan total, and was the largest-single African program through the mid-1970s. As late as 1970, cumulative military transfers to Ethiopia ($163 million) were 45 percent of the African total, and by 1975 cumulative military assistance to Ethiopia ($227.8 million) amounted to almost 70 percent of the sub-Saharan share. Almost three-fourths of these military transfers were in the form of MAP and IMET grants. In addition to Ethiopia's

Table 9–6
Principal Recipients of U.S. Military Transfers to Africa, FY 1950–1980
(million current dollars)

	1950–1955	1956–1960	1961–1965	1966–1970	1971–1975	1976–1980	Total 1950–1980
Total Africa	5.72	39.7	120.6	192.9	191.5	1,329.7	1,880.1
North Africa	.12	5.75	43.4	93.8	77.4	952.2	1,172.7
Africa (percentage)	2	14	36	49	40	72	62
Egypt	.12	.06	16	.02	.03	474.8	475.2
Libya	—	2.6	7.02	31.35	36.6	1.0	78.6
Morocco	—	.39	20.5	48.1	22.8	405.4	497.2
Tunisia	—	2.7	15.7	14.3	18.0	71.0	121.7
Sub-Sahara	5.6	33.9	77.2	99.1	114.1	377.5	707.4
Africa (Percentage)	98	86	64	51	60	28	38
Cameroon	—	—	.25	.03	.03	15.2	15.5
Ethiopia	5.2	32.7	57.4	67.7	64.8	96.7	324.5
Kenya	—	—	—	—	5.6	64.0	69.6
Liberia	.08	.99	3.0	4.0	3.0	4.3	15.5
Nigeria	—	—	.72	.84	11.1	59.3	72.0
South Africa	.24	.09	.42	2.4	3.4	15.2	21.8
Sudan	—	.003	.12	.57	.03	62.7	63.5
Zaire	—	—	11.0	20.4	22.9	48.3	102.6
Subtotal	5.5	33.8	72.9	95.9	110.9	365.7	684.7
Other	.1	.1	4.3	3.2	3.2	11.8	22.7

Source: U.S. Defense Security Assistance Agency, *Fiscal Year Series, 1980*

Notes: Figures represent actual value of deliveries/expenditures, not programmed or pipeline costs.

political and diplomatic importance to the United States, American military interests there included one of the world's largest communication complexes at Kagnew.

A combination of political and strategic considerations also explains the selective distribution of U.S. military transfers throughout sub-Saharan Africa. After Ethiopia, Zaire is the second largest sub-Saharan recipient of U.S. military aid—$102.6 million or 15 percent of the total, which reflects long-standing and important political and economic interests in this populous, resource-rich, and strategically situated nation. The recent emergence of Kenya ($69.6 million), Sudan ($63.5 million) and Nigeria ($72 million) as major recipients of U.S. arms is especially striking. Kenya is important for economic, political, and strategic reasons. Prior to 1980, Kenya was the only East African-Indian Ocean state to allow U.S. overflight and landing rights and navy port calls; the June 1980 Facilities Access Agreement formalized this arrangement as an integral part of the U.S. effort to bolster its military presence and deployment capability in the region. Sudan is the largest African country and the crossroads of the Afro-Arab world. This key Arab ally of Egypt and supporter of the Camp David process has played a moderating role in African and Middle Eastern conflicts. Strategically, Sudan acts as the protector of Egypt's southern flank and the central Red Sea coast, and as a pro-Western buffer state between Soviet-armed Libya and Ethiopia. Nigeria, Africa's most populous nation, also has one of black Africa's largest military forces. In 1979 a civilian government was elected after thirteen years of military rule; in international politics Nigeria is West Africa's most important regional power and a stabilizing force in intra-African affairs. On the economic plane, it represents the largest U.S. investment in black Africa, and is the second largest supplier of crude oil to the United States. It is noteworthy that most of Nigeria's arms imports from the United States ($41 million or 57 percent) were obtained commercially rather than by government-to-government.

Of the three remaining principal recipients of U.S. military transfers, the Union of South Africa's $21.8 million includes $3.15 million in FMS pipeline deliveries after the 1963 arms embargo, and $18.6 million in licensed commercial exports ($15.2 during 1976–1980 alone). These commercial sales include certain U.S. Munitions List articles, such as inertial navigation systems for civilian airlines, data-encryption devices for U.S. corporate subsidiaries, and other nonmilitary equipment for use by nongovernment entities. Liberia ($15.5 million) has long-standing close ties with the United States, including a mutual-defense treaty dating from 1959. Important U.S. communication facilities are located in the country, including the largest Voice of America transmitter in the world, the only OMEGA navigational station in Africa, and U.S. diplomatic telecommunications relays. There are also important U.S. economic interests in banking, investment, and natural resources. In perspective, considering the nature and duration of the United States-Liberian relationship, it is surprising that U.S. military aid has been so small. However, it is important to note that more than three-fifths of U.S. military transfers to Liberia through Fiscal Year 1980 were MAP and IMET grants. Moreover, since the April 1980 coup in Liberia, the United States has undertaken a four-year $43.5 million military-assistance program there. Finally, in Cameroon ($15.5 million) the United States has increasingly important political and economic interests. In 1980 the U.S. Navy made its first port call and the Defense Attache Office was reopened. Cameroon also routinely grants overflight and landing rights to the United States. The Chad civil war and Libyan intervention have unsettled Cameroon's northern border, engaging a mutual concern over regional instability. It is notable, too, that nearly 80 percent ($12.1 million) of Cameroon's arms imports from the United States have been commercial rather than government-to-government.

To complement the preceding discussion of U.S. military transfers measured in terms of dollar values, it is necessary to consider also the content of these programs and the relative standing of the United States as an African arms supplier. Table 9–7 shows the number of students trained under the IMET and FMS programs during 1970–1979. All told, about 230,000 foreign military personnel were trained during this period, mostly in connection with the Vietnam War. About 5,300 Africans received training during 1976–1979, or 1,200–1,400 per year, less than 8 percent of all foreign military training. (Data on the early seventies are incomplete.) In view of the preponderance of U.S. arms transfers to North Africa, it is significant that the 3,981 sub-Saharan students trained during 1976–1979 accounted for three-fourths of all Africans trained. In North Africa itself, Morocco accounted for the bulk of the training, followed by Tunisia, whose program doubled in the late 1970s. In sub-Saharan Africa, Nigeria emerged, in the late seventies, as the principal recipient of U.S. military training. The Ethiopian program, formerly the largest, was terminated after 1977. Of the ongoing programs, Zaire, Ghana, Kenya, and Sudan are the largest. It is also interesting to note the type of training provided. After the elimination of the distorting effect of Southeast Asia during the early 1970s, about one half of all foreign military training was operational, that is, related to weapons, equipment, and combat operations. In Africa, however, only about one-third of the students received operational training.

To gauge the relative standing of the United States among the world's arms exporters, table 9–8 compares the value of deliveries and the number of recipients of the major arms suppliers to Africa in the periods

Table 9-7
Students Trained under IMET and FMS Programs for Africa, FY 1961–1980

	1970	1971	1972	1973	1974	1975	1976
Worldwide	21,847	25,671	52,231	37,401	12,497	8,859	19,804
Africa	786	746	469	315	379	397	1,313
North Africa	423	275	169	67	125	158	238
Egypt	—	—	—	—	—	—	3
Libya	23	—	—	—	—	—	—
Morocco	373	212	105	7	71	93	158
Tunisia	27	63	64	60	54	65	77
Sub-Sahara	363	471	300	248	254	239	1,075
Cameroon	2	—	—	—	—	—	—
Ethiopia	154	140	160	158	148	129	354
Ghana	22	11	9	14	8	41	118
Ivory Coast	8	12	8	2	—	—	—
Kenya	—	—	—	—	—	8	39
Liberia	44	38	36	34	36	20	26
Mali	9	2	2	1	—	—	—
Nigeria	5	108	35	—	—	4	428
Senegal	5	—	—	2	—	—	—
Sudan	—	—	—	2	5	—	—
Togo	—	—	—	—	—	—	—
Upper Volta	—	—	—	—	—	—	—
Zaire	114	160	50	35	57	37	110

Source: U.S. General Accounting Office, *Statistical Data on Department of Defense Tr*

Notes: 70 percent of the training during FY 1970–1975 was for Cambodia, Laos, and Vietnam. For noncomparable FMS data. Last column represents the percentage of students who received managerial/administrative, supply/maintenance, and indoctrination/orientation training and Vietnamese during FY 1970–1975.

Table 9–8
Major Arms Suppliers to Africa, 1961–1971 and 1974–1978

Supplier	Value	No. Recipients
1961–1971		
USSR	$2,618 million	13
France	337	21
U.S.	330	14
U.K.	224	14
FRG	125	17
1974–1978		
USSR	$7,830 million	23
France	1,760	23
FRG	745	16
Italy	560	13
U.S.	540	11
U.K.	270	11

Source: For 1961–1971: U.S. Arms Control and Disarmament Agency, *The International Transfer of Conventional Arms: A Report to the Congress*, House Committee on Foreign Affairs, Committee Print, 93d Congress, 2d Session, April 12, 1974, tables III, A–13 and A–14.

For 1974–1978: U.S. Arms Control and Disarmament Agency, *World Military Expenditures and Arms Transfers 1969–1978*, Publication 108, December 1980, table IV, pp. 160–162.

1961–1971 and 1974–1978. Several points are immediately evident. First, between the 1960s and mid-seventies the United States fell from third to a distant fifth place as an arms supplier to Africa, behind the USSR, France, West Germany, and Italy. Second, in terms of the value of arms supplied, the United States remained among the smallest; indeed, the United States share of the market decreased from 9 percent to only 4.6 percent. Third, comparing the two periods, Soviet arms transfers trebled, French deliveries expanded fivefold, German exports increased sixfold, and Italian sales accelerated dramatically (from worldwide arms exports of $269 million during 1961–1971) to surpass the United States; arms transfers from the United Kingdom remained relatively constant, while U.S. deliveries increased by only two-thirds. Fourth, the number of countries supplied by the United States and the United Kingdom dropped from fourteen to eleven, about half as many as the USSR and France, and fewer than Germany and Italy. On the other hand, the USSR expanded its arms-supply relationships from thirteen to twenty-three countries, while Germany and France remained about the same. Finally, the individual-country data (not reproduced here) shows that during 1974–1978 the USSR was the exclusive or principal arms supplier of nineteen of its twenty-three military customers, whereas the United States had such a relationship only with Kenya, providing about one-half the value of that country's arms.

Table 9–9 shows the actual quantity and type of major weapons transferred to Africa by the major suppliers during the periods 1967–1971 and 1974–1978. Again the relative insignificance of the United States is readily apparent. Although U.S. deliveries nearly trebled during 1974–1978 (246 to 701), the U.S. share of the principal suppliers' total dropped from 6 percent to 4 percent, while Soviet exports expanded sevenfold and French two-and-a-half times; at the same time U.K. major-weapons transfers dropped by 50 percent.

Recently published data on international arms transfers to sub-Saharan Africa in the 1970s indicate that the United States has remained a minor supplier to the region. As shown in table 9–10, the United States delivered only eighty major weapons systems to sub-Saharan countries during 1973–1976. This amounted to less than 2 percent of weapons transfers by the principal suppliers. By contrast, the Soviet Union furnished more than 3,000 such systems, and Western European suppliers about 1,100. Even though U.S. deliveries more than trebled during 1977–1980 to 260, this represented only about 3 percent of those provided by the major arms exporters. In this latter period, Soviet deliveries more than doubled to 6,600 while Western European transfers declined to 980. Looking at the entire eight-year period, 1973–1980, we find that fewer than 3 percent of sub-Saharan arms imports were of U.S. origin. Such a small fraction is inconspicuous in relation to the 80 percent Soviet share.

Since FMS is the largest-single U.S. arms-transfer program, comprising about 85 percent of the value of all military transfers to Africa during 1976–1980, it bears closer scrutiny. Figure 9–1, therefore, depicts cumulative FMS agreements and deliveries during 1960–1980. Agreements show a very slow but steady growth through the mid-seventies, then rapid acceleration as follows: 1960—$5.3 million; 1965—$9.4 million; 1970—$63.5 million; 1975—$428.1 million; and 1980—$4.72 *billion*. FMS deliveries exhibit a parallel pattern: 1960—$4.7 million; 1965—$6.0 million; 1970—$54.4 million; 1975—$114.8 million; and 1980—$1.23 *billion*. Also notable is the fact that the growth rate of agreements has outstripped deliveries. Before 1975 cumulative deliveries were typically about 75 percent of agreements, but after 1975 deliveries fell to between one-quarter and one-third the level of sales commitments. As a result, by 1980 the FMS "pipeline" had reached $3.48 billion.

The changing distribution of cumulative FMS agreements and deliveries between North and sub-Saharan Africa is also of interest. As shown in figure 9–2, FMS agreements with North Africa kept about a 2:1 ratio with sub-Saharan Africa until an abrupt increase in 1980. Figure 9–3 indicates that FMS deliveries to sub-Saharan Africa during the early seventies comprised about one-third of all African deliveries; the portion increased to 40–50 percent during 1975–1978, then dropped to 25–30 percent as North African deliveries surged.

Having reviewed U.S. military transfers to Africa through Fiscal Year 1980, we can now summarize the economic-aid component of the security-assistance program. Table 9–11, therefore, shows U.S. Economic Support Fund programs for Africa during 1961–1980. After dropping from $387.3 million in the early sixties to $117.9 million in the late sixties, ESF allocations for Africa during the 1970s increased to $283.4 in 1971–1975, and then expanded dramatically to more than $4.3 billion during 1976–1980. This rapid growth was due almost entirely to the Egyptian program, which accounted for 92 percent of African ESF aid during the last decade; in fact, during 1976–1980 Egypt alone received about 40 percent of worldwide ESF allocations. The regional pattern in the early sixties shows liberal use of ESF in all five North African states and sparing allocation to only five sub-Saharan states; Zaire received the bulk, $198.3 million or about one-half the African total, and 85 percent of black Africa's share. By the late sixties, the pattern had shifted: no ESF was allocated to North Africa; the sub-Saharan program was cut in half; only six countries received ESF allocations; three of the five former ESF recipients received none; and Zaire and Nigeria together accounted for more than 90 percent of African ESF commitments. The most remarkable features of the early seventies were the reduction in the number of participating countries and the emergence of Egypt as the dominant ESF recipient, Nigeria being the only other African beneficiary of the program. In the late seventies Egypt retained its dominant position and remained the only North African country to receive ESF aid. The sub-Saharan program, although overshadowed by Egypt, also grew more than sixteenfold and expanded its scope to thirteen countries, twelve of which were first-time recipients. Southern Africa also became the principal focus for ESF funds ($249.2 million, or two-thirds of the sub-Saharan share), with an important secondary concentration on the Horn (Kenya, Somalia, and Sudan—$59.5 million).

Against the foregoing background of historical statistics we can conclude this section with a brief analysis of current security-assistance programs. Table 9–12 displays the FMS-, MAP- and IMET-program summary for each African country estimated for Fiscal Year 1981 and proposed for Fiscal Year 1982, by regions. Keeping in mind that FMS cash sales are not reflected here, it is important to note that the proposed 1982 FMS-Financing program for sub-Saharan Africa ($202.9 million) would increase nearly threefold over Fiscal Year 1981 ($73 million),

Table 9-9
Major Weapons Transfers to Africa, by Supplier, 1967–1971 and 1974–1978

Type Weapon	USSR	United Kingdom	France	United States	Total	U.S. (percentage)
1967–1971						
Land armaments	2,000	470	310	170	2,950	6
Naval craft	42	26	45	6	119	5
Aircraft	310	150	270	70	800	9
Missiles	90	—	—	—	90	—
Totals	2,442	646	625	246	3,959	6
1974–1978						
Land armaments	7,600	160	1,135	650	9,545	7
Naval craft	60	—	46	1	107	1
Aircraft	875	65	230	50	1,220	4
Missiles	7,800	100	120	—	8,020	—
Totals	16,335	325	1,531	701	18,892	4

Source: For 1967–1971: U.S. Arms Control and Disarmament Agency, *International Transfer of Conventional Arms: A Report to the Congress*, House Committee on Foreign Affairs, Committee Print, 93d Congress, 2d Session, April 12, 1974, table VI, A–22. For 1974–1978: U.S. Arms Control and Disarmament Agency, *World Military Expenditures and Arms Transfers 1969–1978*, Publication 108, December 1980, table V, p. 164.

Note: Data in both tables include all African countries except Egypt.

Table 9–10
Major Weapons Transfers to Sub-Saharan Africa, by Supplier, 1973–1976 and 1977–1980

Type Weapon	USSR	Western Europe	United States	Total	U.S. (percentage)
1973–1976	3,079	1,099	80	4,258	1.9
Land armaments	2,250	530	60	2,840	2.1
Naval craft	19	39	0	58	0
Aircraft	210	360	20	570	3.5
Missiles	600	150	0	790	0
1977–1980	6,600	980	260	7,840	3.3
Land armaments	4,730	710	230	5,670	4.1
Naval craft	50	40	0	90	0
Aircraft	460	220	30	710	4.2
Missiles	1,360	10	0	1,370	0
1973–1980	9,679	2,079	340	12,098	2.8
Land armaments	6,980	1,240	290	8,510	3.4
Naval craft	69	79	0	148	0
Aircraft	670	560	50[a]	1,280	3.9
Missiles	1,960	200	0	2,160	0

Source: U.S. Congress, Congressional Research Service, *Changing Perspectives on U.S. Arms Transfer Policy*, Report prepared for the Subcommittee on International Security and Scientific Affairs of the Committee on Foreign Affairs, U.S. House of Representatives, Committee Print, 97th Cong., 1st Sess., 25 September 1981, table 7, p. 21.

Note: U.S. data are for fiscal years, and cover the period 1 July 1972 through 30 September 1980: foreign data are for calendar years. Western Europe includes France, United Kingdom, West Germany, and Italy

[a]This figure corrects an apparent arithmetic error in the original table.

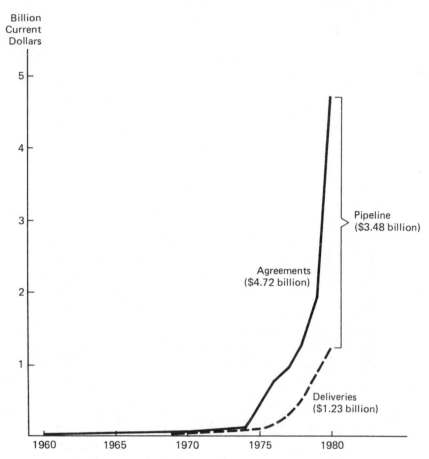

Source: Compiled from U.S. Defense Security Assistance Agency, *Fiscal Year Series*, *1980*.

Figure 9–1. Africa: Cumulative FMS Agreements and Deliveries, FY 1960–1980

while the North African program would almost double from $595 million to over $1 billion. The relative magnitude of the Fiscal Year 1982 sub-Saharan FMS-Financing program can be gauged also from the fact that total FMS-Financing for sub-Saharan Africa through Fiscal Year 1980 amounted to only $345 million. The largest FMS-country programs are slated for Kenya, Liberia, Somalia, and Sudan, while MAP continues to trail off as this historic program lapses. The African IMET proposal would also double between 1981 and 1982 to $12 million, with three-fifths being allocated to sub-Saharan states.

Last, table 9–13 compares the total security-assistance program for

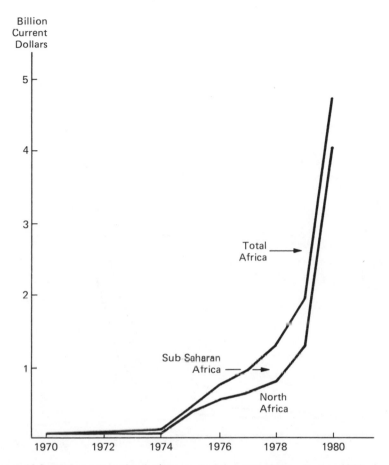

Source: U.S. Defense Security Assistance Agency, *Fiscal Year Series, 1980*.

Figure 9–2. Cumulative FMS Agreements, North and Sub-Saharan Africa, FY 1970–1980

fiscal years 1981 and 1982, both military and economic, by region, for each African country. Although total ESF allocation shows a slight drop in 1982, this is due to the proposed reduction in the Egyptian program from $850 million to $750 million. On the other hand, the proposed ESF allocations to sub-Saharan states represent a 60 percent increase, from $144.5 million to $231 million. Overall, Africa's share of worldwide security assistance is about one-third. The sub-Saharan security-assistance allocations would double between 1981 and 1982, whereas the North African share would increase by one-quarter.

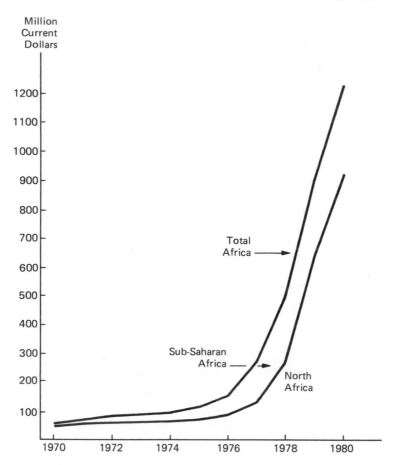

Source: U.S. Defense Security Assistance Agency, *Fiscal Year Series, 1980*.

Figure 9–3. Cumulative FMS Deliveries, North and Sub-Saharan Africa,
FY 1970–1980

Arms for Africa: "Push" or "Pull?"

One of the recurring questions in the scholarly literature is whether international arms transfers are better explained by internal or external
factors. That is, do the national characteristics or attributes of recipients
account for the magnitude and distribution of global arms sales, or do
external environmental and supplier-induced conditions better explain
these patterns? Is demand for arms autonomous, causing supply to vary
accordingly, or do supply-side variations drive demand? In short, do
domestic "pull" factors on the recipient side or external "push" factors
on the supply side explain international arms flows? Do these factors

Table 9–11

U.S. Economic-Support-Fund Programs for Africa, FY 1961–1980

(million current dollars)

	1961–1965	1966–1970	1971–1975	1976–1980	Total 1961–1980
Worldwide	a	3,226	3,686	10,140	a
Africa	387.3	117.9	283.4	4,305.4	5,094
Worldwide (percentage)	a	4	8	42	a
North Africa	153.1	—	261.3	3,939.7	4,354.1
Africa (percentage)	40	—	92	92	85
Algeria	1.3	—	—	—	1.3
Egypt	30.0	—	261.3	3,939.7	4,231
Libya	27.8	—	—	—	27.8
Morocco	76.7	—	—	—	76.7
Tunisia	17.3	—	—	—	17.3
Sub-Sahara	234.2	117.9	22.1	365.7	739.9
Africa (percentage)	60	100	8	8	15
Botswana	—	—	—	39.3	39.3
Cameroon	3.0	—	—	—	3.0
Cape Verde	—	—	—	1.0	1.0
Ethiopia	3.0	.3	—	—	3.3
Guinea	24.0	.3	—	—	24.0
Ivory Coast	—	—	—	—	.3
Kenya	—	—	—	14.5	14.5
Lesotho	—	—	—	5.5	5.5
Liberia	—	—	—	10.2	10.2
Mali	4.0	—	—	—	4.0
Mozambique	—	—	—	1.5	1.5
Nigeria	—	53.7	21.6	—	75.3
Rwanda	—	1.1	—	—	1.1
Senegal	—	.1	—	—	.1

Table 9–11 Continued

	1961–1965	1966–1970	1971–1975	1976–1980	Total 1961–1980
Somalia	—	—	—	5.0	5.0
Sudan	—	—	—	40.0	40.0
Swaziland	—	—	—	12.8	12.8
Uganda	—	—	—	3.0	3.0
Zaire	198.3	54.5	—	42.0	294.8
Zambia	—	—	—	74.0	74.0
Zimbabwe	—	—	—	22.9	22.9
Southern Africa Regional	—	—	—	93.2	93.2
Africa Regional	1.9	7.9	.5	.8	11.1

Source: U.S. Agency for International Development, *U.S. Overseas Loans and Grants*, annual, various issues; FY 1980 data from *Congressional Presentation: Security Assistance Programs, FY 1982*. p. 265.

[a] = cannot be determined due to reporting and aggregating procedures used in various issues of *U.S. Overseas Loans and Grants*.

Table 9–12

Africa: FMS, MAP, and IMET Program Summary, Estimated FY 1981 and Proposed FY 1982
(million current dollars)

	FMS Financing		MAP		IMET	
	1981	1982	1981	1982	1981	1982
Africa	668.0	1,227.9	2.735	.216	6.358	12.055
Worldwide (percentage)	22	30	2.5	a	22	25
North Africa	595.0	1,025.0	.035	.016	2.551	4.6
Africa (percentage)	89	83	1.3	7.4	40	38
Egypt	550.0	900.0	—	—	.846	2.0
Morocco	30.0	30.0	—	—	1.055	1.3
Tunisia	15.0	95.0	.035	.016	.65	1.3
Sub-Sahara	73.0	202.9	2.7	.2	3.807	7.455
Africa (percentage)	11	17	99	93	60	62
Botswana	.5	.5	—	—	.03	.1
Cameroon	1.0	1.5	—	—	.05	.1
Cape Verde	—	—	—	—	—	.035
Congo	—	—	—	—	—	.035
Djibouti	—	1.0	—	—	—	.1
Equatorial Guinea	—	—	—	—	—	.035
Gabon	2.6	2.6	—	—	.05	.1
Ghana	—	—	—	—	.185	.4
Guinea-Bissau	—	—	—	—	—	.035
Ivory Coast	—	—	—	—	.025	.035
Kenya	6.0	51.0	1.0	—	.5	1.3
Liberia	4.7	12.3	—	—	.449	.6
Malawi	—	—	—	—	.02	.05
Mali	.2	—	—	—	.11	.1
Mauritius	—	—	—	—	—	—
Niger	—	—	—	—	.205	.4
Rwanda	1.5	1.5	—	—	.05	.05

Table 9–12 Continued

	FMS Financing		MAP		IMET	
	1981	*1982*	*1981*	*1982*	*1981*	*1982*
Senegal	.5	2.0	—	—	.211	.35
Seychelles	—	—	—	—	—	—
Somalia	20.0	20.0	—	—	.3	.35
Sudan	30.0	100.0	1.7	.2	.65	1.3
Tanzania	—	—	—	—	.06	.075
Togo	—	—	—	—	.03	.06
Uganda	—	—	—	—	.05	.05
Upper Volta	—	—	—	—	.075	.135
Zambia	—	—	—	—	—	—
Zaire	6.0	10.5	—	—	.757	1.56
Zimbabwe	—	—	—	—	—	.1
Southern African Regional	—	—	—	—	—	—

Source: *Congressional Presentation: U.S. Security Assistance Programs, FY 1982.*

[a] = less than 1%.

Table 9–13
Africa: Security Assistance Program Summary, Estimated FY 1981 and Proposed FY 1982
(million current dollars)

	Military Programs (FMS, MAP, IMET)		Economic Support Fund		Total Security Assistance Program	
	1981	1982	1981	1982	1981	1982
Africa	677.1	1,240.2	994.5	981.0	1,671.6	2,221.2
Worldwide (percentage)	21	29	45	38	31	33
North Africa	597.6	1,029.6	850.0	750.0	1,447.6	1,779.6
Africa (percentage)	88	83	85	76	87	80
Egypt	550.9	902.0	850.0	750.0	1,400.8	1,652.0
Morocco	31.055	31.3	—	—	31.055	31.3
Tunisia	15.685	96.316	—	—	15.685	96.310
Sub-Sahara	79.5	210.6	144.5	231.0	224.0	441.6
Africa (percentage)	12	17	15	24	13	20
Botswana	.53	.6	10.0	10.0	10.53	
Cameroon	1.05	1.6	—	—	1.05	1.6
Cape Verde	—	.035	—	—	—	.035
Congo	—	.035	—	—	—	.035
Djibouti	—	1.1	2.0	2.0	2.0	3.1
Equatorial Guinea	—	.035	—	—	—	.035
Gabon	2.65	2.7	—	—	2.65	2.7
Ghana	.185	.4	—	—	.185	.4
Guinea-Bisseau	—	.035	—	—	—	.035
Ivory Coast	.025	.035	—	—	.025	.035
Kenya	6.5	52.3	5.5	10.0	12.0	62.3
Liberia	6.149	12.9	7.0	10.0	13.149	22.9
Malawi	.02	.05	—	—	.02	.05
Mali	.31	.1	—	—	.31	.1
Mauritius	—	—	—	2.0	—	2.0
Niger	.205	.4	—	—	.205	.4
Rwanda	1.55	1.55	—	—	1.55	1.55

Table 9–13 Continued

	Military Programs (FMS, MAP, IMET)		Economic Support Fund		Total Security Assistance Program	
	1981	1982	1981	1982	1981	1982
Senegal	.711	2.35	—	—	.711	2.35
Seychelles	—	—	—	2.0	—	2.0
Somalia	20.3	20.35	—	20.0	20.3	40.35
Sudan	32.35	101.5	50.0	50.0	82.35	151.5
Tanzania	.06	.075	—	—	.06	.075
Togo	.03	.06	—	—	.03	.06
Uganda	.05	.05	—	—	.05	.05
Upper Volta	.075	.135	—	—	.075	.135
Zambia	—	—	20.0	20.0	20.0	20.0
Zaire	6.757	12.06	—	—	6.757	12.06
Zimbabwe	—	.1	25.0	75.0	25.0	75.1
Southern Africa Regional	—	—	25.0	30.0	25.0	30.0

Source: *Congressional Presentation: U.S. Security Assistance Programs, FY 1982.*

vary with recipient-supplier arms-transfer patterns? This section will attempt to answer these questions with regard to Third World arms imports in general and international arms transfers to Africa in particular; the following section will attempt to determine if U.S. military transfers to Africa correspond to the global pattern.

Arms Transfers and Domestic "Pull" Factors

Several recent studies seem to confirm that arms transfers to the Third World are better explained by recipient rather than supplier variables. For example, Leh investigated the possible relationship between arms imports and various physical, demographic, political, military, and economic characteristics of Third World nations.[4] His findings can be summarized as follows. Although geographic location was not a good predictor of arms acquisitions, larger states tended to import larger quantities of arms. Various demographic variables, such as population size, growth rate, and density did not correlate with arms transfers, but level of urbanization did. Nor were political variables such as modernization, ideology, political opposition, and leadership characteristics associated with arms imports. Although military expenditure per capita was not a good predictor of arms transfers, armed-forces-per-1000 and the ratio of military expenditure to government expenditure did correlate. Measures of economic bulk and vigor such as gross national product, GNP per capita, money supply, and imports (and growth rates) also correlated well with arms imports.

On the other hand, Avery sought to explain Third World arms imports as a function of domestic attributes specifically related to political violence and instability, namely armed attacks, deaths from political violence, assassinations, guerrilla war, and riots.[5] Allowing for time lag, he found that all five political-violence indicators correlated strongly with African arms imports. In fact, Africa was the only Third World region in which all measures of political violence predicted arms acquisitions. The very high intercorrelation among these indicators suggests a common underlying dimension and the strength of internal-pull variables in explaining African arms imports. Avery's and Picard's related study of the political economy of arms transfers to Africa used a wider range of pull variables— economic resources, military-strategic factors (civil strife, regional tensions, regime type, and defense expenditure), and domestic-political factors (political instability, decolonization).[6] In this conceptual scheme, the availability of economic resources was the best predictor of arms imports. Military-strategic factors also yielded significant associations with arms transfers, but domestic-political variables did not.

A remarkably high correlation between national wealth and arms acquisitions was also reported in Mullins's study of the relationship between levels of military capability and development in thirty-seven Third World states (including twenty-nine in Africa) during 1957–1976.[7] This relationship remained constant across the sample of cases, notwithstanding variations in level of economic development (GNP), rates of growth of development and military capability, supplier relationships, regime stability, and incidence of interstate conflict. In other words, weapons imports were governed by the economic resources and absorptive capacity of the newly independent states, not by external factors such as availability of arms, suppliers' choices and levels of support for military clients, and foreign conflict.

These findings are corroborated by two other unpublished studies of statistical relationships between several political and economic variables and international arms transfers to Africa. Mintz also showed that most political variables (number of political parties, government expenditure as a proportion of GNP, and years since independence) did not correlate well with levels of arms imports. On the other hand, military regimes, especially those aligned with the Communist bloc, and those with a history of high arms imports, have significantly higher arms-acquisition levels. Indeed, the previous year's arms imports emerged as the best single predictor of subsequent arms transfers. Among the economic variables, level of urbanization, GNP per capita, and energy consumption per capita were not significantly related to arms imports, but GNP and energy production did significantly correlate with armament dependence (GNP was the second best predictor). In brief, African nations that possess and exploit abundant energy resources, which translates into high GNP, and are ruled by military regimes aligned with the Communist bloc, tend to import proportionally more arms than poorer states without energy resources, ruled by civilian regimes that remain nonaligned or Western-oriented.[8]

Finally, Agbese sought to explain arms transfers to African states as a function of several domestic and international economic and political factors, specifically GNP, OPEC membership, regime type, intensity of foreign competition, capital dependence, and dependence on foreign technology.[9] Here OPEC membership was the best single predictor of arms imports, with GNP adding significantly to explanatory ability. Regime type had a positive but weak association with arms-transfer levels, adding very little to the explained variance. Surprisingly, the intensity of foreign conflict had a negative relationship with the value of arms imports, a finding which raised questions about the coding validity of this variable. Dependence on foreign capital and technology also added only marginally to the variance explained.

In summary, these studies show that economic capacity and dynamism (Leh, Avery and Picard, Mullins, Agbese), especially that associated with energy production (Mintz, Agbese) are the most consistent and powerful predictors of African arms imports. Military-strategic factors, particularly the degree of militarization (Leh, Avery and Picard), levels of internal and external conflict (Avery, Avery and Picard), and a past history of high arms imports (Mintz), also correlate well with levels of arms transfers. On the other hand, domestic political attributes generally do not correlate significantly with arms-transfer levels (Leh, Avery and Picard, Mintz, Agbese), except perhaps in the case of military regimes (Avery and Picard, Mintz, Agbese).

Arms Transfers and External "Push" Factors

Having found rather strong positive correlations between international arms transfers and certain national attributes of African states, we must now examine the converse hypothesis that external factors do not significantly explain African arms imports. Interestingly, the few studies available are consistent with the foregoing conclusions. Leh examined the relationship between patterns of regional conflict, bloc alignments, and arms transfers, using Zaire and Zambia as case studies.[10] He found that arms imports depended in part on national military strategy and policy such as diversification of arms suppliers and trade-offs between weapon inventories and sophistication on the one hand, and larger, better trained armed forces on the other. Anticipating a point to be developed later, note that even in this narrowly-focused study, Leh observed that U.S. arms transfers to Africa favor a few friendly states in strategic locations.

Two recent studies by Schrodt of the relationship between arms transfers and international political and military behavior (conflict and cooperation) in the "arc of crisis" from the Horn of Africa to Southwest Asia are also relevant here.[11] Although total arms transfers generally provided the best predictions of a wide range of both conflict and cooperation measures, on the African Horn (Ethiopia, Somalia, Sudan), arms transfers yielded only low correlations with international behavior. Moreover, while the strongest correlations overall were found between arms imports and both political- and military-conflict measures, on the Horn only weak associations were found. Hence the findings of Leh and Schrodt lend support to the contention that international arms transfers to Africa are best explained by internal-pull variables rather than by external-push factors. As we have seen, domestic economic and military-strategic characteristics explain most of the variance in African arms-import levels. Even in the Horn, arms transfers do not correlate strongly with a wide range of international behavior measures.

U.S. Arms Transfers to Africa: What Explanations?

Can U.S. military transfers to Africa be explained by the same factors that account for arms supplies from all sources? Surprisingly, there has been relatively little research and exposition on the subject, and even less systematic analysis: the recent major works in the field of international arms transfers virtually ignore the United States–African military-supply relationship.[12] Early studies by Bienen and Crocker are short wide-ranging discussions of the general objectives and political implications of U.S. military aid to Africa, but make no effort to explain actual patterns of U.S. military transfers to the region.[13] And a more specialized paper by Stitt emphasized the "win friends and influence people" function of the U.S. Army Command and General Staff College (CGSC), concluding that "For the U.S. the African officers attendance at CGSC is an opportunity to influence a potential leader and to gain an inroad for solid diplomatic relations between the two countries. It is also an opportunity to show African officers how a modern military force operates within a democratic nation."[14]

In fact the best overview for many years remained Hovey's early study of U.S. military-assistance programs.[15] His brief treatment of Africa pointed out that the magnitude and distribution of U.S. military aid showed a distinct bifurcation between a large North African program associated with military base/facility-access arrangements, and several small sub-Saharan African programs, often just training, restricted to internal security and civic action rather than external defense, designed to promote pro-Western political orientation, and to prevent arms races or the diversion of resources from economic development.

In the 1970s these general surveys were complemented by a number of empirical studies that provided substantial support for the thesis that political-strategic considerations best explain U.S. arms transfers to Africa. For instance, Peleg's statistical study of international arms transfers to Africa in the mid-1960s concluded that both U.S. and Soviet military assistance correlated with ideological congruence and the strategic importance/location of African recipients, and tended to displace ex-colonial suppliers.[16] A few years later, Dabelko and Baum tested a series of hypotheses about U.S. arms transfers to Africa, specifically that the level of U.S. arms transfers was positively correlated with (1) level of external conflict, (2) level of internal conflict, (3) level of trade dependence on the United States, (4) level of support for U.S. foreign-policy positions at the U.N. General Assembly, (5) nature of regime (military versus nonmilitary), (6) GNP per capita, and (7) military expenditure as a percentage of GNP. Surprisingly, only weak correlations were found with levels of internal and external conflict, and no association was found regarding U.N. voting and military expenditure as a percentage of GNP. The negative correlations with military regimes and GNP per capita showed that civilian regimes in the least developed African countries obtained proportionaly higher U.S. military transfers. Overall, however, only a small fraction of the variance of U.S. arms transfers was explained by the combined effect of the independent variables. The authors thus suggested looking elsewhere for more compelling explanations of U.S. arms transfers to Africa, "possibly in military and strategic reasons" (p. 13).

A final study that sheds light on this issue is Avery's examination of the effect of three types of pull variables on U.S. arms transfers to the Third World during 1964–1973, namely domestic-political conditions (civil strife, political instability), military-strategic factors (external intervention, size of armed forces, defense expenditure), and economic resources (GNP).[18] The size of the armed forces was the best single predictor (half the explained variance) of Third World arms imports from the United States, with civil strife being the only other statistically significant variable (14 percent). However, while U.S. arms transfers to Latin America and the Middle East were best explained (50 percent) by economic resources, U.S. arms exports to Africa were not explained by the model. Avery speculated that these anomalous findings were perhaps due to one or more of the following: (1) U.S. arms transfers to Africa are relatively small in absolute terms, (2) U.S. arms are but a small fraction of most African states' arms imports, (3) there was a high degree of multicollinearity among the African pull variables, (4) other pull factors could better explain U.S. arms imports, and (5) push variables could be more important in the United States–African arms-supply relationship.

The following conclusion emerges clearly from these studies and the data presented in this chapter. Although U.S. arms transfers to Africa are designed to serve a multiplicity of policy objectives, historically the magnitude and distribution of U.S. security-assistance programs in Africa have been determined principally by the *political and military-strategic importance of the recipient to U.S. global and regional interests.* This is confirmed by Hovey and Peleg, corroborated indirectly by Dabelko and Baum, and consistent with both Avery's analysis and the discussion of table 9–6 above. Whereas global arms transfers to Africa are best explained by internal pull variables, U.S. arms supplies to Africa correlate highly with U.S. policy objectives. Rather than responding to African demand in a classical demand-supply-response model, U.S. arms transfers are an instrumentality to further American political and security interests in the region.

Whether or not U.S. arms exports to Africa are an efficacious tool of policy is, of course, an important question too. Do arms-transfer relationships promote peace by maintaining regional military balances, or lead to supplier intervention in local conflicts? Do arms transfers foster political stability and civilian rule, or increase the likelihood of military coups in recipient states? Do arms imports have a net-positive or -negative impact on socioeconomic development? Unfortunately, there has been little systematic comparative research on such questions, and none on the United States–African arms relationship specifically. It is worth noting, however, that most of the literature is polemical, inconclusive, or doubtful that arms transfers are advantageous to either suppliers or recipients.

A brief review of selected works illustrates this point. Sylvan, for example, constructed and tested a model of political efficacy, and found U.S. conventional-arms transfers were "singularly unsuccessful" in achieving American foreign-policy objectives.[19] With respect to the involvement of weapons suppliers in their clients' conflicts, Pearson found no consistent relationship between arms-transfer levels and subsequent military interventions by suppliers; however, when interventions did occur, they were generally in the suppliers' regional spheres of influence and in countries where the interventionist state was the dominant arms supplier.[20] As for the impact of armament dependence on the political stability of recipient states, Rowe's study of eighty-five less developed countries (including twenty-nine in Africa) during 1948–1972 indicated that U.S. arms transfers appeared "to be a contributing factor in undermining civilian elements and increasing the incidence of praetorianism"—hardly a comforting conclusion for American policymakers.[21]

The relationship between arms acquisition and socioeconomic development is even more problematical. Although critics often argue that military procurement impedes and distorts development, several previously cited works show that Third World (and particularly African) arms imports are strongly correlated with economic development. In other words, developing countries generally acquire arms in relatively constant proportion to their available resources. On the other hand, Russett and Sylvan concluded that arms transfers to less developed states entail severe opportunity costs, political and cultural penetration, economic distortion, and marginalization of the labor force.[22] Regarding the larger issue of defense spending, the Smiths have shown that there is no theoretical or systematic empirical relationship between military expenditure and economic growth in the Third World.[23]

Whether these conclusions and evaluations of the impact and implications of such military ties for both suppliers and recipients will be confirmed, and whether they hold for U.S. arms transfers to Africa in particular, must await further research. We have merely raised some of the issues and questions here.

From Carter's "Restraint" to Reagan's "Rapid Response," or Does Rhetoric Matter?

In closing this chapter, it might be interesting and instructive to conjecture about the likely trends in U.S. military transfers to Africa during the next few years. Certainly the advent of the Reagan administration and its public promise of "rapid response" with security assistance to friends in need could not have been further from Carter's policy of unilateral arms-transfer restraint. For a number of resons, however, I think a compelling argument can be made that after all is said and done, in retrospect the arms-transfer records of the Carter and Reagan periods will not look very different.

First of all, it is important to recognize that security assistance programs expanded to unprecedented levels during Carter's presidency despite the policy of unilateral restraint. As the data presented in this paper demonstrate, U.S. arms transfers during the late 1970s accelerated sharply upward rather than slowing or reversing the trend. In Africa particularly, since Carter used arms transfers to counter Soviet intrusions and influence, the inconsistency between the rhetoric of restraint and actual practice became apparent within a few months of his administration.[24] Actual deliveries of defense articles and services to Africa accelerated dramatically: almost $1 billion during 1976–1980 to North Africa (up from a mere $77 million during the previous five-year period); and more than trebled to sub-Saharan Africa, to nearly $400 million during 1976–1980 (see table 9–3 and figures 2 and 3). FMS agreements rose even more sharply during the Carter years: $462 million for sub-Saharan Africa (versus $201 million in the Nixon-Ford period), and $3.5 billion to North Africa (versus $465 million)—a total of nearly $4 billion.

Against this background, considering prevailing conditions, it is likely that the upward surge in African military transfers will continue during the Reagan years. To be more precise, although absolute levels of agreements and deliveries will climb to new heights, the unprecedented growth rate of arms sales to Africa during the late 1970s is not likely to be exceeded by a wide margin during the early 1980s. Among the international factors that will restrain arms exports are high interest rates, current levels of Third World indebtedness, increasing competition of European suppliers (see tables 9–8, 9–9, and 9–10), and the increasing number of Third World arms producers and exporters (for example, Brazil, Israel, India, Korea).[25] Domestic factors will also limit arms transfers, not the least of which are the extensive congressional and statutory controls,[26] and the difficulty in justifying foreign military aid in a period of retrenchment at home.

For Africa, therefore, Reagan's arms-transfer policy will mean more of the same, not a radical departure or sharp increase from trends established during the Carter years.[27] FMS deliveries will continue to rise sharply as the large pipeline of more than $3.5 billion is discharged, and although Africa has received an increasingly larger share of U.S. security assistance in recent years (7 percent of FMS agreements during 1976–1980 compared to 1 percent during the previous decade), U.S. arms transfers to Africa will remain but a small fraction of total African arms imports from all sources. The importance of Africa in U.S. global strategy and regional-security schemes, particularly in northeastern Africa, will doubtlessly continue, and U.S. arms supplies to Africa will continue to be concentrated in areas of special political and strategic importance.

Notes

1. See U.S. Congress, House, Committee on International Relations, *United States Arms Transfers and Security Assistance Programs*, Committee Print, 95th Cong., 2d Sess., March 21, 1978. For an updated survey see Laurel A. Mayer, "U.S. Arms Transfers Data Sources and Dilemmas," *International Studies Notes*, 7, no. 2 (Summer 1980): 1–7. Unless indicated otherwise, statistical data on military transfers cited in this section are derived from these sources or U.S. Defense Security Assistance Agency, *Foreign Military Sales and Military Assistance Facts*, December 1980.

Note that all U.S. dollar values reported and compared in this paper reflect current prices at the time of sale, agreement, delivery, or expenditure, and have not been adjusted to account for inflation or international purchasing power parity. Hence, for example, considering inflation alone, a nominal increase of 60 percent during the decade of the 1960s would represent a real growth of about 20 percent, and a 100 percent increase in the 1970s would mean little or no real growth.

2. Section 38(b)(3) of the Arms Export Control Act of 1976 set a $25 million ceiling. This was raised to $35 million by Section 21 of the International Security Assistance Act of 1979, and to $100 million by Section 107(a) of the International Security and Development Cooperation Act of 1980.

3. In addition to the sources cited above, see U.S. General Accounting Office, *Issues and Observations on the Purposes of Special Security Supporting Assistance Programs,* ID–76–11, 12 September 1975.

4. Robert G. Leh, "The Political, Economic, Military, and Social Qualities of Greater and Lesser Third World Arms Recipients: A Statistical Analysis," paper presented at the Twenty-second annual International Studies Association meeting, Philadelphia, 18–22 March 1981.

5. William P. Avery, "Terrorism, Violence, and the International Transfer of Conventional Armaments," paper presented at the annual Midwest Political Science Association meeting, Chicago, 20–22 April 1978.

6. William P. Avery and Louis A. Picard, "The Political Economy of Conventional Arms Transfers to Africa," paper presented at the 19th annual International Studies Association meeting, Washington, D.C., 22–25 February 1978; "Pull Factors in the Transfer of Conventional Armaments to Africa," *Journal of Political and Military Sociology,* 8, no. 1 (Spring 1980): 55–70.

7. Alden F. Mullins, Jr., "The Development of Military Capability by Newly Independent States" (unpublished Ph D. thesis, University of Michigan, 1979).

8. Alex Mintz, "Political and Economic Explanations of Armament Dependence in Africa: A Cross National Study," paper presented at the Center for the Interdisciplinary Study of Science and Technology Lecture Series, Northwestern University, Evanston, Illinois, October 1979.

9. Pita Ogaba Agbese, "Correlates of Arms Transfer Behavior in Africa," unpublished master's thesis (Northwestern University, 4 May 1981).

10. Robert G. Leh, "Weapons Transfers in Africa, with Emphasis on Bloc and Front-line Example States," paper presented at the annual Midwest Political Science Association meeting, Chicago, 20–22 April 1978.

11. Philip A. Schrodt, "A Pilot Study of the Statistical Relationships between Arms Transfers and International Behavior in the Arabian Sea Area," paper presented at the twenty-second annual International Studies Assn. meeting, Philadelphia, 18–21 March 1981; "Arms Transfers and International Behavior in the Arabian Sea Area," unpublished paper, Northwestern University, June 1981.

12. For example, Andrew J. Pierre, ed. *Arms Transfers and American Foreign Policy* (New York: New York University Press, 1979) contains chapters on the Persian Gulf and Latin America but no other regions. Pierre's new book, *The Global Politics of Arms Sales* (Princeton, N.J.: Princeton University Press, 1982), devotes only a short section to

sub-Saharan Africa (pp. 255–271), in which a few pages touch on U.S. arms supplies. Uri Ra'anan et al., eds. *Arms Transfers to the Third World: The Military Buildup in Less Industrial Countries* (Boulder, Colo.: Westview Press, 1978) includes several papers on U.S. arms transfers, none relating to Africa. Likewise, Stephanie G. Neuman and Robert E. Harkavy, eds. *Arms Transfers in the Modern World* (New York: Praeger Publishers, 1979) has eighteen topical essays but no country/regional papers. Among the eight papers in Cindy Cannizzo, ed. *The Gun Merchants: Politics and Policies of the Major Arms Suppliers* (New York: Pergamon Press, 1980), George E. Hudson's deals with Soviet arms policy toward Africa, but none address U.S. military transfers to the region; nor do any of the nineteen contributions in Asbjorn Eide and Marek Thee, eds. *Problems of Contemporary Militarism* (New York: St. Martin's Press, 1980) focus specifically on Africa or U.S.–African military ties.

Other general works give only a nod toward Africa. Philip J. Farley et al., *Arms Across the Sea* (Washington, D.C.: Brookings Institution, 1978) devotes four pages (91–94) to Africa, specifically limited to Ethiopia–Somalia and the Horn, while Geoffrey Kemp's 80-page *Arms Traffic and Third World Conflicts,* International Conciliation, No. 577 (New York: Carnegie Endowment for International Peace, March 1970) gives Africa somewhat more attention (pp. 58–64), particularly on arms-control prospects. Mary Kaldor and Asbjorn Eide, eds. *The World Military Order: The Impact of Military Technology on the Third World* (London: Macmillan Press, 1979) contains one paper on the French counterinsurgency in Algeria and one on arms transfers and repression in South Africa, but none on U.S. military transfers to Africa. Finally, Basil Collier, *Arms and the Men: The Arms Trade and Governments* (London: Hamish Hamilton, 1980), a sketchy history of international arms trade in the twentieth century, is virtually silent on Africa; and Russell Warren Howe's journalistic *Weapons: The International Game of Arms, Money and Diplomacy* (Garden City, New York: Doubleday, 1980), despite its 798-page bulk, includes only passing references to Africa, all the more surprising in view of the author's prolific writing on African affairs.

13. Henry Bienen, "Foreign Policy, the Military, and Development: Military Assistance and Political Change in Africa," in *Foreign Policy and the Developing Nation,* ed. Richard Butwell, ed., (Lexington, Ky.: University of Kentucky Press, 1969), pp. 69–111; Chester A. Crocker, "Motivations for External Military Assistance to African States: A Policy Perspective," paper presented at the eighteenth annual African Studies Association meeting, San Francisco, 29 October through 1 November 1975.

14. Major Wilbert Stitt, Jr., "The African Officer and the Command

and General Staff College Experience," paper presented at the eighteenth annual African Studies Assn. meeting, San Francisco, 29 October through 1 November 1975.

15. Harold A. Hovey, *United States Military Assistance: A Study of Policies and Practices* (New York: Frederick A. Praeger, 1965), pp. 104–112.

16. Ilan Peleg, "Military Assistance to Black Africa: The Ex-Colonial Variant," unpublished paper (Northwestern University, August 1973).

17. David Dabelko and Edward Baum, "U.S. Military Transfers to Africa: An Examination of Alternative Hypotheses," paper presented at the eighteenth annual International Studies Assn. meeting, St. Louis, Mo., 16–20 March 1977.

18. William P. Avery, "Recipient Influences on U.S. Arms Trade with the Third World," *Mondes et Developpement*, no. 18 (1977): 342–359.

19. David J. Sylvan, *Arms Transfers and the Logic of Political Efficacy*, Military Issues Research Memorandum ACN 78041, Strategic Studies Institute, U.S. Army War College, Carlisle Barracks, Pa., 10 July 1978.

20. Frederic S. Pearson, "An Analysis of the Linkage between Arms Transfers and Subsequent Military Intervention," paper presented at the twenty-second annual International Studies Assn. meeting, Philadelphia, 18–21 March 1981; Occasional Paper 8102, University of Missouri—St. Louis, March 1981.

21. Edward Thomas Rowe, "Aid and Coups d'Etat: Aspects of the Impact of American Military Assistance Programs in the Less Developed Countries," *International Studies Quarterly*, 18, no. 2 (June 1974): 239–255.

22. Bruce M. Russett and David J. Sylvan, "The Effects of Arms Transfers on Developing Countries," commissioned research report prepared for the United Nations Group of Governmental Experts on the Relationship between Disarmament and Development, Yale University, July 1980.

23. Dan Smith and Ron Smith, "Military Expenditure, Resources and Development," commissioned research report prepared for the United Nations Group of Governmental Experts on the Relationship between Disarmament and Development, Birkbeck College, University of London, April 1980.

24. See Herbert Y. Schandler et al., *Implications of President Carter's Conventional Arms Transfer Policy*, Congressional Research Service Report 77–223 F, 22 September 1977, pp. 34–38.

25. David J. Louscher, "The Future of Arms Transfer Restraint,"

paper presented at the twenty-second annual International Studies Assn. meeting, Philadelphia, 18–21 March 1981.

26. See Michael D. Salomon, ''The Congressional Role in Arms Transfer Decisions: Contribution or Intrusion,'' paper presented at the twenty-second annual International Studies Assn. meeting, Philadelphia, 18–21 March 1981.

27. For a more extensive review, comparison, and critique of Carter's and Reagan's policies, see U.S. Congress, Congressional Research Service, *Changing Perspectives on U.S. Arms Transfer Policy,* Report prepared for the Subcommittee on International Security and Scientific Affairs of the Committee on Foreign Affairs, U.S. House of Representatives, Committee Print, 97th Cong., 1st Sess., 25 September 1981.

Part IV
Conclusion

10 Arms Transfers to Africa in the 1980s

Bruce E. Arlinghaus

As the preceding chapters indicate, the demand for and the supply of conventional arms for African nations is likely to continue and perhaps increase over the next decade. While these trends are easily discerned from prior data, the ebb and flow of the international trade in armaments is a much more dynamic process. Because of the political importance and significance attributed to these transfers by both supplier and recipient nations, changes in leadership may cause radical redefinitions of both the ends and the means of foreign policy, which will drastically alter or reorder the relationships in that marketplace. There are, however, several conclusions that may be drawn regarding the supply of arms to Africa:

The Soviets and French will Continue to Dominate, but Decline over Time

The Soviet Union has been the principal supplier of weapons to Africa, and is likely to continue as such over the next decade. This is simply because military assistance represents the only foreign-policy instrument with which the Soviets have been in any way successful in Africa.[1] Beset by their own domestic-economic difficulties, the Soviets can little afford extensive economic assistance, and have little credibility as a model for economic development. On the other hand, the Soviets enjoy a reputation as an arms supplier that provides military assistance that is roughly 50 percent cheaper, with deliveries of equipment that are 50 percent faster and significantly less complex than those of their competitors.

Yet the perception of their equipment as "simple, rugged and reliable"[2] has worked to their disadvantage, since many African nations—the Nigerians in particular—are seeking more advanced systems, and this has caused them to lose sales or that they are required to demonstrate a "willingness to supply expensive advanced weapons systems on short notice.[3] Financial difficulties aside, this development has only served to exacerbate the "ugly Russian problem"[4] in which Soviet efforts to manipulate and control recipient nations through spare-parts diplomacy and a reluctance to pass on technology and training antagonize and alienate potential allies.[5] Further, there seems to be a growing awareness on the part of many African leaders that Soviet arms and military assistance in excessive amounts are not what they need to resolve the social and economic problems that confront them. As one official in Equatorial Guinea is reported to have said: "You can't eat guns."[6] Although the Soviets have apparently responded to these changes to some degree, their eroded credibility has caused many Africans to question exactly what they, and their Cuban and East European allies, are doing for Africa.[7]

While Soviet arms transfers are beginning to decline, the initial perception that the Mitterand government would drastically curb French arms sales appears unfounded. Despite the Socialist party's rhetoric regarding "less arms, more machine tools,"[8] the political and economic realities of French involvement overseas have caused the Mitterand government to reassure its African allies that it would continue to honor all arms sales and overseas agreements, and that its aid commitments would be met or increased.[9]

Sales by Secondary Suppliers will Remain Relatively Constant

Although also troubled by political second thoughts regarding its role as a major supplier of arms to the developing world—in particular, Africa and the Middle East—the West Germans are unlikely to reduce their arms transfers. Such debates are likely, however, to restrain any significant increases in arms supplies, especially to those areas perceived as trouble spots.[10] While British and Italian arms transfers to Africa can be expected to increase, especially since the former nation's decision to reduce the size of its own defense establishment will provide it with a wealth of surplus equipment for sale,[11] it is to the United States that many look to fill the vacuum created by either a Soviet or French decline in arms sales.[12] Although there was a definite shift in policy—the Reagan administration view of arms sales as an important policy instrument, compared to its treatment as exceptional in the Carter era[13]—both administrations have tended to behave pragmatically. Sales increased steadily during the Carter years, more than many expected, and the policy of the Reagan administration has been to consider each sale on a case-by-case basis.

The Slack in the Market will Be Taken Up by New Third World and European Suppliers

Arms exports to Africa and the developing world generally can be expected to continue to increase over the decade, and this growth, together with those markets lost by the Soviets and the French, will be taken over by a new set of suppliers, seeking stronger ties with the nonaligned world, markets for fledgling armaments industries, improved balance of payments and, of course, political influence. While the traditional European suppliers, Belgium, Austria, and others are seeking to increase their market share, many are beset by the same political problems as are France and West Germany.[14] The greatest growth, then, can be expected among the newly industrialized countries, and those already possessing sizeable defense industries: Brazil, Argentina, South Africa, Israel, India, Yugoslavia, North and South Korea, and Taiwan.[15]

Brazil[16] is an excellent example of a newly industrialized country that has, through development of its own defense-industrial base, begun exporting military hardware to absorb excess capacity and to improve its balance of payments—particularly with oil producers such as Iraq and Nigeria. The Brazilians seem to combine the best of both the Soviets and the French—simple, durable, and relatively inexpensive equipment supplied discreetly with few, if any, questions asked. Add to this its own status as a nonaligned developing nation and the concomitant absence of political linkage or leverage accompanying its sales and it is readily evident why Brazil has become one of the world's top ten arms suppliers (over $1 billion annually), and their growth is likely to continue.[17]

Arms sales are only a part, however, of the expanding economy of Brazil, whose products are being aggressively marketed in Africa.[18] But more important than the transfer of military-end items is the potential for technology transfer, especially for Nigeria, which is looking to Brazil to make it into the "India of Africa".[19] This suggests the fourth trend in arms transfers.

African Nations will Seek to Develop Indigeneous Defense Industries

There are several reasons for this development, not the least of which is the symbolic value of such capacity for deterring enemies and lessening dependence on suppliers of arms and military assistance. Not only do defense industries lessen the impact of spare-parts diplomacy, but they also are tangible evidence of sovereignty and independence in foreign affairs.[20]

For Africans, the most visible evidence of this has been the growing South African military-industrial complex that has effectively insulated them against political leverage in the form of arms embargoes.[21] Yet in their attempt to keep up with the Afrikaaners, many African nations appear to ignore the critical diversion of financial and human resources that such a program represents.[22] In addition, such development is not possible without the assistance—in the form of technology transfer, licensing, and coproduction agreements—of the same industrial states that demand political influence for arms already. Since they are likely to demand such leverage or linkage when asked to aid in the development of defense industries, it is no wonder that Nigeria has turned to Brazil and elsewhere, to get the same assistance as South Africa has received from France and Israel.[23]

Given that Nigeria and a few other African states are only beginning to develop defense industries, and that most other African nations lack the money to even consider such a step, a final conclusion is in order.

Most African Nations will Continue to Buy Arms on Credit

Despite their desires to become militarily self-reliant, most African countries will continue to buy arms on credit, if only for the financial leverage it provides them. But for many countries—Zaire and Sudan in particular—such a strategy has its limitations. Senegal, Sierra Leone, Liberia, Togo, Central African Republic, Uganda and Madagascar have also had to have international debts rescheduled, and it is unlikely that many others have the wherewithal to dramatically increase military expenditures or arms purchases on anything other than the most concessionary terms.[24]

Conclusions

It is this element, the financial dependency of African states, that will continue to determine the pattern and scale of conventional arms transfers in the region. Since they cannot meet their own perceived defense needs without arms, yet cannot afford to purchase them on a cash basis (comparable to most Middle Eastern nations), they will be forced to acquire arms from those states able and willing to grant them military-sales credits. Although the nonoil producing African nations might prefer to purchase Brazilian or other nonaligned arms, they will most likely be forced in most instances to make their purchases from the more traditional suppliers, East and West.

In addition, these simple facts of international financial life will reinforce supplier-nation confidence in the ability of arms transfers to influence African nations. Since the demand for arms is so great, even in the face of enormous political and economic costs, the supplier nations must respond. Any attempts to limit arms sales to Africa will be interpreted as a lost opportunity to influence a region of growing strategic importance to both East and West. While nonaligned suppliers may exploit this competition for their own economic benefit, the only realistic source of a reduction in military assistance and arms transfers lies with Africans themselves, and a redefinition of sovereignty that deemphasizes military force and defense capabilities.

Notes

1. Alvin Z. Rubinstein, *Soviet Foreign Policy Since World War II: Imperial and Global,* (Cambridge, Mass.: Winthrop Publishing, 1980).

2. Edwin W. Besch and Ronald E. Fischer. "Soviet Weaponry: Simple, Rugged and Reliable," *Army* (February 1982): 18–24.

3. "Soviet Third World Arms Sales Increased, CIA Reports," *The Washington Post* 11 December 1980, p. 27.

4. Gavriel D. Ra'anan, *The Evolution of the Soviet Use of Surrogates in Military Relations with the Third World, With Particular Emphasis on Cuban Participation in Africa* (Santa Monica, Calif.: Rand Corporation, 1979) Paper No. P-6420, p. 33.

5. Jay Ross, "Ethiopia Leans Uneasily on Soviets as Reliable Source of Arms," *The Washington Post,* 31 December 1981.

6. Tom Gilvoy, "Red Star Dims in Africa," *The Christian Science Monitor,* 27 May 1981.

7. David Binder, "Soviet Cuts Arms Aid in Favor of Economic Pledges," *The New York Times,* 21 October 1979, p. 24; "Angolans Begin to Ask Just What Cuban Soldiers Are Doing for Them" *The Christian Science Monitor,* 29 December 1981.

8. "Mitterand Writes a Cheque for Foreign Arms Makers", *The Economist* (May 23, 1981): 67–8; Lamiri Chironf, "The French Debate: Arms Sales," *Adieu Report* (July/August, 1981): 15–17. See also "Will Mitterand Really Crack Down on Weapons Exports?" *World Business Weekly* (20 July 1981): 22–23.

9. Richard Eder, "Mitterand Tells the Africans France Will Keep Up Its Aid," *The New York Times,* 4 November 1981, p. A15; Samuel F. Wells, Jr., "The Mitterand Challenge," *Foreign Policy,* no. 44 (Fall 1981): 57–69.

10. "West Germany: Who Wants to Sell Arms?" *The Economist* (13 January 1979): 42–3; "West Germany Debates Role of Arms Industry, *The New York Times,* 11 August 1980, p. D1; Udo Phipp, "Terman Arms Exports: The Debate Warms Up," *International Defense Review,* 14, no. 4 (1981): 417–20; Bradley Graham, "West Germany

Probes Arms Shipments to Trouble Spots," *The Washington Post,* 9 August 1980, p. 20.

11. Martin Edmonds, "The Domestic and International Dimensions of British Arms Sales, 1966–1978" in Cynthia A. Cannizzo, ed. *The Gun Merchants* (Elmsford, N.Y.: Pergamon, 1980) pp. 68–100; "Want a Navy Cheap? British Cuts Could Mean Big Sales." *Baltimore Sun,* 4 August 1981, p. 4.

12. "Arming the World," *Time* (26 October 1981): 28–41.

13. Compare the texts of both policy statements, Office of the White House Press Secretary, "Statement by the President on Conventional Arms Transfer Policy," May 19, 1977 and "Text of President Ronald Reagan's July 8, 1981, Arms Transfer Policy Directive."

14. Murray Seegen, "West European Arms Industry Seeks to Concentrate Firepower," *The Lost Angeles Times,* 19 July 1981, p. 1F; Gary Yerkey, "European Armsmakers Aim for Third World", *The Christian Science Monitor,* 12 March 1981, p. 1, and "Belgium Embroiled in Controversy Over Sale of Military Hardware to Foreign Governments," *The Christian Science Monitor,* 6 January 1981, p. 10; Jack Cooley, "Austria Increasing Sales to Mideast's Third World," *The Washington Post,* September 1980, p. 17, "Arms Exporter Faces Challenge in Neutral Austria," *The New York Times,* 15 March 1981, p. 20.

15. Judith Miller, "Third World Lands Join Ranks of Arms Exporters, *The New York Times,* 13 December 1981.

16. "Brazil: A Major Contender in the Arms Business," *Business Week* (31 July 1978).

17. *The Wall Street Journal,* 19 March 1981, p. 31, "Gabon to Receive Brazilian Armoured Vehicles," *Defense Africa* (September/October 1981): 28.

18. "Brazil and Cuba Court Africa," *South* (November 1980): 15–18.

19. John Ostheimer and Gary J. Buckley, "Nigeria" in Edward Kolodziej and Robert Horkavy, eds., *Security Policies of Developing Countries,* (Lexington, Mass.: D.C. Heath and Co., Lexington Books, 1982) pp. 285–303.

20. Baldez Fja Nayar, "Political Mainsprings of Economic Planning in the New Nations," *Comparative Politics,* 6, no. 3 (Fall 1974); Michael Moodie, "Sovereignty, Security and Arms" *The Washington Papers,* no. 67 (1979).

21. Caryle Murphy, "Embargo Spurs S. Africa to Build Weapons Industry" *The Washington Post,* 7 July 1981; "Pretoria Produces Most of Its Weapons at Home", *The Chicago Sun,* 28 February 1982.

22. "Big Cuts Ordered in South African Defense Contracts," *Financial Times,* 22 December 1981.

23. Drew Middleton ''South Africa Needs More Arms, Israeli Says''
The New York Times, 14 December 1981, p. A9. It is ironic that growing
Afro-Arab solidarity, and African dependence on Arab oil has caused
Israel—one of the primary sources of military and technical assistance
immediately following African independence—to become a pariah state
more closely allied with South Africa.

24. See ''A Nightmare of Debt: A Survey of International Banking'',
The Economist (20 March 1982).

About the Contributors

David E. Albright is currently professor of national security affairs at the Air War College, Maxwell Air Force Base. Previously, he worked as research associate and editor of the project on the United States and China in world affairs at the Council on Foreign Relations in New York, and as senior text editor of *Problems of Communism*. He has written extensively about the Communist states and Africa. Among his works are an edited volume titled *Communism in Africa* and a forthcoming coedited volume titled *The Communist States and Africa*.

Cynthia A. Cannizzo is affiliated with the Strategic Studies Program at the Arctic Institute of the University of Calgary. Prior to this appointment, she was a research Fellow at the Centre for the Study of Arms Control and International Security at the University of Lancaster and the Mershon Center at the Ohio State University. She has written extensively on arms transfers and edited *The Gun Merchants* (1980).

Regina Cowen received the B.A. in international relations from the University of Keele in 1979, and since then has worked as a research assistant at the Centre for the Study of Arms Control and International Security at the University of Lancaster. She is currently completing her doctoral dissertation on the structure of the West German defense industry and its implications for arms transfers.

Roger E. Kanet is professor of political science and a member of the Russian and East European Center of the University of Illinois, Urbana-Champaign. He is the author of numerous articles dealing with Soviet and East European foreign policy. His three most recent edited books are *Background to Crisis: Policy and Politics in Gierek's Poland* (1981), *Soviet Foreign Policy in the 1980s* (forthcoming), and *Soviet Foreign Policy and East-West Relations* (forthcoming).

Edward A. Kolodziej received the doctorate from the University of Chicago in 1961. He has written extensively on French foreign policy and arms transfers, and has recently coedited with Robert Harkavy, *Security Policies of Developing Countries and American Security Policy and Policymaking* (Lexington Books, 1982). He has taught at the University of Virginia and the University of Illinois, where he is currently a professor and codirector of the Office of Arms Control, Disarmament and International Security.

Bokanga Lokulutu is a graduate student at the University of Illinois and research associate of Dr. Kolodziej.

Edward J. Laurance is a graduate of the U.S. Military Academy and holds advanced degrees in political science (Temple University, 1971) and international relations (University of Pennsylvania, 1973). He is currently professor in the Department of National Security Affairs at the Naval Postgraduate School, Monterey, California. The author of many articles and studies concerning arms transfers, he is currently engaged in research on the U.S. Congress and American defense policy.

Joseph P. Smaldone is chief of the licensing division, Office of Munitions Control, U.S. Department of State. He has taught at the U.S. Naval Academy, and holds a doctorate in African history. He has written extensively on arms transfers to Africa, past and present, including *Warfare in the Sokoto Caliphate* (1977) and ''Soviet and Chinese Military Aid and Arms Transfers to Africa: A Contextual Analysis.''

George T. Yu is professor of political science at the University of Illinois, Urbana-Champaign. A 1961 graduate of the University of California, Berkeley, he is the author of many articles and books on the People's Republic of China and its activities in the developing world, including *China and Tanzania: A Study in Cooperative Interaction* (1970) and *China's African Policy* (1975).

About the Editor

Bruce E. Arlinghaus, Captain, U.S. Army, is assistant professor of anthropology and political science in the Department of Social Sciences at the U.S. Military Academy, West Point, New York. After commissioning through R.O.T.C. at Ohio State University, he was named a university Fellow at Indiana University, receiving the M.A. (1973) and the Ph.D. (1982) in anthropology and African studies. While assigned to the Third Infantry Division in Europe (1974–1978), he served as the antitank platoon leader and as a rifle-company commander in a mechanized infantry battalion. He is currently engaged in research on the impact of high-technology arms transfers on economic development and political stability in sub-Saharan Africa.